BIRDS OF A FEATHER

Alan Balter

PublishAmerica

Baltimore

First printing

ISBN: 1-59129-882-2
PUBLISHED BY PUBLISHAMERICA BOOK
PUBLISHERS
www.publishamerica.com
Baltimore

Printed in the United States of America

For Barbara
My precious wife and best friend.

Prologue

Richard is our son. He is mentally retarded.

Fifty years ago, Richard would have been called "feeble-minded." Before that, he would have been an "imbecile." Now, the preferred terms are "developmentally delayed" or "cognitively challenged." Euphemisms come and go with each generation, but, no matter the terminology, our son will be mentally retarded for as long as he lives. He will be 20 on his next birthday.

On the first day of Richard's life, his mother and I were told he was a mongoloid. The nurses put him in an isolated section of the hospital nursery, away from the viewing windows, so nobody could see him. Until we insisted, they didn't bring him to my wife for feedings. The doctor urged us to put him in an institution. "These things are always difficult," he said, "but the separation will be easier if you do it immediately, before any bonding occurs." Then, he went home to play with his children.

We chose to ignore the good doctor's advice. Instead, we brought Richard home from the hospital and never looked back. He was cute, he had all his parts, and he had that delicious smell only newborns have. Months passed and we bonded like hell. Like all new parents, we had our share of sleepless nights. We worried, we were tentative, and we were exhausted, but my wife and I learned to take care of our infant son. It has been said that when the going gets tough, the tough get going.

We joined our local Association for Parents of Mentally Retarded Children. It was helpful to talk with other parents. They recommended pediatricians and experts on infant stimulation. They showed us activities we could do at home to enhance Richard's development. They lent us their support and their books. We read everything we could find about Down syndrome, another of those preferred terms. It wasn't easy reading.

The books said Down syndrome is one of the most common types of mental retardation. Overall, it affects about one out of every 700

5

babies, but the probability is much greater in mothers who are 35 or older when they conceive. The chances of Down syndrome increase as fathers get older, as well. We were busy with our careers.

As the result of a genetic error, children with Down syndrome have an extra chromosome, 47 rather than the usual 46, in each of their cells. On intelligence tests, they score lower than 98 percent of children their age. In school, they have problems learning to read, write, spell and compute. Their intellectual and academic limitations make it difficult for them to grow into independently functioning adults, either socially or vocationally, should they live that long.

The books said children with Down syndrome are at risk for serious medical problems and physical disabilities, too. These include congenital heart defects, respiratory disorders, visual and auditory problems, inner ear infections, short stature, leukemia, and many others. Indeed, physical examinations of groups of children with Down syndrome have identified more than 50 harmful characteristics affecting every major organ system in the body.

During early childhood, they are slow to master basic self-help skills–important developmental milestones like speaking, toileting, feeding and dressing themselves, and walking. As young adults, they aren't able to find adequate jobs or keep them, prolonging their dependency on parents or guardians. As they reach middle age, a disproportionately high incidence of early onset Alzheimer's Disease has been noted. Their life expectancy has increased during recent years but remains far below average.

All that stuff was in the books.

As we read, my wife and I learned some of the history of mental retardation, as well. Instances of abusive treatment have been well-documented. Not long ago it was acceptable to house mentally retarded people in large institutions, often located in isolated rural areas. There, away from public scrutiny, they were crammed into wards with 100 roommates, give or take a few. This unnatural way of living made it easy for them to imitate each other's deviant behaviors. Thus, they grew ever more deviant. Together, they became institutionalized.

It was acceptable for them to be deprived of any form of recreational or training program. They were kept indoors, stagnating on their backs, bedsores festering, all the while staring at blank ceilings until the next attendant came to change their diapers. Sometimes, the next attendant, often a person working for minimum wage and unemployable elsewhere, was late or neglected to come to work at all, so the "retardates," as they were called, played with their feces and smeared it on the walls. Or, they ate it.

It was acceptable for them to be stripped naked and strapped upright to the walls of a special bathing room with seven of their mates. The room was flooded, shoulder high, for their weekly bath. After a few minutes, the dirty water was flushed, and attendants dried them and dressed them in their next outfits. Whether their clothes were the right size or even gender appropriate didn't matter much. They simply wore whatever items of clothing were on the top of the pile.

It was acceptable to sterilize them without consent, too. "Eugenics" it was called, a method for improving the human race by the calculated selection of parents. The idea was to make it impossible for mentally retarded people to have children, thus effectively eliminating their kind in the relatively brief span of a few decades. Sieg Heil!

Depriving people who were mentally retarded of any semblance of dignity was justified by assuming they were so lacking in awareness as to be oblivious to their surroundings and treatment. What the heck. If they don't know what's going on, what difference does it make? Right? One must wonder how it can be that a house pet, say a cocker spaniel, is aware of its surroundings and treatment, but a person, even a person who is mentally retarded, isn't?

"Surplus population" is a term that was appropriate. In the bad old days, the mentally retarded were treated as if they were a freakish overstock, a mutated species somewhere between the great apes and modern man on the phylogenetic scale, to be discarded, mistreated, or, at best, ignored.

More recently, there has been some progress. Greater public

awareness of mental retardation, often brought about by the efforts of parent advocacy groups, has resulted in some good things. Many of the old institutions, "human warehouses," as they were, have been closed, and smaller, community based facilities have taken their place. As a way of replacing institutionalization with a more natural, family style living arrangement, only small groups of people, usually no more than twelve, live under the same roof. They live in rooms, not wards, and parent surrogates assist in providing for their needs.

There are better educational and vocational training programs for the mentally retarded, as well. Congress has passed legislation making it mandatory for public schools to provide special education services for the mentally retarded from the time they are three until they are twenty-one years old. As a result, more capable teachers and counselors are working in the schools. Programs stress the importance of regular interaction between mentally retarded children and their intellectually normal classmates. The federal government and private agencies have granted more funding for research on causation, treatment, and prevention.

However, in spite of the progress, myths and misinformation have endured. There is the notion, for example, that people who are mentally retarded have criminal tendencies. They have brute strength and are prone to violence. They are easily frustrated and unable to control their emotions. They are incapable of appreciating the current or long-term consequences of their behavior. They are lazy and shiftless, lacking in initiative and perseverance. Emotionally, they are "flat"; that is, they seldom demonstrate either happiness or sadness. They are pleasant, affectionate, and forever childlike in their relations with others.

The nonsense goes on and on: They are sexually promiscuous and irresponsible. They contribute an excessive number of defective children to the population. They have a very high tolerance for pain. Unable to delay gratification, they seek to satisfy their needs immediately. At the same time, they are insensitive to the needs of others. They are inflexible, stubborn, and slow to learn from experience. If they work at all, they can only succeed at jobs involving the simplest, most repetitive tasks.

It's enough. It's time to dispose of the myths and misinformation at last. Meet our son Richard.

CHAPTER I
Richard

Some people still call me Dicky, but my real name is Richard. I'm a grownup guy, nineteen and a half years old, so I don't like it too much when people call me Dicky. My real name is Richard. Everyone should call me Richard.

Not too long ago, exactly 26 or 28 days before today on my calendar, I moved to this new place to live. A group home is what you call it. So far I like living here pretty much. There's a lot of other people that live here too, exactly 13, if you count every single person besides me. Some of them are my age, and a couple are a little younger than me. Most are a little older, though. Every now and then, mostly when I'm all alone trying to fall asleep at night, I miss my mom and dad and the house where I used to live, but I'm doing pretty good at my new house. I mean, it's not like I'm terrible homesick or nothing. Homesick is what little boys get.

I'm not sure if it's true, but one time my best friend Billy told me you only get three wishes in your whole life. Not two wishes or four wishes, but exactly three wishes in your whole life. Billy said it was a good idea to be very stingy with your wishes. You don't want to use them up too fast. Usually, I listened to what Billy said, 'cause he was older than me. He was a real smart guy too, one of those very brainy guys that got good grades and made the honor roll at his school all the time. There was no honor roll at my school. When your teachers don't give you a report card with grades on it, then your school doesn't need to have an honor roll. That's just the way it is.

Even if it's not true that you only get three wishes, I'm going to pretend it is anyway, 'cause grownups that are going to be 20 years old on their next birthday should still have hopes and dreams. I think a grownup guy should always have hopes and dreams, no matter how old he is. I mean, even a geezer, which is another word for a very old person with wrinkles, should still have hopes and dreams.

That's what I think, all right. So here I go with my first wish. You can never tell when a wish will come true.

My first wish is that I didn't look like me. I know I can't do too much about how I look, but that doesn't mean I have to like it. I don't even like to see myself in a mirror unless I really have to, like maybe when I shave off my whiskers or comb my hair in the morning. And even then, I try to finish up as fast as I can. You probably wouldn't like it too much neither, if you looked like me.

My eyes are kind of slanty, so when I laugh or smile, they look like slits. My nose is flattened out and takes up way too much room on my face. And, my mouth doesn't look so good, neither. My tongue is too big, and there are some cracks on the top of it. A lot of times, 'specially when I'm not thinking about it, my tongue will hang out to the right side of my mouth. Sometimes it will hang out of the left side, but usually out of the right side, and never out of the middle.

Mom and Dad always tell me to keep my tongue in my mouth, but I still forget to do it a lot. I forget a lot of things I guess, at least compared to other grownups that are going to be 20 years old on their next birthday. But, I remember a lot of things, too. A lot of things I forget, and a lot of things I remember. That's the kind of guy I am.

I had a bunch of juicy pimples all over my face when I first got to be a teenager. I've noticed that some teenagers get pimples and some don't. The lucky ones don't, and the unlucky ones do. I think my doctor, the one that knows all about bad stuff that can happen to your skin, called them acmes or something like that, but I just called them pimples, 'cause that's what they were. I mean, why not call them what they are, which is pimples, instead of some other name, like acmes, that means the same thing but some people might not know the meaning of right away, 'specially if they were lucky and never had any?

Anyway, Mom got me some medicine at the drugstore, and I was supposed to smear it all over my pimples every night, last thing before I went to sleep. I never liked how it smelled, and it messed up my pillow too, but most nights I smeared it on anyway, 'cause a guy doesn't want to go through life with juicy pimples all over his face. So, if you're just getting to be a teenager and you have some pimples that aren't going away all by themselves, ask your mom to get you some medicine at the drugstore. Then, be good and listen to the doctor and your mom and dad. Smear a lot of it on every single night, and don't forget.

After exactly 11 or 13 tubes of that smelly medicine, my pimples finally dried up and fell off. I've still got a lot of scars on my cheeks, though. They're real doozies, giant red scars that are easy to see, so anyone that looks at me can tell I used to have a bad case of pimples. It's sort of a silly thought that most grownups probably wouldn't have, but sometimes I wonder exactly where dried up pimples go after they fall off. When you think about it, everything has to be somewhere in this world of ours.

I keep an extra tube of that medicine in my top dresser drawer just in case my pimples decide to show up again. They probably won't, 'cause you usually don't get them so much when you're a grownup guy like me. By the way, if you don't want a messy pillow, you could try sleeping on your back.

My hair started to fall out when I was still in high school, and now, except for a few long ones that I comb over the top of my head and some fuzz around the sides and back, it's just about all gone. I figure the hair that fell out of my head and didn't grow back probably went to the same place as my pimples, although I can't be too sure about it.

Usually I wear one of my sailor hats so people won't be able to tell I don't have too much hair. Sailor hats are way cool. I have two of them just in case one might be in the wash, 'cause it's dirty. Or, it's always possible I could lose one. You can never tell when you might lose one of your sailor hats, so it's a good idea to have a spare. It's the same thing for tires.

Getting back to how I look, it's not that I'm pure ugly or nothing like that. I mean, people don't scream and run away from me like I'm a monster man or a freak of some kind that you usually see next to the lady with a beard or the dog with two heads at the circus. But,

I know I'm not one of those handsome type guys, neither. Let's just say I'm plum positive that nobody from Hollywood is ever going to ask me to be a movie star. You could bet all your money and then some on that, and, to tell you the honest to God truth, the rest of me doesn't look all that much better than my face.

I'm only five feet and two inches tall, which isn't very tall for a grownup guy. And, I have this bad habit of not standing up too straight, which makes me look even shorter. Mom and Dad always remind me to stand up straight and tall. They want me to stick my chest out, pull my shoulders back, and keep my chin up. I'm supposed to stand at attention like I'm one of those soldier guys, even though I've noticed sailors and marines stand up pretty straight, too. So do policemen.

Mom and Dad usually remind me about standing up straight right after they tell me to put my tongue back in my mouth. Most parents are like that, you know. They always want you to look your best. I don't mind. It's not easy being someone's parent, 'cause of all the worrying they have to do. I tell my mom and dad not to worry about me too much, but they keep on doing it anyway.

I don't have any real hard muscles on my body like a lot of other grownup guys, neither. My skin just sort of hangs down around my stomach, 'cause I weigh too much and I'm flabby, which is another word for having loose skin. It's real hard for me to lose any weight, though, 'cause eating is one of my favorite things to do. I like to eat just about everything except asparagus, broccoli, and brussel sprouts, and if they're floating around in some cheese sauce, I don't mind chowing down on them, neither.

Now, I'm not saying that vegetables are anywhere near as tasty as a delicious double cheese pizza with mushrooms, onions, green peppers, and Italian sausage on the top of it or one of those delicious foot long Polish sausage sandwiches with mustard, pickle relish, grilled onions, tomatoes, and a mess of cheese fries, but they're still good enough to eat, and they're healthy for you, too. I've noticed that most things that are healthy for you don't taste quite as good as pizza or Polish sausage.

Boy oh boy; it makes my mouth get real juicy just thinking about all that delicious food. Well-done steaks and lobster tails with a lot of butter for dipping make my mouth real juicy too. By the way, when I was still a little kid, I used to play a trick on Mom and just eat the cheese sauce. Sometimes, she let me get away with it, but most of the time she didn't.

I don't know about other people, but brussel sprouts give me a ton of gas. So do asparagus, broccoli, and baked beans now that I think about it. Some food gives you gas and some doesn't. I'm not sure exactly why; that's just how it is, I guess. *Vrrooom.*

Another reason I weigh too much and I'm flabby is 'cause I can't go to the health club and work out like a lot of other guys that are trying to firm up their muscles and lose some weight. There were some bad things wrong with my heart and lungs right after I was born, so I'm usually not supposed to do hard exercises too much. Tough is another word for hard. So is strenuous, which is a bigger word I like to say sometimes instead of hard or tough, 'specially when I'm talking about different kinds of exercises.

My doctor, the one that knows all about hearts and lungs, always warns me to take it easy after he listens to my heart beating along, steady as she goes, through that metal thing that he presses against my chest that has the rubber ends sticking into his ears. I can never remember what you call that thing, but it's made out of some kind of silver metal and it usually feels pretty cold on my skin. It's not the kind of cold that's icy or nothing; it's more like chilly, or maybe closer to nippy, I would say.

Besides the stuff I've already told you, there are a few more things about me that aren't too good, neither. Another doctor, sort of an old geezer that knows all about ears, noses and throats, says that the holes that go in from my ears are way too skinny. So, ever since I was a baby, I've always had a lot of ear infections. Boy oh boy. I can tell you for sure that an ear infection really hurts like crazy. You don't ever want to catch one if you can.

Maybe an ear infection isn't as bad as getting your finger slammed in a car door or getting a sharp stick poked into one of your eyeballs, but it's almost as bad as that, and it's way worse than a sore throat or a stomach ache. And, as long as I got on the subject of aches, I've noticed that toothaches can hurt pretty bad too, 'specially when the ache is in one of those boulders, I think you call them. They're those big choppers that are way in the back of your mouth where you usually might forget to brush after each meal or even three times a day.

Anyway, when I was a little kid with all that goop clogging up my ear holes, I guess I didn't hear as good as I should of, so now, all these years later, when I talk out loud, some of my words don't come out sounding exactly like they're supposed to. If you don't hear so good when you're a little kid, chances are you won't talk so good when you're a grownup. Fact is, how you talk depends on how you hear. That's why most people that are deaf don't hardly talk at all, except for some funny sounds that other people usually can't understand. That's the way it is, no matter how hard they try.

Most people that have been around me for a while and know me pretty good can understand what I'm trying to say without much trouble. Still, I usually don't like to talk out loud too much, unless I really have to, like when someone asks me a question and they're waiting on me for an answer. If you want to have good manners, sometimes you just have to speak up, even if you would rather keep on being quiet.

Another thing that I don't like too much is my hands. They're pretty small for a grownup like me. My pinky fingers are crooked, and they point in towards the palms of my hands. And, I only have one crease in the middle of my hands instead of three creases that people are supposed to have. You're probably counting the creases in your hands right now, I bet. Like I said, you're supposed to have three of them, just in case you're worried about being normal and want to check out your creases. Go ahead; I don't mind waiting 'til you're done counting.

If you're done counting now, the next thing you should know is I have some funny looking feet, too. Maybe I shouldn't even waste time talking about them, 'cause I've noticed that a lot of guys besides me, even guys with handsome faces and hard muscles on their bodies, have feet that are funny looking. That doesn't make me feel any better about mine, though. I have these big, wide spaces between my first and second toes. It looks like two of my toes are missing unless you take the time to count all ten, not that you would ever want to. I mean, normal people don't usually go around counting other peoples' toes, mostly 'cause the answer's always going to be five at the end of each foot, which comes out to be ten on both, just the same as it is with your fingers. It works out perfect.

So now you know why I don't like to go to the beach too much where you usually have to take off your shoes and socks. Or, if I do go, I make sure and dig my feet down under some sand so nobody can look at my toes. But, the rest of me sticks out, plain as day, for everyone to see. Seems like some things you just can't hide, no matter what.

Well, now that you know what I look like, which isn't too great you have to admit, it's time for my second wish. There's no reason my second wish can't come true just 'cause it isn't the first one on my list. Fact is, I think my second wish probably has a better chance of coming true than my first one. You can never tell about wishes.

My second wish is that I could learn how to read. Boy oh boy. When I was a kid, I tried to learn how to read a lot of times, almost without a break, but even with special tutors that came over to my house after school and sometimes on Saturday morning too, I never got all that good at it. Seems like what I learned from my tutor at one lesson I would already forget by the time the next lesson rolled around. So, there I was, right back where I started, still being pretty crummy at reading.

After trying to learn to read so many times, a lot of grownup guys would just give up. Not me though. I'm just going to keep on trying, 'cause when the going gets tough, the tough get going. Dad always says that a lot. I think he might of learned it from his football coach in high school. The coach used to yell it at all the guys when their team was losing a game. I'm not so good at football, and I don't like it very much when people yell at me. People should just talk soft instead of yelling.

Fact is, I'm finally starting to get a little better at reading, 'cause I practice every night, even if I'm sick with a cold or something. I can read some words, like the names of streets, and avenues and boulevards, real quick when I see them. I mean, they just pop right into my head in a flash. And I'm getting to the point where I can sound out a few other words, too. If you know which sounds the letters stand for, then alls you have to do is blend the sounds together, one letter after the next in the right order, until you read the words. That's how it works. By the way, blend is another word for putting stuff together, like when you add the "f" sound and the "a" sound and the "t" sound all together, the total is fat.

'Course, I know that words in a book or a magazine are supposed to mean something, maybe even tell you a story. They could tell you about romantic love stories between a man and a woman or about being a brave hunter looking for some lions and tigers to shoot in the dark jungles of Africa or about the first spaceman that landed on the moon or other kinds of adventures that would be very exciting to have. So, if you can read, it's like being able to have those adventures without even leaving your house, and if some part of the adventure scares you, alls you have to do is close up the book. Now, that's way cool, you have to admit.

Sometimes I see little kids that are way younger than me already reading and writing like it's a snap for them. I mean, they just go along reading and writing as easy as breathing in and out, it seems to me. When I see those little kids already doing what I can't do so good yet, I usually get down on myself for a while. About half way between sad and ashamed is how I feel. And, when I get that feeling is when I usually forget to stand up straight and keep my tongue in my mouth.

When I was in grade school, the teachers didn't even try to teach me to read or write. They put me in what they called a "special" classroom without any books or pencils and paper to practice on. It never made much sense to me why the teachers thought that class was so special, and it still doesn't. I mean, when you think about it, what's so special about a classroom that doesn't even have books or pencils and paper to practice on?

The teachers at my school said I was trainable mentally handicapped, which are just some fancy words for dumb. "Children like your son can grow up to be lovable, pleasant, and happy people, but in school work, mongoloids never make it to the first grade level," they told my parents. Well, I would say I'm mostly pleasant, and sometimes I'm happy all right, but I'm not too sure about the lovable part. Maybe I'm lovable sometimes, but most of the time I'm probably not, except to my mom and dad. They love me a lot. That's how moms and dads are, most of them, anyway, would be my guess.

'Course, now people say I have "Down syndrome," like having something with a different sounding name really makes any kind of a difference. I mean, why should I feel any better about having Down syndrome now that I'm a grownup guy that's going to be 20 years old on his next birthday than I used to feel about being a mongoloid when I was just a little boy?

I think people should spend more time teaching us how to read and write better or even just making friends with us instead of worrying so much about what to call us. What I'm saying is that it doesn't matter to me all that much whether you call me a mongoloid or a guy with Down syndrome. You could pick whichever one you like the most. Or, maybe you could stop worrying about it so much and just call me Richard. Everyone should call me Richard.

Fact is, just because a grownup guy has Down syndrome and can't read or write so good doesn't mean his head is empty and there's nothing he wants to say. My head is always filled up with stuff. Some of what I think about is probably silly stuff; you know, the kinds of thoughts that little kids usually have, but I have some pretty smart thoughts too, the kind that other grownups that don't have Down syndrome probably think about.

Even though I don't talk so clear, I still would like people to know what I'm thinking about and how I'm feeling inside. A lot of people are usually too busy with their work, or no one is around that wants to listen, but I'm still sure there must be someone that would be interested in getting to know a grownup guy with Down syndrome like me. So, I'm going to go ahead and tell everything I remember about me. I might as well go all the way back to the beginning, 'cause that's usually the best place to start, 'specially when you don't want to leave out anything that might be interesting. That's what I think, all right.

I bet you're probably wondering what happened to my third wish, 'cause so far I only told you about two of them, and I still have one more to go. Well, alls you need to do is keep on listening. You can never tell when you might hear some more interesting things about me. I mean, you never know; my third wish could be a real doozy, so I'll just keep you waiting in suspense for a while. That's the kind of guy I am.

Anyway, when Mom and Dad were young, way before they got married and had me for their one and only son, they lived next-door to each other. It was an apartment building where exactly 14 or 16 other families lived. All the kids of those families played in a big back yard that had some grass growing in it behind the building. They played games with each other like Kick the Can, Ring Allevio, and Red Rover Come Over.

On rainy days, they took turns going to each other's apartments to play inside games like Monopoly and Sorry. I know how to play both of those, except Monopoly has a lot of rules that can be a little confusing every now and then. The little green ones are the houses and the big red ones are the hotels, and when you pass Go, you get some play money. At the end, the person with the most money wins. There's a lot of other rules to playing Monopoly, but it's always the person with the most money at the end that wins.

I'm pretty good at playing Checkers, too. It doesn't matter if you're red or black; you should never move your men in the back row. That's the secret to winning. You can never tell when you might have a game of Checkers with someone and you'll need to know the secret of winning. So, no matter what, don't move your men in the back row is what you always want to remember.

To get back to the story of Mom and Dad that I was starting to tell you about, they usually hung out together when they were kids. At school, both of them got real good grades all the time without a miss. Dad was on the football team, 'cause he could run fast and throw far, and Mom won the school spelling bee and the Good Citizenship Award. By the time they got to be teenagers in high school, they were already going steady, which is another way of saying they were sweethearts to each other and nobody else could butt in.

After they graduated from high school and went to college, they decided they wanted to be attorneys, which is another word for lawyers. So, after four years at regular college, they went to a special college for three more years, and that's where they learned how to be lawyers. What's really way cool is that during all those years at high school, regular college, lawyer college, and even now when they're pretty old, not that they're geezers or nothing even close, they've stayed sweethearts to each other. Parents that are pretty old can still be sweethearts to each other you know; it's not just for young people.

Even though Mom and Dad are pretty old now, they still work as lawyers. Every day except Sunday, they go to their office, way uptown on the top floor of a tall skyscraper. Both of their names are printed on one of those glass doors that you can't see through, right across from where you get off the elevator. One of the men that works the elevators is Charlie. He's a real nice guy, and he talks to me a lot.

A lady that's a receptionist sits at a desk behind the glass door. Her job is to answer the telephone and decide when it's time for the people that come for an appointment to go in for their talk with Mom and Dad. After their talk, Mom and Dad send a bill to the people that tells them how much money they owe. By the way, Charlie likes to tell me jokes. Once he said his job had a lot of ups and downs. I figured it out pretty quick. Think it over in your mind for a second or two, and you'll get it, too.

I think Mom and Dad are very good at being lawyers. They must be pretty near the best lawyers in the whole city, 'cause they sure make a lot of money. I would say they make thousands and thousands of dollars, maybe even a million dollars. I never figured out exactly why, but sometimes, when my dad is talking about all his money, he calls it dinero, buckeroos, or even clams.

By the way, no matter how tall a building is, it could never really scrape the sky, 'cause the sky doesn't have a top to it. It just keeps on going up forever and ever, way higher than outer space even. I'm thinking that maybe the sky really does have a top to it somewhere, but spacemen just haven't discovered it yet. Until they do, what goes up always comes down. Dad always says that, too. He never told me where he learned it, but it probably wasn't from his football coach would be my guess.

Anyway, my parents made enough money to buy this big house in a fancy suburb. It's the house where I grew up. They bought some real nice modern style furniture for all of the rooms. The house has a living room, dining room, family room, library, and den on the first floor. Most of the bedrooms are on the second floor, and underneath everything is where the basement is. It's the kind of basement that's all finished up with carpets on the floor and panels on the walls. Sometimes my parents invite some friends to come over, and they have parties down there. That way the rest of the house doesn't get too worn out or used up even.

An attic on the top floor is where my room was. It was a nice room to have all for myself, 'cause it was very big and it had lots of windows for the sun and moon to shine in. I took good care of my room, too. I don't like a messy room, 'cause it makes me sort of nervous. Fact is, I really hate it when there's any mess around. Dad taught me there's a right place for everything and everything should be in the right place, so that's how I kept my room. I've heard a lot of guys don't keep their rooms too tidy, but for me, neat and clean is the only way to be, all right.

Mom and Dad belong to a country club where they go to play golf and tennis and swim and eat supper with a lot of other pretty old people from the neighborhood that have a lot of dinero and big houses, too. I never figured out why it's called a country club, 'cause it's right here in the same suburb where we live. I mean, if the club was somewhere way out in the country, I would understand it better is what I'm saying.

Mom and Dad sure take a lot of vacation trips, too. They've gone on trips to the Grand Canyon and Las Vegas and other places all over the United States of America, and they go on boats and airplanes to foreign countries like France and Germany and Italy. Those are some foreign countries way on the other side of the Atlantic Ocean. I never figured out exactly why, but Dad calls it the "Big Pond."

It's easy to tell how far away Mom and Dad go by looking at the globe of the world in the den. It's one of those globes of the world that lights up in the dark. Dad leaves it on at night just in case someone wakes up from being hungry and wants to go to the kitchen for a snack without bumping into any modern style furniture. You can never tell when you might stub your toe on a chair or something and not be able to fall back asleep, 'cause it hurts too much.

When I was just a kid, Dad noticed I was very good at maps, almost the opposite of being very bad at reading, I guess you could say. I'm not exactly sure, or even a little bit sure, of why it is, but alls I have to do is look at a map one time and I have a perfect picture of it that stays in my head forever. The pictures are in Technicolor, too.

A lot of times Dad and me play a game with a map that shows the streets around where we live. He points to a place on the map, and, in a flash, I tell him how to get there; you know, like what streets to take and whether to turn left or right. I just close my eyes and there it is, easy as pie for me to see, and I never forget it, neither. I've been thinking that maybe everyone, even guys like me with Down syndrome, has one special thing they're very good at, and I guess that maps must be my special thing. I been wondering what's so easy about pie, too.

Mom and Dad always brought me cool presents when they came home from their trips. A few times it was a T-shirt with some French or Italian words on it, but most of the time it was a picture book. I usually liked the book better than the shirt, 'cause I could learn a lot of stuff from it. That's how I learned a lot about Paris, which is the biggest city in France. The people that live there say "wee" when they mean yes and "mercy" when they mean thank you. 'Course, they can say whatever they want, except why not just say yes and thank you in the first place when that's what you mean? There's this world famous tower in Paris where folks go to look out over the whole city. I'd sure like to climb to the top of that tower some day, even though I usually get that funny feeling in my knees that you get when you're way up high, looking over a ledge of a tower and thinking about falling off.

There's this big museum in Paris, France, too. I forget the name of it, but it's so big it takes up a whole block. Inside, there's a lot of statues of famous dead people and a lot of art pictures, too. In one of the books Mom and Dad brought home for my present, there's a picture of this French beauty queen whose name is Mona Lisa. Mona Lisa is so famous that nobody ever has to say her last name. I think she must be dead by now, but I'm not exactly sure how she died. Maybe she just got old and died while she was sleeping in her bed, which isn't a bad way to die, when you think about it.

I forget the name of the guy that painted Mona Lisa too, some guy from Italy I think, but I sure like looking at Mona's beautiful face in my picture book. She looks peaceful and she's almost smiling, but not quite. Her picture is way more beautiful than this other guy's art pictures of a bunch of men and women with their faces split in two and their eyeballs and noses sticking out from the wrong places. If you ask me, I think that other guy must of been drinking way too much pure booze when he drew up those pictures. Split faces. What was the matter with him? And, whoever decided his pictures were good enough to be hanging on the walls of a famous museum must of been drinking some of the same booze. Boy oh boy.

When my parents went on trips, I stayed home with Mamie and Winifred. They're the maids that live at the house. Actually, Mamie is the maid and Winifred is the cook. We call her Winnie. She's a big, fat lady, 'cause she likes to eat what she cooks so much. She's nice, though. I've noticed there are a lot of fat people that are nice. Maybe some of them aren't so nice, but most of them are. 'Course, there are a lot of skinny people that are nice, too. Come to think of it, if a person is fat or skinny, or even somewhere in between, like medium, probably has nothing to do with if they're nice or not. And, it doesn't matter if you have pimples, neither. That's what I think, all right.

Seeing that they were so busy with their lawyer work, it wasn't until Mom was exactly 40 or 42 years old that her and Dad decided they wanted to have a baby. Since Mom was already pretty old at the time, I guess older than most women that decide they want to have a baby for the first time, her doctor said she should have a special test that would tell if I was growing just like I was supposed to inside of her. If the test showed that I was a mongoloid or had some other kind of bad problem that wasn't normal and couldn't be fixed, the doctor could stop me from getting born. I'm not sure exactly how a doctor stops a baby from getting born, but I've heard they can do that. It's called an abortion.

Mom and Dad wanted to have a baby no matter what, so they decided to skip the test. Sometimes I wonder if they might be sorry Mom didn't go ahead with the test. Sometimes I'm sorry she didn't go ahead with the test. Then, I'd be an abortion, which I guess is like being nobody at all, or at least I wouldn't be a guy with Down syndrome. Who knows? I might even be an attorney that has a ton of clams and his own private receptionist to answer the telephone. Or, at least I might be a kid in school that made the honor roll all the time. You can never tell who you would turn out to be if you didn't turn out to be you. That's just common sense.

It wasn't very long after I was born, maybe just a couple of hours, that the doctor told my parents I was a mongoloid. Mom told me they put me in a room all by myself at the hospital, and, at first, they didn't even bring me in to meet her and Dad. The doctor thought it would be better for everyone that way. He told my parents he knew of a nice place for me to live where good and kind people would take care of me. It's called an institution.

The doctor told Mom and Dad they should put me in that institution place right away, before we started to get to know each other. I guess that if you don't start getting to know someone like your mom and dad, then you're never going to miss them, and maybe they will never get around to missing you, neither. It's like everyone just lives happily ever after, 'cause nobody gets too sad from missing anyone.

'Course, Mom and Dad didn't do what the doctor told them to. They decided to keep me and get to know me. They took me home from the hospital where I was born, so I never went to that institution. I'm sure glad about that. "There's no place like home, even though it's humble." That's what Dad always says, 'specially after him and Mom come home from one of their long trips across the Big Pond.

Before I moved to this new house, I used to worry about where I would live when my mom and dad died and went to heaven above. If I had a brother or sister, I could of lived with one of them, but Mom and Dad didn't have anymore babies after me. I thought about staying with Winnie and Mamie, but they're pretty old, too. Like I said, I used to worry about it a lot. I mean, a guy always wants to know where he's going to be and who he's going to be living with, 'specially if they're not going to be his mom and dad.

Dad says I was almost five years old before I started to talk. You probably know that most kids are already talking full speed ahead by then, but I've usually been slower to do things than most kids. That's how it was, not just for talking, but for sitting up, rolling over, crawling, and then walking and running, too. Dad would get down on the floor with me and do all kinds of exercises to make my muscles strong enough for walking and running, but even so, it took me a very long time to stand up and get moving. He said it was a lot like that little kid story where the slow turtle wins a running race against the fast rabbit, except this time, the fast rabbit never took a nap and the slow turtle (me) never caught up.

About the same time that I finally started to talk, I started to hear about going to school. At first, I really didn't know what school was, except a place your mom takes you and leaves you with a teacher and some other kids to learn stuff during the day until it's time for you to come back to your humble home again after school is over each day. The time that I started going to school is when I really started to know that I was pretty different from most of the other kids. Boy oh boy; I guess I stuck out like a sore thumb, not that I ever had one. I had a sore pinkie finger once though, after Mom slammed a door on it. It was an accident that she didn't mean to do on purpose.

The other kids that lived in my neighborhood went to the grade school just a few blocks from our house. Their grade school was almost brand new, and it had a playground that was way cool with swings, slides, and those monkey bars that you climb all over and fall off of if you're not too careful. There's a big, open field around it for playing games and sports, too. Except for a few of the kids that lived a little too far away and got to ride on the big yellow school bus, they all walked right past my house every morning on their way to grade school and every afternoon on their way back home.

I thought that when I started going to school, I would just walk right along with the neighbor kids. But, I couldn't go to the same school as the other kids. Instead, I went to school at a church where there was a classroom in the basement for me and some other trainables. There were no swings or slides or playgrounds outside, neither. I did get to ride on a yellow school bus, but it was smaller than the regular one, 'cause it only had seats for exactly 12 or 14 kids, and no standing was allowed. About four or five of those kids looked just like me. We looked like we were all brothers and sisters, even twins, with all those slanty eyes, wide noses, and hands that were missing two creases.

Mom and Dad tried their best to find fun things for me to do after school and on Saturday and Sunday. The doctor said I could play some sports if I didn't strain myself too much, so they signed me up for soccer, baseball, and swimming. I wasn't much good at any of those sports, at least compared to the other kids my age. Swimming was my worst, but I was pretty bad at soccer and baseball, too. You have to run fast as a whistle when you play sports, and I never could run very fast. A trot is usually as fast as I go, 'cause my legs start to hurt and I run out of air pretty quick.

The other kids knew I couldn't run so fast and I wasn't so good at sports. When there were games in the neighborhood, nobody asked me to play unless they needed someone to chase after a ball or to be the finish line in a race or something like that. You only have to trot when you chase after a ball, and when you're the finish line in a race, you don't get tired and out of air, 'cause you're not supposed to move at all.

Once, the neighbor kids let me be second base in their baseball game. It wasn't much fun just standing there for the whole game and watching guys run past me to third base. My job was to just be quiet and not move, not even an inch, until the game was over. I never once got a turn to bat or a chance to catch the ball. I almost forgot to tell you that first base was the crabapple tree and third base was the Miller's garbage can.

After a while, the only boy from the neighborhood that played with me was Billy. I'll tell you about him, 'cause he was my best friend until he moved pretty far away. Fact is, he was my only friend back in those days. My parents and Billy's mom and dad were good friends, too. They all went to the same high school and college. Billy's parents lived right across the street from us, and they visited with my parents all the time. They went to movies, out to supper, and even went on vacation trips with Mom and Dad.

Billy and me were born at the same hospital. He's a year older, 'cause he was born first. Whoever is born first is the oldest; that's how it works. Even though Billy was older than me, you could say we grew up together from the time we were very little kids. It's just that after a while, Billy grew up much faster than me. I tried my best to keep up with him, but then I just knew he was a faster grower.

He was one of those handsome type of guys too, the type of guy that doesn't mind looking at himself in a mirror. He had a big wave in the front of his hair that he liked to comb a lot to make it look just right. He was tall and didn't stoop over too much, and he had big round eyes and the right sized tongue, without any cracks on the top of it that I ever noticed. In the summer, he hardly ever wore a shirt, 'cause he had a good built, not too fat and not too skinny. And, he didn't mind walking around barefoot, neither. He looked a lot more handsome than me all right, plum handsome you could say, but that didn't stop him from being my best friend.

What a good friend he was. We hung out together so much that he could understand the words I said with hardly no trouble at all. After Dad got plum tuckered and gave up, Billy finally taught me how to ride my two-wheeler. Boy oh boy; he just kept at it, holding me up and running alongside of me, until I learned how to balance myself and stopped falling off every single time. Billy cheered for me the first time I made it to the end of the block. Then he hugged me and patted me on the back. Most kids, except your best friend, usually don't cheer for you or give you pats on your back or hug you too much.

Billy and me did a lot of other things together, too. We took hikes through the woods, went fishing, had sleepovers, and dressed up for Halloween. When he came back from his Boy Scout meetings, he would come right over to my house and show me everything he learned, like how to tie special kinds of knots in a rope or how to find out where you were if you ever got lost in the woods or some other scary place like that. I hardly ever got lost though, 'cause I was so good at maps.

Like I said, I wasn't good at sports like Billy was, but I would go to his football, baseball, and hockey games with our dads, and I would cheer for him and give him pats on the back and hugs, even if his team lost the game. When we got a little older, Billy asked me to stop hugging him so much. That was OK; I mean, older guys don't usually want to hug other guys so much. I kept on going to his games though, even after my dad didn't want to go anymore. That's the kind of guy I am.

When Billy got to be a teenager, a lot of girls started coming over to his house. When you have Down syndrome, girls hardly ever come over to your house. They usually don't like you too much, even before they get to know you. At least, that's how the girls were that came to my best friend Billy's house. I heard them ask him why he always hung around with me, and I heard them use words like "retard" and "mental." I saw them make funny faces and hang their tongues out of their mouths, too. That used to hurt my feelings a lot. My friend Billy always stuck up for me. He told those girls to stop doing those things, and after a while, they usually did. They still didn't like me, though.

A lot of times, after Billy's girlfriends left, he would come over to my house just to hang around and have a talk. He told me all kinds of stuff about how they played with his hair, kissed on the lips, stuck their tongues into each other's mouths, and touched each other in different places. He even told me what a boner was. I pretended it was way cool, but I really didn't understand it that much at the time. Now I do, though. I know all about that kind of sexy stuff. You could ask me anything.

Fact is, nobody ever kisses me on the lips except my old Aunt Shirley, and her lips are usually pretty wet from spit. She has a lot of hair above her lips too, almost like a guy that forgot to shave off his whiskers for about a week or two. And, sometimes she smells of booze or onions. It could be garlic, but I think it's onions. About the only good thing you could say about kissing Aunt Shirley is that it doesn't last nearly as long an earache. You could say that kissing Aunt Shirley is something I'm not too crazy about, all right.

Come to think about it, I wouldn't mind kissing some other grownup girl on the lips, though. I'm not too sure about the tongue part, but I would probably give it a try if I ever had the chance. Maybe I'd let the girl stick her tongue in first, just to see if she knew about it and wanted to try it out. That would be good manners, I think. By the way, when two people kiss and they put their tongues into each other's mouths, it called a French kiss. I guess some guy from Paris, France and his girlfriend must of invented it and showed other people how to do it before they ate any onions or garlic. After that, people from all over the world that weren't even from France were happy to give it a try.

A little while later, Billy's dad got a new job, and their family moved to another suburb that was pretty far away, almost on the edge of the Pacific Ocean. Dad showed me where it was on a map of the United States of America, and he told me that if you flew on the fastest jet airplane there is, it would still take almost four hours to get there, even if the plane was right on time. If you drove in a car, it might take as long as five or six days, 'cause you have to sleep at night on a long car trip. Or, I suppose you could sleep during the day and drive at night. Either way, it was just as far away though, exactly nine states to the left, if you fly as straight as a crow, like Dad says all the time.

I was very sad when my best friend Billy moved away. Truth is, I cried like crazy, but I didn't let anyone see me. Billy said he would write me letters, and he did for a while. I was plenty happy when Mom read the letters Billy wrote me. Then, she would write down what I told her to say back to Billy and give my letter to the postman, after I licked the stamp and stuck it on my letter, of course.

I got to thinking it would be way cool if the people that work at the Post Office or wherever they make stamps would put some good tasting stuff on the back of them; you know, the part that you lick just before you stick it on your envelope and send away your letter. That way you would come away with a nice taste of chocolate or strawberry or even well-done steak or lobster tail on your tongue instead of what you get now, which doesn't taste too good, 'cause it's kind of bitter. I'm going to tell the postman about my idea, just to see what he says. He might like my idea. You can never tell when a postman might like your idea. By the way, I've seen lots of crows that fly crooked, so I'm not exactly sure why Dad says that all the time.

Anyway, about a couple of years after they moved near the edge of the Pacific Ocean, Billy and his mom and dad came back to our suburb for a visit. I remember how excited I was while I was waiting for my best friend to come over and hang around with me like he used to. Boy oh boy; I bet I went to the bathroom at least around six or eight times while I was waiting for Billy that afternoon. When I get excited like that, I usually have to go to the bathroom a lot. Dad told me it's normal.

When Billy finally got to my house, was I ever surprised at how tall he was. I mean, I had to bend my neck almost all the way back just to see his face. We started to talk about stuff from when we were little kids, but it was hard, almost like we didn't know each other as

31

good as we used to. Billy smiled a little when I showed him I could still make the knots he taught me. So, it's not like we were perfect strangers or nothing, but it just didn't seem to be the same between us like it used to be in the good old days.

Billy went away to college after a while, and he stopped sending me letters. Mom and Dad told me that when you go to college, you get very busy with all the hard books your professors make you read, so you might not have much time for writing letters to a guy that used to be your friend. It makes me sad when I think about it, but I guess friends usually don't last forever. Even best ones. When you're a grownup guy, you just have to get used to those kinds of things and stop crying so much. It's better to get busy doing something else, maybe clean up your room or straighten out your closet or anything else you can think of to get your mind off why you're crying. Professors are the same as teachers, except they teach in a university, which is another word for a college.

I went to grade school in the same church basement until it was time for me to graduate and go to high school. Then I went to a bigger church that was on the other side of the suburb where we lived. That church had a basement, too. Some of the same kids I went to school with since first grade came to the bigger church with me. And, we met a lot of new kids that came from their own suburbs, too. I'd say there must of been exactly around a hundred of us all together going to high school at the bigger church, and I'm telling you, it was some kind of a group all right. You should of seen them. Boy oh boy.

There were a lot of kids with Down syndrome like me, and there were a lot of kids that weren't like me. Some of them had to sit in wheelchairs with their skinny legs all wasted away from not standing up and walking around on them. If you don't use it, you lose it. Dad always says that, too.

A couple of kids couldn't move their arms neither, but they could still make their wheelchairs go back and forth, in different directions, by breathing into a tube that was attached to their wheels. Now, I'm not saying I ever figured out exactly how those wheelchair tubes worked, but I thought it was way cool to be able to make your chair move around like that, just by breathing in and out.

I could hardly stop from staring at those kids, even though Mom and Dad always taught me it's not good manners to stare at a person that happens to be a cripple. If you want to have good manners, you should just smile and say hello, try to be nice, and wait for a crippled person to ask you for help if he wants any, or she wants any if the crippled person is a girl. That's the way not to hurt anyone's feelings, which you never want to do to a person, whether that person is crippled or not.

Fact is, I always wanted to have a turn on one of those wheelchairs and try breathing into a tube myself, but I never worked up enough nerve to ask. And, come to think of it, even if I had the nerve to ask, where would I put the crippled kid when I was using his chair? It's not like they have a second chair, like a spare, that they carry around to use when someone wants to take a test drive in their first one. Also, it's probably not such a good idea to breathe into someone else's wheelchair tube with all the germs and diseases that a lot of guys might be carrying around on them. You can never tell what you could catch, although I doubt if it would be an earache.

Some of the other kids could walk pretty good if they used a cane or crutches, and some were very good at walking, even running, without needing a cane or crutches at all. A couple of them had giant size heads with eyes that sort of popped out under their thick glasses. Some others had tiny little heads, and they couldn't talk at all, just make sort of grunting noises that usually didn't sound too good.

This girl Audrey had a doozy of a scar on her head, 'cause she had about half of her brains taken out. I don't know why a girl would ever need to have half of her brains taken out, but that's what I heard. Honest to God. I guess she's only about half as smart as she used to be, and it could be that she wasn't all that smart to begin with. Anyway, after meeting my new classmates in high school, I didn't mind looking at myself in the mirror all that much. At least, for a while. Boy oh boy; they were some bunch, all right.

If you think my classmates didn't look so terrific, the way they acted wasn't so great, neither. I'm telling you they acted different enough to get your attention right quick. You could even say they acted peculiar, which is another word for very strange. What I'm saying is a lot of my classmates did stuff I never forgot, and I still can't figure out to this day. I mean, one morning Victor banged his head so hard on the bus window that he cracked the glass. After he quieted down, he just sat there rocking back and forth in his seat, saying all kinds of real nasty swear words, and rubbing his head the rest of the way to school.

The next day, and every other day after that, Victor had to wear a football helmet all the time so he wouldn't hurt his head if he took to banging it on a window again or maybe even against a brick wall, which is so hard you can't break it, at least with your head. Some of the kids, the ones that could talk, started calling him Jim Brown. But, Victor didn't pay any attention to that. He just kept on rocking and swearing. It could be that Victor didn't even know that Jim Brown was a great football player, maybe the greatest that ever lived since grownup guys started playing football. So, most people know who he is, except for Victor, maybe.

Carmella was a girl that had the very bad habit of biting on her fingers and hands. She would go at it, just gnawing away like crazy with her teeth that I don't think she brushed too often, 'cause they looked sort of half way between green and yellow to me. They came in all different sizes and were crooked, too, instead of matching up nice and straight like normal teeth are supposed to do.

All the time she was doing her gnawing, she'd be making these slurping sounds, until she started to bleed all over her clothes and the kid sitting next to her. After that, the teachers tied mittens on her hands, even on warm days in the springtime of the year. But, that didn't stop Carmella. She kept on gnawing, right through her mittens. When her teeth got tired, she would wave her hands back and forth really fast in front of her eyeballs and giggle like some kind of a wicked witch out west that was in the Wizard of Odds or some other movie like that I sort of remember.

It's pretty hard to talk to a girl when she's doing that kind of strange stuff. Pretty soon, kids stopped trying to talk to Carmella at all and even stopped sitting next to her. You can't really blame them. I mean, it's not that Carmella was a bad person or smelled bad from body odor or nothing, but nobody wants to get to high school with someone else's blood all over their shirt and pants. Mamie wouldn't like it when you got home, neither. I mean, she has enough dirty laundry to do already without having to mess with your bloody shirts and pants.

There was this kid Vladimir, too. I think he was born in one of those foreign countries across the ocean that Mom and Dad go to on one of their many vacation trips, but wherever he came from, he was pretty strange, too. He could hardly see, even though he wore the thickest glasses you ever saw, thick as the glass on top of one of those modern style coffee tables in your living room. And, I don't think Vladimir could talk the English language; at least, he never did that I could hear. On the school bus every day, he would mostly just hum some musical tunes and pick his nose a lot. He did loud belches, too, 'specially when big trucks or other busses drove by.

What Vladimir could do besides pick and belch was play the piano. Fact is, he was as good at playing the piano as I was at maps. Like Dad says, Vladimir could really "tickle the old ivories." Boy oh boy, it was really something to see, or I guess something to hear would be a better way to put it.

Whichever way you want to put it, the teacher would play a song on the record player only one time, and I'm talking about one of those classical tunes that you never heard even once before in your whole life on the radio or TV, and Vladimir could play it right back perfectly, with both hands, and with no mistakes at all, at least that I could tell. He'd just be sitting there at the piano, smiling this wide grin, moving his head back and forth, doing a belch now and then, and all the time playing his perfect classical tunes. Vladimir couldn't do much else besides play the piano, though. I know for a fact that he still needed help to tie his shoestrings, zip his zipper, button his buttons, and blow his nose, for example. And his desk; boy oh boy, what a mess. I don't know how anyone could stand having a desk as messy as Vladimir's. It looked like a hurricane or some other kind of giant windstorm like a tornado blew right through it. *Vrroom.*

A couple of times, Vladimir wet his pants while he was playing the piano. His pee was making a fair sized puddle on the floor, and some of the other kids were laughing about it. It didn't bother Vladimir though, 'cause he kept right on playing until the end of his tune, like nothing was happening at all. Like I said, he sure was a strange one, all right. By the way, I think playing the piano is a good thing to be able to do; I mean, I wouldn't mind being able to tickle some of the old ivories myself, but not if I had to be as strange as my classmate Vladimir.

I used to think the strangest of all my classmates was Penelope. Mostly, I called her Penny for a nickname. I probably shouldn't of, 'cause when you think about it, Penny is sort of a little girl's name in the same way that Dicky is a little boy's name, and I didn't want to hurt her feelings or nothing. I kept reminding myself to call her by her real name, even though Penelope isn't any kind of name I ever liked that much. And anyway, it really didn't matter if I called her Penelope or Penny, 'cause she would never talk to me anyway, no matter what name I tried. Fact is, she would never even look at me, except sometimes out of the sides of her eyeballs.

Maybe some of the other kids at school didn't think Penny was the strangest of all our classmates; I mean, some of them might of thought Vladimir or Carmella was the strangest kid out of our group of pretty strange kids. I'll tell you some things about Penny, and maybe you could decide for yourself. Just go ahead, 'cause Dad taught me that everyone gets to have their own opinion, even if it's not the same as his or mine.

So like I was saying, Penny never talked to me. Even if I went right up close to her and asked her, in my best manners and with a nice quiet voice, how she was feeling or if everything was cool or something like that, she just wouldn't answer me. If I stuck out my hand for a shake or asked if I could help carry her books, she didn't pay any attention to me, neither. It was like I wasn't even there, indivisible you could say, even though I was standing right next to her. Or, if I was visible, which would mean she could see me, she acted like I wasn't even a person, but more like a wall or maybe a coffee table or a kitchen sink.

At first, I thought Penny was afraid of me or didn't like me for some reason, but after a while, I noticed that she didn't talk to anyone else, neither. I got to thinking that maybe she was just terrible bashful, which is another word for shy. Then I thought that maybe she had some awful disease of the mouth when she was still a little girl and a doctor that knows about mouths had to take her tongue out, and so that's why she couldn't talk, even if she wanted to.

Honest. I really thought Penny didn't have a tongue until one morning on the school bus, I happened to take a quick peek over to where she was sitting. During my peek, which turned out not to be such a quick one, I saw her lean forward in her seat and stick her tongue out. Then, she licked the silver handle that sticks up from the top of the seat. It's that handle that you're supposed to grab on to so you don't fall down if you break the rules and stand up while the bus is still moving.

Another thing that was pretty strange about Penny was that she never smiled, at least that I ever saw. Even guys like me with slanty eyes that turn into slits can't help but smile once in a while. I mean, you may hear a dirty joke or see something funny on TV or think about the time your teacher farted by mistake in class, and so you've just got to smile or even laugh out loud. You can't help but giggle is what I'm saying. But not Penny. She just sat there all day long, mostly twirling her charm bracelet over and over in front of her eyeballs like she was one of those machines I think you call a robot or a mechanical man. I never heard anyone say mechanical woman, which is what Penny would be called, of course.

One time on the way to school, our bus passed some construction guys that were fixing up holes in the street. A couple of those guys were using those air hammers, I think you call them. They make a real loud racket while they're busting up the street. It was loud enough to wake up the dead, like Dad always says when he hears something making a real loud racket.

When Penny heard all that noise, it was like she had a fit, although I think panic would be a better word for it. She put her hands over her ears and squeezed real tight, and she had this scared look in her eyes like something terrible was happening. She did the same thing when a fire engine went by and the siren was going off. It was almost like someone was beating her up or she was just waking up from a terrible bad dream of some kind. That's how scared she looked. Honest.

Penny held her nose a lot of times, too. We would be riding along on the school bus, and everything seemed fine to me. But, the next thing you know, there she goes again, all of a sudden squeezing her nose shut with her fingers like she smelled something rotten or maybe even some skunk smell in the air. 'Course, I took a whiff or two to find out what it was that was bothering her, but I didn't smell a darn thing, at least nothing that smelled bad.

Now, the strange thing was that in a minute or two, the bus always came to one of those tar wagons or a garbage truck or some smoke that was blowing over from a factory or something else that was stinking up the air. You could bet all your money on it. It's like Penny had a sniffer as powerful as one of those police dogs the sheriff and his posse use to catch some bad guys that just broke out of jail or robbed the bank. Bloodhounds, I think you call those dogs, even though smellhounds would be a much better name, seems to me.

The last thing I want to tell you about Penny, at least for now, is that she is the most beautiful girl I've ever seen in my whole life. Her hair is yellow and it hangs down to the middle of her back. She has a perfect, small nose that doesn't take up too much room on her face, and her eyes are colored the kind of blue you can see when you look up at the sky on a summer day and there's no clouds. The skin on her face doesn't have any pimple scars, so it looks real smooth, and it's probably soft to feel if you ever got a chance to touch your fingers on her cheeks. 'Course, I've never seen Penny's teeth, 'cause she never talks or smiles, but I would bet you anything that they're real straight and pure white instead of crooked and ugly 'cause they're half way between yellow and green.

Penny is so beautiful that whenever I saw her, I always got this weird feeling in my stomach. It's one of those hard feelings to tell you about except it's not any kind of pain or ache. It's more of a funny feeling, almost like your stomach is turning over inside of you for a second or two. Maybe you get that feeling in your stomach sometimes, like when you see a girl that looks like an angel. The funny feeling usually goes away pretty quick, and when it does, you can't make it come back, even if you want to.

Getting back to high school, most of the subjects we had were the same subjects we had in grade school. The truth is I was bored stiff most of the time. There were a few days that I even fell sound asleep, right there at my desk. Or, if I wasn't sleeping, I was busy daydreaming and not listening to one word teacher was saying. I bet you would fall asleep or stop listening to your teacher too, if most of what you heard in school was the same old stuff, year after year, over and over and over again.

I'm telling you that it doesn't take more than two or three times before you get sleepy when teacher starts talking about community helpers like the brave fireman and the friendly policeman again. Learning how to make change for a dollar, 'specially when you can't even use real money, will get you to yawning pretty quick, too. But, most boring of all was learning about the holidays. I mean, how many times can you hear about Christopher Columbus and his three boats on the way to discover the United States of America, about George Washington that never told a lie about a cherry tree, and about the Pilgrims that ate a Thanksgiving dinner of wild turkey and corn on the cob with some friendly Indians before the sandman catches you and you're dozing off into dreamland again?

When we weren't learning that kind of stuff over and over again, we learned about habits of good grooming all the time; you know, like how important it is to take a shower or bath every day, to brush your teeth after you eat, to keep your hair combed, to put on clean underwear, to wear neat and clean clothes, to stop picking at your pimples, and to put deodorant under your armpits. Fact is, that stuff made me just as sleepy as talking about Christopher Columbus, 'cause

I already had good grooming habits. When you're the kind of guy that likes a neat and clean room of his own, chances are you're going to keep yourself neat and clean, too. I been wondering why people always get stiff when they get bored.

There was one subject in high school when I never fell asleep, though. It was in sex education class. Boy oh boy; I never got even a little bit sleepy in that class, and if I was sleepy when I got there, I woke up quick as flash, just as soon as teacher started talking about that stuff. Mr. Farber, the gym teacher, taught the boys all about sex, and Mrs. Collins, the guidance counselor, taught the girls all about sex.

I guess the teachers thought it wouldn't be a good idea to teach sexy things to the boys and girls all together at the same time, except when you think about it, men and women in the real world that are finished going to high school are supposed to do sexy things with each other at the same time. I mean, from what I learned in sex education class and from my dad and my best friend Billy too, unless men and women do sexy things together, at the same time, after a while, there won't be enough boys and girls to have a sex education class in high school. I figured that out all by myself. Like I said, sometimes I have smart thoughts, just like other grownups that don't have Down syndrome.

'Course, one of the things I learned in sex education class was how a man and a woman make a baby in the first place. We learned that right after learning the grownup names for a man and a woman's private parts, not that I didn't already know them from some private talks I had with my dad. Mr. Farber had this black and white movie that showed us how the man's sperms shoot out of his penis (Billy called his a wanger most of the time) and swim around in the woman's vagina looking for one of her ovums to latch on to.

There's thousands of them, maybe even millions of those sperms, all swimming around in different directions as fast as they can, trying to beat the other sperms, it looked like to me. It's like a swimming race, and the prize for the sperm that swims the fastest is an ovum, which is another word for egg. Then, when the winner gets his ovum, he grabs ahold of it real tight, and pretty soon the sperm and the ovum begin to divide up and make the different parts of a baby, like the head, and the brain, the stomach, the eyes, the elbows, and the toenails.

Just nine months later, here comes another little kid into the world, with exactly the right amount of parts, as well as a nice little wanger, if it's a boy of course, all attached exactly to where they're supposed to be. I mean, you get a whole, brand new baby that begins from just one sperm and one ovum. Now, that's way cool, you have to admit.

I learned a couple of other interesting things in sex education class, too. I must admit I don't understand these other things as good as I should, but I'll try my best to explain them anyway. These are some things about how I got to be me; you know, first a little kid that was a mongoloid and now a grownup guy with Down syndrome. So here I go trying to explain these other interesting things.

Most of the time, when people have more of something, like more brains or more money or more hair than other people, they think it's a good thing, and they like it. I mean, you never hear people wish they were less smart or less rich or they had less hair, except maybe if it's a woman like my Aunt Shirley, the one with too much fuzz growing over her lips. Sometimes, though, it's better to have exactly the same amount of something that other people have. Not more and not less, but exactly the same amount of something that other people have.

Fact is, I'm not exactly sure what chromozones even are except these real tiny things that live inside your body. Mr. Farber told us you get them from your parents when they make you, and they're so small that they don't even show up on an X-ray picture. There's no way you can even tell they're in there without the most powerful telescope. But, what I do know for sure is that chromozones are something you don't want to have more of than other people.

Mr. Farber explained that you're supposed to have exactly 46 of those chromozones in every part of your body. Not 45 or 47, but exactly 46. My classmates and me that have Down syndrome all have one chromozone too many. It's that one extra one that somehow makes us all look like we belong to the same family and have a lot of problems like bad hearts and lungs and ear infections and makes it harder for us to learn to read and write. I don't think those extra chromozones have anything to do with getting acmes, 'cause I've seen a lot of kids with juicy pimples on their cheeks that don't have Down syndrome.

Like I already told you, I usually don't like to talk out loud too much, but when Mr. Farber got done explaining all that chromozone stuff to us in sex education class, I went right ahead and asked him why the doctors just don't take out the extra ones. I mean, everyone knows that doctors learn how to take stuff out when they go to doctor's college. They can take out what's called a tumor when a person has a bad sickness like cancer of the brain or take out an appendix that's causing a person to have a bad bellyache. So why not take out those extra chromozones if they're going to cause you so many problems, I wanted to know?

Mr. Farber said that so far that isn't possible and that once a person has those extra chromozones, he's going to have them forever, or at least until he dies. Teacher said that maybe in some future years down the road a piece when doctors understand more and more about Down syndrome, they might be able to fix it up or even stop it from happening in the first place. I think that will be a very good thing for guys that have Down syndrome in some future years, but for the time being, like right now this very second, it sure doesn't help me, not even one little bit. Not even a tad or a smidgen, which are words Dad says when he means a little bit. By the way, doctors know how to put things in too, like a new kidney or a new liver if one of your old ones happens to break down and stop working too good.

So anyway, once you have Down syndrome, it looks like you're stuck with it until you die and go to heaven above. As long as I got on the subject, Dad told me there are some people that don't believe in heaven. They think you don't go anywhere after you die. It's like the lights go out and you just aren't anymore. 'Course, there's no way of knowing for sure, 'cause Dad said nobody has ever come back from heaven yet to tell us what it's like up there or even if there is anything up there at all except empty sky with no top to scrape. Fact is, I'm going to keep on believing there is a heaven anyway, 'cause I think everyone that gets to go there gets to be perfect. What I'm saying is that I think nobody that goes to heaven has Down syndrome. On the way up there you get fixed. God finally takes out your extra chromozones and you're normal, in a flash, just like that. I mean, you're probably reading all kinds of hard books, just like Billy reads at college, even before you land up there and have a nice howdy do with your first angel. That's what I think, all right.

There was one more interesting thing Mr. Farber told us about guys with Down syndrome. At first, I didn't believe him, but I asked Mom and Dad about it at home, and they told me the same thing. After that, I believed what teacher told us. When your mom and dad tell you the very same thing that your teacher tells you, the chances are pretty good that they're all telling you the truth.

What Mr. Farber said is that if you're a grownup guy with Down syndrome like me, you can't make any babies of your own. You can go ahead and do sexy things with a woman all right, together at the same time and all that, but when you're done with it, no matter how hard you try or how many times you try, or which of the many positions you're in, there's never going to be a baby of any kind coming into the world nine months later.

At first, when I found out about not being able to make a baby of my own, it bothered me some. I got to thinking about why I couldn't make a baby. It's not that I was thinking it would be so great to have a baby of my own, with the diapers you have to change, all the crying they do, and all the other stuff you have to do to take care of them, but I was still curious to know why I couldn't make one.

Fact is, I was getting pretty tired of finding out about stuff I couldn't do. First I couldn't walk when I was supposed to, and then I couldn't talk like I was supposed to, and then I couldn't play sports too good, and then I couldn't go to a regular school, and then I couldn't read or write. That's a whole lot of things I couldn't do like other guys, and then I found out I couldn't make any babies, neither. Boy oh boy. Sometimes things don't work out too fair in this world of ours. And that's the honest to God truth, all right.

For a while, I didn't know if I should ask my dad or Mr. Farber to explain the reason I couldn't make a baby. I was real embarrassed to talk about it with anyone, 'cause talking about sexy things like making babies is sort of a secret, or you could say a private thing that a person usually doesn't bring up too often, even if that person talks perfectly clear.

And, another reason I was embarrassed to talk about it, to tell you the truth, is 'cause at first I thought that maybe I couldn't make a baby 'cause of my wanger, which happens to be very small, at least compared to my dad's or my best friend Billy's or Mr. Farber's, although I can't be too sure about the size of teacher's wanger.

I finally decided not to ask my dad or Mr. Farber. Instead, when I was all alone with my doctor, the one that does regular check ups, I asked him to explain why I couldn't make a baby. My doctor told me that it had nothing to do with the extra small size of my penis. Instead, he said that guys with Down syndrome usually don't have enough sperms inside of them, and the ones that they do have are usually not fast enough swimmers to catch up with an ovum. It made good sense to me; I mean, like I already said, I was never a very good swimmer that could catch up to anyone, neither.

After my doctor explained why I couldn't make a baby, we went ahead with some more interesting talk about sex education. I found out that a woman with Down syndrome could make a baby of her own, but it doesn't happen all that often. And, when it does happen, there's a very good chance that her baby will have Down syndrome, too. It's like if your mom or dad have curly hair, the chances are pretty good that you will have curly hair, too. I never liked curly hair all that much, but come to think of it, curly hair would sure be better than no hair at all. I mean, straight or curly hair, what's the big deal, as long as you got some.

The last year in high school is when you're a senior. It was a lot different than the first three years when you're not. What happened that was so different is that the seniors, at least the ones of us that didn't act up with any sort of bad behavior problems like banging their heads or chewing on their hands got to leave school for about half of the time and go to the workshop where you usually weren't bored so stiff most of the time.

The workshop was in this big building right next-door to the church. Some of us went in the morning, before lunch, and some of us went in the afternoon, after lunch. And, no matter what time of the day we went, the best thing about the workshop was that we got paid for working there.

Now, I'm not saying we got paid a lot of money, like thousands of dollars or nothing. I mean, it wasn't near enough to buy a fancy house full of modern style furniture or a shiny new car, but it still felt pretty good to have some of my own money instead of just getting my allowance from Mom and Dad every week. When your parents just keep giving you an allowance every week, it makes you feel like you're still a Dicky.

There were counselors at the workshop that taught us how to do certain jobs. The jobs were usually easy to do like stuffing toys into boxes or letters into envelopes or putting the right amount of screws into plastic bags. Once, we even got to make the pillows that you get if you ever fly on an airplane and you want to take a nap. That was the job I liked the most, maybe 'cause I was pretty good at it. The truth is I could make more pillows than anyone else in the whole place. My record was four pillows, without a single mistake, in just one afternoon. So, somewhere up in the sky, on one of those super fast jet airplanes, maybe there's four people that are napping on pillows with tags on them that say: "Made by the one and only Richard, the best pillow maker at the workshop." 'Course, there might only be two people if they're each hogging my pillows.

After about an hour or so at those jobs, I could usually do what I was supposed to do without even thinking much about it. I didn't mind when that happened, 'cause I could do my job and still daydream about what to do with all the money I was making. Mom and Dad said it was my money so I could spend it on whatever I wanted, except they told me I had to put a little of it, like maybe around half of it, into the First National Bank. That's the same bank where Mom and Dad put all their money, too. I found out there is a Second National Bank, just in case you were wondering about it like me. I don't know anyone that puts any money in it though; maybe people only go there when the First National Bank is full up.

It's a good idea to save around half of your money in any National bank, no matter what number there is in front of it. You never know when an emergency will come up and you might need some of the money you got saved up. Or, you might know someone, a friend or someone, that needs the helping hand of a loan until they get some of their own money. Also, a bank is usually a safer place to keep your money than maybe in one of your dresser drawers or under your bed where a robber could get at it real easy and steal it when you're out having pizza or bowling or something like that.

Another thing I learned is that a bank gives you extra money just for letting them keep what you put in. What you put in is called a deposit, and the extra money they give you for keeping it safe is called interest. They keep adding that interest on to all of the deposits you already made. Pretty soon you could save up some big money. You have to admit that it's pretty nice of a bank to give you extra money that you don't even have to work for.

So, what I did every two weeks was take this green bankbook they give you to the lady that stands behind the bars at the counter at the First National Bank. She's called a "teller," which I haven't figured out the reason for yet, except maybe you tell her things. Anyway, I sign my paycheck and give it to her with a deposit slip, which tells exactly how much money I'm putting in, and then she adds on my interest and puts a new amount into my green bankbook. I tell her thanks, and I'm on my way, still thinking of the money I'm saving up and all the things I might do with it.

I'll tell you one of the things I've been thinking about doing with some of the money I've been saving up in the bank. Here comes my third wish, at last. You probably remember that a guy gets exactly three wishes in his life, but until right now, I never got around to telling you my third one yet. Sometimes, you don't want to tell a person everything at the same time, like all at once. You could say I was keeping you in suspense so you would stay very interested in everything I'm telling you.

My third wish was that Penny would finally talk to me and smile. I daydreamed about her smiling and talking to me at work all the time. I had dreams about her smiling and talking to me at night, too. I wished that Penny would talk to me and smile at last, 'cause if she only did those things, I would be very happy, probably as happy as I've ever been in my whole life, I would say.

In my dreams, I took some of my money out of the First National Bank and asked Penny to come with me for some fun. We went to a movie that showed some aliens from outer space attacking the earth or maybe some good guys and bad guys fighting each other, and then we went to a restaurant for a large pizza with whatever she would like on top and some Cokes. I had some funny jokes and stories ready to tell her in perfect speech, and on the walk home, we held on to each other's hands. When we got to her front door, we gave each other a hug and a kiss on the cheek, like good friends usually do.

After our hug and kiss on the cheek, Penny finally smiled and said thank you, out loud I'm saying, for the good time she had. Then, she gave me her telephone number, and I called her up when I got home and talked to her some more in my perfect speech. She told me to call her up on the telephone any time I felt lonesome for a friend and missed her or if I had a new joke that would cheer her up. That was my dream, all right, and that was my third wish.

Anyway, except for my dream, the closest I ever got to having a girl for a friend in high school was at one of the social events that the workshop had every couple of weeks. After work, mostly on a Friday night, we went bowling or roller skating and then for some pizza or cheeseburgers to eat. Sometimes, if there was enough snow on the ground, we went sledding. It wasn't like a date or nothing, 'cause everyone went in one big group and nobody was really matched up with anyone else. You didn't get to walk anyone back home, neither. But, at least there were girls and guys all together at a place that wasn't school, and it was usually pretty much fun, all right.

We tried what's called square dancing a couple of times, and I could never figure out why they called it that instead of circle dancing, which is closer to the shape you're actually in when you square dance. It seemed to me the kids that liked square dancing the most were the kids in wheelchairs. They really liked huffing and puffing into their tubes and moving around to the music.

Fact is, I thought square dancing was kind of hard to do with that guy yelling out all those fast instructions about who you're supposed to be dancing with and how. After just a couple of spins around the floor, dough see doughs, you call them, I couldn't remember exactly what I was supposed to do in square dancing. So, I usually stopped my dancing pretty soon and went over to the sidelines to watch Victor in his helmet and remind him not to bang his head on anything too hard. He usually said he wouldn't.

Well, one Friday night after work, the social event was bowling. Some counselors always came to watch us, and they would usually bowl right along with us. We would split up into teams and keep score to see which team won. Most of the time I wasn't that good at bowling, but that time I got six strikes in a row. Honest. I mean, those strikes just kept on happening, one right after the other, until I got six in a row. I got a couple of spares too, which are almost as good as strikes, but not quite.

The counselor that was keeping score said mine turned out to be exactly 222. Boy oh boy; it was like a miracle or something. Mine was the highest score of the night, way higher than anyone else's, even the counselors'. I was very happy when I found out that my team won, and I couldn't wait to get home and tell Mom and Dad how good I did at bowling. It was like I was the champion bowler of the United States of America or maybe even the whole world.

When the bowling game was finally over and I was still feeling pretty good, I was sort of surprised when Penny came over and sat down next to me on the bench, where you change into your regular shoes before you go home and tell your mom and dad how good you did at bowling. Penny sat down sort of close to me on the bench, which made me feel a little nervous, mostly 'cause I was worried that my sweaty feet might not smell so good after being cooped up in those bowling shoes, that were a little too tight, all night. Nobody wants to smell your feet, 'specially if they're stinky, 'cause they been cooped up in too tight bowling shoes all night.

I got the feeling Penny wanted me to know how proud she was that I made the highest score in bowling that night. She stopped twirling her charm around and around in front of her eyeballs like she usually did, and she looked right at me. She even rubbed her hand on my face. She put her fingers right over where the giant red scars are from the pimples that I used to have, and she did it real gentle, I thought, almost like she was thinking she could make the scars go away.

I got that real funny feeling in my stomach I already told you about, and I was hoping as hard as I could that Penny would smile and talk to me at last. I was hoping she would tell me the reasons why loud noises bothered her so much and why she always put her tongue on the metal handle of the seat. Sometimes it makes you feel better if you tell people your reasons for doing or not doing certain things. But, Penny didn't talk to me or even smile, so I had nothing to do except finish lacing up my regular shoes. Then, it was time to go home.

Anyway, before you know it, my last year in high school was almost over. One day, a photographer guy came to school with his big black camera and bright lights. He took our pictures for the yearbook. Actually, he took four pictures of each of us seniors so you could look carefully at all four of them with your mom and dad and decide which was the best one for the yearbook. A guy always wants to look his best in his high school yearbook. Many years later, some guys might want to drag out the old yearbook and show their graduation picture to their children. You can never tell when a guy will want to show someone his graduation picture, even if it's not to his children.

Fact is, I didn't think any of my pictures looked all that good, even though Mom and Dad liked a couple of them. Finally, we just picked the one that showed my eyes the best. I had sort of a little smile on my face, instead of a big one, so my slits didn't show too much. Mom and Dad ordered one big graduation picture of me for their dresser and some smaller ones that parents carry around in their wallets. You should see how beautiful Penny looks in her picture. It's almost as beautiful as she looks in real life, but not quite. It's right behind mine in the yearbook, on the very next page.

There was a graduation ceremony at the church that was a pretty nice thing to go to. It was in the part of the church where people usually come to pray on Sunday. We got to march real slow down the aisle with our partners, two at a time, while one of the teachers was playing that classical music tune you always hear at graduations. I still don't know what the name of that classical tune is, but Vladimir probably does.

Everyone was wearing a dark blue cap with some strings hanging down and a gown to match, which looked kind of silly, if you ask me, but since everyone was wearing the same cap and gown, everyone looked kind of silly, not just me, so I didn't mind it too much. Penny was my partner for walking down the aisle. I liked that part more than anything.

Mr. Higgenbottom was the principal, which is another word for the chief or the boss of the school. When he finished making his speech about being a good citizen, which wasn't all that interesting, he called out each of our names. We got to walk up on the stage, right under the place where Jesus, the Son of God, is nailed to that big cross, and get our diplomas from high school. A diploma means you're done.

Even though Mr. Higgenbottom made sure to remind all the parents and other people that were sitting in the pews not to clap until after everybody had their names called out, nobody paid that much attention to him. What happened instead was that all the parents clapped for their own kid at the very second they heard their kid's name. Sometimes, parents don't have such good manners, neither.

I could tell that Mr. Higgenbottom didn't like all that clapping very much, 'cause pretty soon his face got really red and the veins started popping out on his forehead. Victor's parents clapped the longest, and Carmella's mom and dad did some long clapping, too. I noticed Carmella didn't wear her mittens, and Victor didn't wear his helmet, neither. That seemed like a nice thing to me. Nobody should have to wear a football helmet or mittens to their high school graduation ceremony.

When our graduation ceremony was finally over, the teachers served fruit juice and cookies to everyone that wanted some. Most of the parents knew each other pretty good, 'cause the school had a parents' group that moms and dads belonged to for meetings. It was nice that almost everyone knew each other, 'cause I didn't have to introduce my mom and dad to anyone else's parents. I know that introducing people is good manners, but it still makes me feel a little nervous. I usually forget the rules, like exactly what words to say and whose name you're supposed to say first.

Mom and Dad told me they were proud as punch, which is very proud, that I was graduating from high school, and they wanted me to have two special treats. First, they gave me a new color television set for my room. It was an excellent present, 'cause sometimes the TV shows I liked to watch weren't exactly the same ones that my parents liked. When I got my own TV, I just said, "Excuse me" and went up to my room to watch whatever I wanted. It was nice to have some privacy, and anyway, the picture on my new set was way better than the one Mom and Dad watched in the family room. 'Course, Mom and Dad could of watched my TV whenever they wanted to, but usually I had it all to myself.

The second treat that Mom and Dad gave me for my graduation from high school was to take me to my favorite restaurant after the juice and cookies which I didn't have too much of. I mean, why ruin your appetite on juice and cookies when your parents just told you that you're going to Bonofaccio's Italian Kitchen for a well-done steak which is probably number one on my list of favorite things to eat? It's either well-done steak which is my number one favorite or lobster tail with that buttery sauce they give you for dipping; I can never decide which.

The coolest thing about Bonofaccio's Italian Kitchen was that for guys like me that can never seem to make up their minds whether to eat well-done steak or lobster tail, you can have both on the same plate. It's called surf and turf, 'cause a lobster is a fish that swims in some water that's called surf and a steak is part of a cow that walks on the turf, which is another word for ground.

First, you take a nice size bite of steak and then you take a nice size bite of lobster. Or, you can start with the lobster if you want to. Either way you start, you keep going on and on until there's nothing left on your plate but lobster juice and steak sauce. Boy oh boy. Dad always says I don't leave anything on my plate but the pattern; you know, the lines and circles and stuff that are painted on the plate, although sometimes it's just pure white with no pattern showing.

'Course, no one can ever tell what the future will bring, so there was no way I could of known what was going to happen at Bonofaccio's Italian Kitchen on graduation night. Boy oh boy, it was really something. What happened changed my life around, and that's the honest to God truth. I know you're in a hurry to hear about it, so I'll tell you about that night at Bonofaccio's. Like I already said, there's a lot of things I forget, but not that night at Bonofaccio's. I remember it like it was yesterday.

CHAPTER II
Penelope

A person comes close, and Penny feels vibrations. She hears a humming sound. She smells your scent, and she sees your aura. If you're in pain, she knows where it hurts. A person touches her, and Penny hears your thoughts. You're thinking Penny is pretty. You're thinking Penny is strange. You've never known anyone like her. You're uncomfortable, anxious, even a little frightened. You're hoping she'll go away and leave you alone. Pretty Penny does peculiar things.

She stares at shiny objects. She spins them between her fingers. She licks cold metal. She plays with fire. She blows out candles and breathes the smoke. She never laughs or smiles or talks. Woolen clothes and rushing water hurt her skin. She doesn't like being touched. She smells music. She can taste it, too. She sees out of the sides of her eyes. She hears snowflakes and dust landing. She remembers her birth and being suckled. Penny is so peculiar a person has a name for her. You call her autistic.

Penny was a beautiful baby. She looked at her mother's eyes. She smiled and spoke to her mother. She loved her mother. Then, Penny stopped looking and speaking, and she broke her mother's heart. It's not your fault, Mom. It was never your fault. Penny still loves you. She loves you more than ever.

Penny's mother and father didn't know what to do. They took her to doctors, but they didn't know what to do, either. Most of the doctors had never seen a child like Penny, because there aren't many children like Penny. Just one out of every 500 children is like Penny. She's part of a very small minority group. Help fight segregation. Invite peculiar Penny to dinner. A person should give Penny soft food for dinner. Hard food makes too much noise when she chews, and it feels like stones in her mouth.

Then, Penny and her parents went to a famous and learned professor who called himself a psychiatrist. He told Mother it was all her fault. She was aloof and mechanistic, more like a machine than a mother. She was cold; a "refrigerator woman," he called her. Subconsciously, she resented being pregnant, and she rejected pretty Penny from the moment she was born. Penny sensed her mother's rejection and withdrew into herself.

The famous and learned professor said all those things about Penny's mother. He said them with absolute conviction after he had known her for less than an hour. What a perceptive man he must have been. Or, maybe he wasn't.

The professor had an impeccable reputation. He was the foremost authority in his field. He professed at a prestigious university, and he wrote scholarly books. People are quick to assume that such an accomplished person must be right about everything. Penny's parents assumed he was right. Other parents of autistic children assumed he was right. Everyone but Penny assumed he was right. She knew of his accomplishments and reputation, but she was suspicious. His aura was very dim, almost invisible.

Penny's mother took the blame. Then, the famous professor convinced her parents that Penny wouldn't get better unless she left her home and family. The professor wanted her to live at his special school. His school was in a big city, far from Penny's home. Penny would have to be separated from the people she loved. The professor had a curious word for busting up families. He called it a "parentectomy."

Penny knew her mother and father were desperate. They were ready to try anything that might help her. They wondered what kind of parents they would be if they didn't do what the professor advised. So, they helped her pack her belongings. They said goodbye and sent her to the professor's far away school. After all, such a perceptive man must be worthy of trust. Or, maybe he wasn't.

It was two months before Mother stopped weeping during the day. She never stopped at night. Father put on a brave front, but inside, he was melancholy. Their child was gone; he missed her; he felt a terrible sadness. Penny was hundreds of miles away; still, she knew how her parents suffered.

There were no classrooms, no desks, and no blackboards at the professor's special school. Some days the teachers didn't prepare any lessons, and the students didn't follow any rules. The air felt thick and brown, polluted, and it smelled like rubbing alcohol. Penny lived at his school while the professor and his band of assistants practiced their "psychiatric stuff" to make her less peculiar. When that didn't work so well, they practiced child abuse.

Penny lived at the professor's school for two years. She lived with other autistic children who came from all over the country. Their parents were desperate and willing to try anything, too. When Penny and her mates weren't being practiced upon, they had plenty of time to wonder what their refrigerators were doing. For two years, Penny never saw her parents. Not once. Even written correspondence was forbidden. The professor excised Mom and Dad from her life, just like he said he would.

Penny got no better, so Mom and Dad started questioning the professor. They didn't like his answers. They stopped trusting him, and they decided to bring Penny home. With all his insight, or perhaps his desperation, the professor wanted Penny to stay at his place for two more years. "These things take more time," he said.

Mom wasn't willing to give him more time. "You've had our child long enough," she said.

The professor insisted. Foremost authorities get to be adamant. He looked surprised when Dad narrowed his eyes and quietly told him to go to hell. Dad wanted to hurt him. Penny saw and smelled her father's rage. It was red-orange, and it reeked of burning rubber. The professor stopped being adamant.

A few years later, the famous and learned professor from the prestigious university got depressed. No one knows for sure why he committed suicide. Maybe other people grew suspicious. Maybe other people stopped trusting him. Maybe he felt guilty, because he had not always been kind to children. Maybe he could no longer stand knowing the truth--that underneath his skin there was a mean and bigoted man, a man who wasn't a psychiatrist at all, a man who was an impostor, a fraud, a man who built his impeccable reputation on a foundation of lies. Whatever the reason, the professor did himself in; he bought the farm, a person might say.

Or, a person might say he performed a "selfectomy."

The professor was wrong about everything. Penny's mother was a brave, sweet woman who loved her as much as any mother ever loved her child. She loved Penny from the first, fiercely, without reservation, never stopping, not for a second. Every day and every night of her life, she got on her knees and prayed for Penny to get better. Refrigerator woman indeed. You cannot break a refrigerator's heart.

Now, at last, the doctors know better. They know it's not mechanistic mothering or any other psychological factor that makes Penny the way she is. Many doctors think certain chemicals may be out of balance in Penny's brain. Other doctors think parts of Penny's brain may be damaged. Some of them are beginning to think Penny's problem is genetic. Research is finding out that many children with autism have abnormal chromosomes, just like children with Down syndrome.

It will probably be a while before the doctors discover the exact cause. Perhaps they will discover more than one cause. But, until the doctors finish their good work, at least a person can stop blaming Penny's mother. Penny's mother never did anything wrong. It's not your fault, Mom. It was never your fault. Penny still loves you. She loves you more than ever.

Penny remembers everything that has ever happened to her. There is a storage bin in her brain with unlimited capacity, a wide entranceway, and no exit doors. She recalls sequences of events in precise order, exactly as they occurred. Her memories come as they please, sometimes triggered by a song, a smell, colors, textures, or even a taste. And, there are no abridged versions. Penny wishes her bin weren't so full, but the memories are stubborn. They linger, all the way back to her beginning.

Penny remembers her birth. There is liquid. There is pushing and pressure on her head and shoulders. There are moans, woman screams, and man talk. There are silver instruments, blood, green gowns and masks. It's very cold and she's quivering. There are hands on her, and air fills her lungs. She's warmer under a light. A woman in white clothes has a moist, warm cloth. She cleanses Penny of fetal residue and covers her with a blanket. Another woman reaches for her. There is mother smell and warm milk. Silk is the feel of her. Sweet is the taste of her. It is when Penny starts to love her.

Penny remembers being an infant. Gramma Marie is a large woman, big as a giant, she thinks. Gramma enjoys picking her up and cradling her in her arms, but Penny hates being touched. Gramma's arms are huge, pink worms about to swallow her. She feels like she's trapped in a small space and suffocating. Gramma stops picking her up when Penny arches her back and spits like a cat. Gramma clucks her tongue and thinks Penny is an odd little girl. Penny hears what Gramma Marie is thinking.

Penny hates the feel of her pajamas too, especially the woolen ones she has to wear when it's cold. The pajamas are sandpaper on her skin. Her skin screams. They're high pitched, tinny screams, muffled, almost inaudible, like the sound ants make when a person steps on them. If she can't pull off her pajamas, she feels weak and dizzy. She sees spots in front of her eyes, and she throws up. Mother finds pretty Penny in the morning, partly naked and shivering in her crib. Penny is investigating her vomit with her fingers, nose, and tongue.

Penny talks when she's nine months old. By her first birthday, numbers and letters fascinate her. She can count to 20, and she knows the names of the letters of the alphabet and the sounds they make. Penny reads the letters and counts the flowers on her birthday cake. The family is amazed. "Maybe she's a genius," they say. Gramma Marie thinks geniuses are usually a "little off." Soon, Penny stops talking, except to echo a few words that others have said. "Hello pretty Penny," she says, over and over again, like a parrot. Then, she stops talking altogether.

Penny remembers being a young girl. She thinks everyone hears and sees the way she does. How is she to know what is normal when she has never experienced what is normal? Now, Penny knows better.

She knows her hearing, vision, and other senses are terribly acute. "Hypersensitive" is the word the doctors use. The doctors are just beginning to learn how terrible it is. It's as if she hears, sees, smells, touches, and tastes too well. So, in Penny's world, there is no respite. It's like an assault.

A person tries to enter Penny's world with a question. At the same time, a clock is ticking. A faucet is dripping. Some children are playing outside, a truck is rumbling down the street, the wind is blowing some leaves, the kitchen windows are rattling, an ambulance is wailing, the refrigerator is humming, some clothes are tumbling in the dryer, the telephone is ringing, the toilet is running, and a dog is barking. Penny hears everything around her, but she doesn't respond to your question. Your voice is just one more sound competing for her attention, no more or less important than any of the other background noises. They're all persistent assailants in the same assault.

Most nights, Penny doesn't fall asleep easily. To her parents, the house is still. They don't hear the foundation settling, the nails loosening, or the floors sinking. They don't hear the bugs gnawing or the mice nibbling. They don't hear their eyelashes blinking. They don't hear dust landing on their dressers and night stands. But, in Penny's world, it's never silent. She even hears the air moving through the room.

It's not only sounds from outside that keep her awake, but sounds from inside her body as well. She hears her heart beating and blood coursing through her veins. She hears her intestines growling and her bile oozing. She hears her lungs expanding and deflating. Noises from swallowing bounce off her temples. She hears too well. She hears what other people don't. In Penny's world, there is no escaping things. She gets no rest.

High and low voices bother Penny. Mom's woman voice rings in her ears and hurts. Dad's man voice echoes like a cannon. He talks and she covers her ears. Father thinks Penny is afraid of him. He reaches out to hold her, but Penny cries and cowers in a corner, face to the wall. Father can't know it's just the sound of his voice that frightens her. Late at night when they're alone, even dads cry. They do it because their little girls won't come to them, and they can't figure out why.

Penny's eyesight is perfect, but her perception isn't. There is a large maple outside Penny's window, but she's unaware of the trunk, the branches, and its overall shape. She misses the essence of the tree, because she's riveted by the individual leaves. There is an ocean wave heading onshore. She doesn't perceive it as a swell of water, because she focuses on the individual droplets. There is a person standing next to her. She doesn't recognize your face, because she fixates on your pores. Penny is slow to perceive your whole, because she can't get past your parts. A person shouldn't take it personally.

Penny can't sleep because of the sights. She's on her back in bed, and she opens her eyes. She sees specks of light moving against the blackness of the ceiling. She's floating weightless through space, among the stars. Or, tiny fireflies are hovering above her glass casket. In fact, they're just dust particles reflecting the night light.

She closes her eyes, and the lights remain, pulsating in a thousand different hues. They fade to black and reemerge as neon lights or pasta primavera or faces of dead relatives or the shape of Peru or anything else trapped in her storage bin. Penny sees too well. She sees what other people don't. She gets no rest.

A person approaches Penny from behind, and she knows. There is the humming as you draw close. And, there is her eerie peripheral vision. She's like an insect that can rotate its eyes 360 degrees. Her side vision is so good, she can see you without making eye contact. It's one of the reasons she doesn't look at your eyes. Another reason is that she doesn't want to see inside of you.

Penny sees sounds. Sounds have flavors, they smell, she can feel them, and they move, too. Beethoven's Fifth Symphony is green. It feels cool and smooth, like satin on her skin. The music smells like wet grass, and it tastes like pears. It moves at a moderate pace, in rhythmic waves, from left to right. Dylan's Subterranean Homesick Blues is red. It feels hot and gritty on her skin. The music smells like garlic, and it tastes like barbecue. It moves in fits and starts, from right to left, with occasional spikes when it's loud.

Penny plays with dangerous toys. She lights matches and holds the flame under her hands. She snuffs candles with her fingers and inhales the smoke. She cuts her hands and arms on broken glass. She climbs to the rooftop and walks along the edge. She climbs a tree and sits on a high limb. She won't stop, even after she falls and hurts herself. A person thinks Penny is unaware of danger.

Penny likes to feel clean. She takes a bath in the morning and another at night. She won't take a shower, because the rushing water hurts. Hundreds of hypodermic syringes pierce her skin. The water roars like wild animals off in the night. She soaks for a long time in her bath, and she moves her hands through the water. With the movement, she sees the colors of the rainbow reflected in the water. Green makes her buoyant. Blue quiets the sounds in her head. Purple makes her sleepy. Red gives her energy. She likes the colors.

Penny remembers her adolescence and high school. Peculiar kids like Penny don't go to regular high schools. They go to church basements and sit in classrooms with other peculiar kids. The teachers call them special education classes, but the kids don't. They call them retard classes, crip classes, and weirdo classes. But, there are books, lessons, and rules in Penny's classroom. Teachers analyze her assignments, not her. Teachers are kind, and they tell the truth. They don't touch. She likes it much better than the dead professor's school.

There are seven students in Penny's classroom. They're all members of the same minority group. Two of her classmates speak. Three of them use sign language. Most of them are very skilled at reading facial expressions and body language. A few, like Penny, are able to sense what others are thinking. So, in one way or another, they manage to communicate, not always with their teacher, but at least with each other. As time passes, they grow close. Of course, there is an occasional squabble as there is in every classroom, but, for the most part, Penny and her classmates get along fine. Together, they understand how it is to be peculiar. The weirdos pull for each other, don't you know?

Penny has no awkward phase like a lot of adolescents. She grows taller by several inches, and her hair reaches the middle of her back. In the summer, she enjoys being outside in the sun. The rays enter her body and mingle with her blood. They warm her and lift her mood. Her skin darkens and her hair lightens. Often, strangers stop what they're doing to look at her. They're amazed at how beautiful she is. They cannot know how peculiar she is.

Penny's body fills out to perfect proportions. She changes from a girl to a woman, and she begins to have sexual feelings. During nights when she is able to sleep, she has erotic dreams. At first, they embarrass her, but she comes to enjoy them. Sometimes, if she awakens too soon, she wills herself back to sleep to continue her dreams. She smiles and laughs in her dreams, and she speaks. When she can sleep no more, she gets out of bed, takes her bath, and puts on her clothes. She's ready for school with time to spare--all dressed up and mute.

Riding the school bus is hard for Penny. There are too many people in too small a space. The morning rush hour is noisy, and she has nowhere to go to escape the din. Cars, trucks, and buildings rush by and make her dizzy. The smell of gasoline fumes and garbage cans makes her sweaty and nauseous. She feels trapped, like she's back in Gramma Marie's arms, about to be swallowed. To relax and feel better, she licks the metal handle on top of the seat. It's cool and soothing on her tongue, like snowflakes. Twirling her charm counter clockwise makes her less dizzy. Having Richard nearby helps her feel better, too.

Richard is a boy with Down syndrome. Some people used to call him a mongoloid, because his eyes are slanted. Penny would like to know if boys in Mongolia who happen to have round eyes are called Caucasoids. At school, they call Richard mentally retarded. He goes to another of those special education classes in the church basement. His classmates are other boys and girls who are called mentally retarded, too.·

Penny wonders how anyone can be sure Richard is mentally retarded. Is he mentally retarded because he can't read? Is he mentally retarded because of the way he speaks? Maybe Richard is mentally retarded because of the way he looks. Is everyone with slanted eyes and scars on their cheeks mentally retarded? People should know more about a boy than how he looks and how he reads and how he speaks before they call him anything. There are other, more important things to know. In some ways, maybe Richard is a genius.

Penny knows Richard better than the people at school know him. She knows he is a kind and gentle boy who cares about her and the others who ride the bus. He wants to talk with her and make her smile and laugh. He wants her to be his good friend. He likes her long, yellow hair, and he wants to touch her face. Richard doesn't like how he looks, but deep inside of him, even deeper than his chromosomes, there is a beautiful boy. Outside of him, he has the brightest aura Penny has ever seen. There is light wherever Richard goes.

Penny remembers going to the workshop next to her school each afternoon. At first, leaving her classroom and going to another place makes her uncomfortable. Any change in routine makes her nervous. After a while, though, she doesn't mind going to the workshop. Making pillows is very tedious work, but she likes being able to start and finish something on the same day. Richard goes to the workshop every day, too. He always manages to get the workstation next to hers. He pretends it's an accident, but Penny knows better. She doesn't mind, though. She likes being close to Richard. And, he keeps everything so neat and clean.

The counselors work alongside the students. They help Penny and her schoolmates learn their jobs. On Friday afternoons, when school is over, there are special events. Often, they go roller skating or square dancing. When it snows, they go sledding. Penny loves the feel of the flakes on her face, and she wishes they wouldn't melt so quickly. She opens her mouth and swallows as many as she can. She imagines they stay whole in her body. They make her feel calm and clean inside, as if she were new.

It's peaceful at the sledding hill, quiet when the wind stops, and pretty. If Penny stands away from her classmates, she can hear the snowflakes landing. A person might be surprised to know that no two snowflakes make exactly the same sound.

The counselors take them bowling, too. There are enough players for three teams, and there is a contest to see which team gets the highest score. Penny and Richard are together, and their team wins. It's because Richard keeps knocking down all the pins at once. He has a higher score than anyone else that night.

Schoolmates and counselors cheer for Richard. He is happy and proud of himself when his team wins. This is the first time in his whole life he's won anything. He can't wait to get home to tell his mom and dad.

Penny is proud of Richard, too. She sits next to him on the bench while he changes his shoes. She wants Richard to know how she feels, so she moves closer to him. It's warm around him. She reaches through his aura. She touches both of Richard's cheeks, and she moves her fingers over his scars. Penny looks straight into Richard's eyes, and she touches him again. He is a kind and gentle boy.

It's nearly time to graduate from high school, and a photographer comes to school. Later, Richard is happy when he shows Penny their yearbook. Her picture is one page after his. They're exactly back-to-back, so if a person cuts out Richard's picture, Penny's is on the other side. In the yearbook, they are very close, as best friends are supposed to be.

The students wear blue caps and gowns to their graduation ceremony. Richard and Penny march down the aisle of the church together. The music is soft, green, and beautiful. It smells like sweet peas. They see their parents smiling. Richard holds on to Penny's arm, and he is careful to stay in step. He keeps time in his head, all the way to their seats. He stands up straight, and he keeps his tongue in his mouth, too.

All the parents applaud when the principal calls their children's names. For the moment, the moms and dads are joyous. They're thinking of how difficult it has been for their children and how far they have come. They're thinking of how difficult it has been for them, too. And, they're worried about what will come next. Most parents stop worrying quite so much when their children grow up, but parents of peculiar kids never do.

After graduation, Penny and her parents decide to go out to dinner to celebrate the occasion. Mom and Dad ask Penny if she would like to invite some classmates and their parents to join them. She feels shy with people she doesn't know very well, so the three of them go to a restaurant by themselves. They go to Bonofaccio's Italian Kitchen where the bread and pasta are soft.

Penny and Mom walk into the restaurant, and Dad looks for a parking place. While they're waiting for a table, Penny is surprised to see Richard and his parents seated at a booth toward the back. Richard sees her, too. He gives her thumbs up, a big smile, and he waves with both hands. Penny gives him a little wave back.

Dad comes in, just as some people are getting up from a table in front. The table is next to a wide window overlooking the street. A busboy clears the table and brings fresh linen, silverware, plates, and glasses. Dad helps Mom and Penny with their chairs, and they all sit down. Penny feels good inside. She's happy to be with her family. They have loved her from the first. They have loved her, no matter what.

Mom and Dad hold Penny's hands and tell her how lovely she looks. Dad tells Mom and Penny about his day at work. He's enthused about a new design project he's starting. The waiter brings menus. Dad orders a bottle of Mom's favorite wine and some Italian bread with cheese and tomatoes on top. The food and drink come. Dad proposes a toast in honor of Penny and to everyone's good health. "Here's to our high school graduate and to our family's health and happiness for many years to come," he says.

Then, Penny's life changes forever.

Penny is startled by screeching sounds, a thud, and the roar of an engine. She sees a motorcycle sliding across the street on its side. It leaves a trail of orange and yellow sparks before bouncing off a parked car and stopping in the middle of the street. A bus jumps the curb and lurches across the sidewalk. It flattens a no parking sign and a fire hydrant. The bus driver is wrestling with the steering wheel.

The horn is blowing. There is panic on the driver's face. He's afraid. The bus is only a few feet away. One of the headlights is blinking. The other is broken and spewing vapor. The bus smashes through the window, and pieces of glass are whizzing around. So are building blocks and metal. Penny is flying through the air. She lands on her back. Her face and chest hurt, and people are screaming. The horn is still blowing, and there is the smell of gasoline and exhaust fumes.

The engine keeps roaring, and the bus keeps lurching. Penny crawls toward her mom and dad. They're under the bus. One tire, still turning, crushes her mother's chest. Her eyes are vacant, staring at nothing. Another tire crushes her father's head. His face is gone. Penny sees his brains--white, gray, pink and red globs--mixed together with hair and bone and tomato and cheese bread, all floating in a pool of blood. Penny sees it all. She sees too well.

Penny feels nausea and noises building in her belly. She feels spasms in her throat. Dreadful shrieks and pitiful gurgles rise from her belly and come out of her mouth, the first sounds she has made since she was one. Penny is repulsed by her sounds. It's sour in her mouth and she dry heaves. She is hot and sweaty. She feels filthy.

There is liquid. There is pressure on her head and shoulders. There are moans, woman screams, and man talk. There are steel instruments, blood, and a man with a green mask. She is cold and quivering. A woman in white clothes is washing her under a warm light. Mother is holding her close and giving her warm milk. Where is the silky feel of her? Where is the sweet taste of her? Please Mother, let me smell you. Please Mother, just one more time.

Richard is next to her, on his knees. He tries to help, but he doesn't know what to do. Nobody knows what to do. Penny can't bear the screaming. Then, she hears a siren. An ambulance is coming. She covers her ears to shut out the sounds. Four men run into the restaurant. They pull her parents from under the bus. They cover them with sheets. Richard tries to block her view, but she sees the men stuff her mother and father into rubber bags. They zip the bags and carry her parents away. Mother's pearl necklace and bits of Father's brains are still on the floor. A fly lands on a red glob.

Penny's head hurts. She has never felt such horrific pain. It comes in alternating waves, from ear to ear, then front to back. At first she gasps; then she screams; then it hurts so much, she can only whimper. It hurts so much, she wants to die. Please Mother, let me die.

There is an electrical storm in Penny's brain. It feels as if her neurons are being ripped apart and rearranged. Her arms and legs twitch spasmodically. Her breathing is shallow and quick. The back of her head bangs on the floor. Saliva drips from her mouth. Mucous drips from her nose. Urine drips from her bladder. Her lips and fingertips turn blue. She sees two of everything. She hears two of everything.

Finally, Penny faints, and when she awakens, she sees and hears nothing. What has happened is so hideous, her senses rebel. To shield her from any more horror, her hearing and vision shut down. She is blind and deaf. It's over pretty Penny, at least for now. No more. Bonofaccio's Italian Kitchen is mercifully silent and dark. No more. Then, she faints again. She welcomes the void.

Penny wakes up in a room she doesn't know. The blinds are drawn, and the walls are green. A television sits in a niche across the room. A telephone and a pitcher of water are on the table next to her. A voice is asking someone named Dr. Sullivan to report to the emergency room. A no smoking sign hangs on one wall, and a picture of Mary and the Christ child hangs on another. He died for our sins. Or, maybe He died for nothing.

Penny is in a bed that isn't hers. Next to her, a second bed is empty. There are bandages on her face, and her cheeks hurt. She breathes and her chest hurts. A nurse takes her temperature and adjusts a tube running into her arm. Richard and his parents are in the room, too. Penny's parents are surely with the angels.

Richard holds Penny's hand and whispers a prayer. Penny squeezes his hand. Big tears fill his eyes and wet his cheeks. He's never felt so sad, even when his friend Billy moved away. He's wondering if pretty Penny will have scars on her face. He's thinking there's no chance she'll ever smile or laugh now. He's worrying about what he would do if his mom and dad were killed. He is a kind and gentle boy. Penny is so tired she wishes she could sleep forever. It would be so much easier. She has a fitful sleep, but only until the next morning.

Richard and his parents are in her room when Penny wakes up. They encourage her to eat. The toast is soft and buttery, and she forces some down. Her teacher and a social worker from the hospital come in. Everyone is thinking about Penny. They're very sad for her, and they want to make her feel better. But, they must talk to her about funeral arrangements for her mother and father. There are no relatives to help, so Richard's parents and the social worker will take care of everything.

For two days before the funeral, Penny stays at the hospital. A doctor gives her medicine to ease her pain. He changes her dressings and holds a mirror so she can see her face. She doesn't like what she sees. Pretty Penny isn't. She's thin and there are black circles under her eyes. There's blood in her eyes, too. The doctor shows her stitches in her cheeks. He says she may have some scars, but they'll probably be hard for anyone to see. She doesn't care about the scars. Richard has some, too. She takes pills that make her drowsy again. She doesn't care about anything.

Penny fades in and out of sleep. It's hard for her to separate her dreams from what actually happens. She knows Richard comes to see her, and so do his mother and father. They bring her sweet smelling flowers, sympathy and get well messages from her schoolmates, and fresh clothes. They bring her a pearl necklace. They talk to her, and they hold her close. Penny doesn't mind when they touch her. It's very strange, but she likes it when they touch her.

The next morning a man in a black suit and tie drives to the hospital in a black limousine. He takes Penny, Richard, and his parents to the funeral chapel. On the way, they pass a fire engine, speeding in the opposite direction. The siren is loud. Richard and his mom cover their ears, but Penny doesn't. It's very strange, but the noise doesn't hurt anymore.

Two plain wooden coffins have flowers around them. Pictures of her mother and father are on top. All of Penny's classmates are at the chapel. So are some neighbors and people from dad's office. A nice man speaks, and there is soft music from an organ. The music has no color. It doesn't smell or taste, either. In her mind, Penny says goodbye to her mother and father. Every one of her classmates hugs her. The weirdos pull for each other, don't you know?

It's cool at the cemetery. A light breeze is blowing. The nice man says the Lord's Prayer and more kind words. Some other men lower her mother and father into the ground. Penny feels the noises building in her belly again, but she keeps them down. Her ribs hurt when she sobs, but she can't stop. Richard helps her shovel some dirt on top of the coffins. There is nothing more to be done. It's time to leave.

During the ride back to the hospital, Penny wonders what will happen to her. Where will she live, and who will take care of her? She feels abandoned. In the midst of these good people, she feels alone and afraid. It's not your fault Mom. It was never your fault. Penny loves you more than ever.

Richard brings her magazines and snacks. He talks to her, and she understands his speech. He tells her about working full time at the workshop. He's earning more money, so he has more to put in the bank. He has a new job, putting cans of dog food into boxes, and it's pretty boring. He tells her what their classmates are doing. He reminds her of the times they went bowling and sledding. When he has nothing more to say, he sits on the chair next to her bed and holds her hand. Penny rests easily when Richard comes for visits. She feels better when he is close to her.

Penny's face and ribs heal well enough. She stops taking medicine for her pain. It's almost time to leave the hospital and go to a new place to live. The social worker knows of a group home. Young people live there. Maybe it's a place for kids with dead parents. Richard's mother and father ask Penny if she'd like to visit. Penny knows that wherever she goes, she will not be coming home after two years. Not this time.

The group home is a short ride from the hospital. It's on a pretty street with trees on both sides. At the treetops, the branches bend to touch each other, so it's like driving through a green tunnel. The house is big, old, and cheerful looking. It's built of tan bricks that might have been yellow when the house was new. The shutters and doors are royal blue. The roof is blue too, and attic windows, shaped like eyes, overlook the street and yard. Someone has painted eyelashes and eyebrows over the windows.

Rocking chairs with purple and yellow pillows and a swing big enough for four people are on the front porch. The back yard smells of lilac. A brick patio and a barbecue grill take up part of the yard. Flowers and a vegetable garden take up another. A small wishing well sits off to one corner. Two wooden ducks, painted to look like an old man and woman, stand on either side of the well. Carolyn and Tom Doherty welcome Penny to their home. As best they can, they would be her substitute parents.

The Dohertys are friendly people. Tom is tall and muscular. He has ruddy cheeks, freckles, a lot of red hair hanging over his forehead, a hook in his nose, and the whitest teeth Penny has ever seen. He has a dimple in his jaw, and when he smiles, which is often, there are deep creases at the corners of his eyes. For a man his size, his voice is very soft, hardly above a whisper, and surprisingly high pitched.

Carolyn is short, just a little more than five feet. The top of her head reaches the second button on Tom's shirt. She is a very pretty woman with a slim, shapely figure and green eyes. She doesn't wear makeup, and she keeps her straight, black hair in a ponytail. Like her husband, she has a ready smile and brilliant teeth. Her voice is soft too, but low pitched and mellow. She would sing low notes if she were in a choir.

Penny feels comfortable around Carolyn and Tom Doherty. She likes this big man and little woman whose voices somehow got mixed up. Penny can tell they love each other very much. She can tell they like each other, too.

Carolyn and Tom tell Penny they're sorry for her loss and ask if she'd like to come in to look at their home. A person can climb four steps or wheel up a ramp to get inside. There is a large foyer with an elevator at the back. The living room, dining room, and library are on one side of the foyer. A big bedroom, family room, kitchen and pantry are on the other. Two young people are busy making bacon, lettuce, and tomato sandwiches. Two others are setting the table. They stop working and say hello to their guests.

All the furniture is big and cushy. Pillows of every color are on davenports, love seats, easy chairs, and on the floor. Even the tables have pillows on them. Tom notices Penny looking at all the pillows. He gives her a little nudge on the arm and says, "I like having soft things in our house--the sofas, the chairs, the floors, and most of all, my Carolyn." Carolyn rolls her eyes and tells him to shush. It's very strange, but Penny almost smiles.

There is a finished basement with a television set, a pool table, a game table, and an old-fashioned jukebox. Tom has fixed it so a person doesn't have to put in any coins. A white, shaggy rug is on the floor. It's so clean, thick and fluffy it reminds Penny of new snow. The walls are knotty pine, and a corkboard has messages tacked to it. Pictures of young people with Carolyn and Tom hang everywhere. Beanbag chairs, the kind that are big enough for two and fit to your shape when a person sits, are all over the floor. A long bar, with shelves for glasses, runs along one of the walls. There are soda dispensers over a sink and stools to sit on. Above the bar, there is a neon sign. The words "Absolutely No Belching" are flashing. Again, Penny almost smiles.

Upstairs, there are six bedrooms. Boys live on one side of the elevator, and girls live on the other. Denyse is by herself, in the first room, next to the elevator. She's painting a picture. She stops her work and introduces herself. She's very friendly, even though she looks at Penny out of the sides of her eyes. Like Penny, she's very pretty. She's also very talented. Denyse shows Penny her painting. A little girl with a sad face is standing alone on one side of a wire fence. Some boys and girls with happy faces are playing games on the other. The fence looks way too high to climb.

Back in the living room, Carolyn holds both of Penny's hands. Carolyn asks if she'd like to stay with them. Penny looks into her eyes. In her head and in her heart, Penny knows this is a good place. She knows she can't go home. She feels more tears coming. Carolyn tells her it's OK and holds her close. Carolyn knows how sad, frightened and lonely Penny is. She smells good to Penny, different than her mother, but still good.

Later that evening, Richard, his parents, and Denyse help Penny move into her new home. After she's settled in, Richard's mom and dad sit with her a while. There are some things that need to be taken care of. Someone needs to look at the police report of the accident and talk with representatives of the bus company. Penny must find out whether her parents had a will, life insurance, and investments. She needs to decide what she wants to do with her parents' house, furniture, and other belongings. Penny can't deal with all of those things by herself, so she's pleased and relieved when Richard's parents offer to help.

Some time passes and so does a little of the horror. There are some images Penny will never forget--the bus looming over them and the broken glass and bricks, the tires and Mother's empty eyes, sweet Father without his face, rubber bags stuffed with bodies, and coffins in the ground. But, like her body, her mind is healing well enough too, and the memories are a little less vivid and constant. She can look at Mother's picture without weeping. She can think of Father and see his face. She wears a pearl necklace. Slowly and bravely, she starts the next part of her life.

Denyse helps Penny learn the routine. All the young people take turns with household chores, grocery shopping, and cooking. Tom is the carpenter and chief maintenance man, and Carolyn is the head cook and gardener, but Penny and Denyse and the rest of their housemates help, too. Work schedules vary, so it's usually four or five people at a time for breakfast and lunch. Everyone is home for dinner though; 14 people, often more because of guests, all sit together and eat at the big table in the dining room.

It takes a while for Penny to feel comfortable in such a large group. Soon, however, she tolerates it easily; in fact, she begins to like the company. Her housemates come in all shapes and sizes, and they have all kinds of problems. A blind girl lives in the room next door. Her roommate can still see, but her vision is getting worse each day. A girl in a wheelchair lives next to them. Her roommate walks on artificial legs. Two boys who have no hair live in the room just past the elevator. Another boy has cerebral palsy, and his roommate is a little person. Two more boys who look a lot like Richard share the room at the end of the hall. Everyone seems friendly, except one of the bald boys who is a little crotchety and mostly stays to himself. He's having a bad time with his chemotherapy.

One evening after dinner, Tom and Carolyn talk with Penny about working during the day. They encourage her to go back to the workshop, at least until she's ready to begin looking for a different job. Penny has been thinking about it herself. She thinks it's a good idea. She wants to get out more and get busy. She's anxious to see Richard and her schoolmates. She has missed them, especially Richard.

The next morning Penny wakes up early to get ready for work. In her bath, she moves her hands through the water, but she doesn't see any colors. She moves her hands again, faster this time, but the colors are gone. Penny lets the water out of the tub and stands. She lathers her body with lavender soap and takes a hot shower. She feels unusually clean.

After breakfast, Tom drives her to the workshop. On the way, they pass a construction crew fixing the street. Jackhammers slam into the concrete, but the noise is tolerable. A few blocks down the road, they stop for a red light. Tom's car is directly behind a garbage truck. Penny doesn't notice until the light changes.

They pass Bonofaccio's Italian Kitchen on the right. The no parking sign and fire hydrant have been replaced, and new windows have been installed. A janitor sweeping the sidewalk stops his work so a deliveryman can carry trays of bread inside. "Some things are so easy to fix," Penny says. She says the words out loud. She likes the sound of her voice. She says the words again.

Two counselors are waiting in front of the workshop to welcome Penny. Richard is standing between them. He has a big smile on his face, so big that Penny can't see his eyes. She can tell he wants to hug her, but he hesitates. He's probably not sure if it would be good manners. So, Penny opens her arms and hugs him. Richard squeezes her just hard enough to make her feel good. He tells her how happy he is to see her.

Penny smiles and says, "Thank you for being my best friend."

Richard is stunned. His mouth drops open, and his tongue falls out. Penny is so delighted at his reaction she laughs out loud. It's a nice tinkling sound. Richard doesn't know what to make of it, so he just keeps hugging Penny and patting her on the back. He seems very happy.

Richard and Penny go into the workshop together. As always, he takes the workstation next to hers. During the day, Richard looks over to her whenever he can. Each time, Penny looks right at his eyes, and she smiles at him.

In the weeks that follow, Richard and Penny spend more time together. Penny invites Richard and his parents to the group home for supper. They meet Denyse and the rest of Penny's housemates. Richard seems comfortable with everyone, especially the guys with Down syndrome. They spend some time looking at each other's palms.

After dinner, Richard's parents stay and have a private talk with Penny. They have some business and legal matters to discuss with her. Richard's mom has talked with the head of the company where Penny's father worked. He put her in touch with her parents' attorney. It seems that Penny's mom and dad had large life insurance policies, which, in the case of accidental death, pay double their face value. They had a large savings account and some investments too, mostly in stocks and bonds. Together, they are worth many thousands of dollars.

Richard's mom has a lady friend in the real estate business. She is anxious to put the house up for sale and arrange to auction whatever furniture and personal belongings Penny doesn't want. The rest she can put into storage and save for later.

Richard's dad has contacted the police and the bus company. It turns out that the bus driver had been drinking the night of the accident. Rather than drag things out in a lawsuit they had no chance of winning, the bus company has offered to settle the case immediately. Richard's parents think the offer is fair.

The money from the bus company, the insurance policies and investments, and the proceeds from the sale of the house is a huge amount, more than Penny will ever be able to spend. In fact, Richard's parents show Penny how to invest the money so she will have more than she needs just from the interest. Peculiar Penny is a very wealthy person.

At the workshop each day, Richard and Penny share lunch. They go bowling after work. They see pictures about aliens from outer space at the movies. They go for pizza, and Richard insists Penny choose the toppings. Richard holds her hand and walks her home. He takes her to her first baseball game. They visit her parents' graves.

Penny and Richard take their coffee breaks together. They sit in the lounge and have colas or root beer. They're happy to be with each other, and they talk easily. One day, Penny asks Richard when he will move to a different house, away from his parents. He's older now, and maybe he needs to be on his own. She thinks it would be good if Richard came to live with her at the group home.

CHAPTER III
Richard

I remember that night at Bonofaccio's Italian Kitchen like it was yesterday. Mom and Dad took me, 'cause they knew it was my number one choice for celebrating something special like graduating from high school. Actually, we went there so many times, even when we weren't celebrating something special, that Mr. Carmine Bonofaccio, the guy that owned the Italian Kitchen, knew us like we were part of his family, or at least old friends that he liked a lot.

Mr. Bonofaccio usually met us at the front door of his restaurant, and this time he was right there, too. He was waiting for us with a big smile on his face, the kind that stretches to both ears. He said "bono sera" in the Italian language, which means good evening. Mom and Dad must of told him the reason for our celebration, 'cause he said he was very proud of me for graduating from high school. He said that part in English.

You can probably tell I've learned some foreign language words. I can say thank you in French and good evening in Italian. Those are some foreign language words that a person with good manners should always know. You can never tell when you'll need to say thank you to a French person or good evening to an Italian person. I can say "Ola" too, which means hello in the Spanish language, just in case you ever run into a Spanish guy and want to give him a polite howdy do. When you're done talking to him and you still want to be polite, just say "adios mi amigo." That means "goodbye my friend." It's a good thing to be polite to everyone. That's the kind of guy I am. By the way, Spanish works with guys from Mexico, too.

Anyway, after the very friendly greeting at the front door of his Italian Kitchen, Mr. Bonofaccio shook Dad's hand and mine, too. It was one of those hard handshakes that a lot of grownup guys do, the kind that almost makes your knuckles crack. You're supposed to squeeze back and keep smiling anyway so nobody knows your hand hurts like crazy.

Then, Mr. Bonofaccio sort of bowed to Mom and kissed her hand. He gave her a big red rose, a real doozy all right, and he told her she was very beautiful. "You are more beautiful than a rose in the springtime," were the exact words he said. I said those exact words over and over in my head until I knew them by heart, 'cause a guy can never tell when he might have a big red rose and want to tell a girl how beautiful she is in the springtime.

I think a lot of Italian guys have real good manners, 'specially when it comes to sweeping the ladies off their feet. Dad said Mr. Bonofaccio was a smooth operator, the kind of guy that's a real Romeo, all right. You've probably heard the story of Romeo and his girlfriend Juliet, the one and only sweetheart of his life. It's one of those very sad type of stories, a real tragedy, you could say, 'cause they all die in the end. By the way, I noticed that a lot of the ladies at Mr. Bonofaccio's restaurant had red roses just like the one Mom got.

We sat down in a booth near the back of the restaurant, not all the way in the back, but a little closer to the back than the front, I would say. I usually like a booth better than a table, 'cause the seats are made out of leather instead of wood. 'Course, leather seats are much softer than wood seats, which makes them much more comfortable to sit on. And, a guy doesn't want to sit on an uncomfortable seat, 'specially when he's celebrating something special like his graduation from high school.

Mom and Dad were reading the menu deciding what kind of delicious dinners they wanted to eat. There was no way I had to worry about reading or deciding though, 'cause I already knew exactly what I wanted. Boy oh boy. I'm telling you I was daydreaming about surf and turf ever since Mom and Dad told me we were going to Bonofaccio's. It's a good thing they didn't tell me until after Mr. Higgenbottom made his speech at the graduation ceremony, 'cause when you think about graduation ceremonies, it's not so easy to pay attention to a principal's boring speech about the golden rule and being a good citizen in the community when you have well-done steak and juicy lobster tail running through your mind every second or two.

Dad ordered up some appetizers to start us off. They were these round, sort of crusty appetizers, made out of a light brown color, and some of them had these skinny things, like strings, hanging down. What you do is slide them around in some tasty red or white sauce before you pop them into your mouth. I was popping those guys in there pretty quick all right, one with the tasty red sauce and the next one with the tasty white sauce, trying to decide which sauce was the tastiest, until Mom told me what I was eating.

You could of knocked me over with a feather when I found out I was chowing down on some squid, which is another word for octopus. To me, an octopus is one of the ugliest looking fishes in the whole ocean. They usually have those big heads, shaped almost like a pumpkin, with huge eyeballs staring out at you. They have a lot of arms, as many as eight I been told, and they're all covered up with suckers so they can latch on to you and suck out your blood. Or, if their suckers aren't working too good, they can still wrap three or four arms around your neck. Then, they squeeze out all your air and strangulate you to death. An octopus can be a pretty mean critter, all right, 'specially when they're still alive and kicking.

When I was first thinking of all that ugly stuff in my mind, I wanted to stop eating those squids real quick, no matter what color dipping sauce I liked the best. But then I got to thinking that a lobster is pure ugly to look at, too. And, even with those long things waving around, feelers I think you call them, and those nasty looking claws trying to pinch on to you, I sure didn't mind chowing down on them, at least the tail part. I mean, it's not like a squid or a lobster that you order up in a restaurant is still alive and flipping around on your plate or nothing. So, I stopped thinking about how ugly squids are and got right back to popping them into my mouth. "Through the lips and over the gums, look out stomach, here she comes." That's what Dad always says when he's in the middle of chowing down on something that's really tasty.

While we were waiting for the waiter to bring the entree, which is another word for the main dish, Dad asked if I would like to try a sip of his wine. It was the kind of wine that's dark red. There's another kind of wine that's white for people that don't like the dark red kind too much. There's pink wine, too, that you get when you mix the red kind with the white kind.

Dad said it would be OK for me to have some wine, since I was a high school graduate, so I just went ahead and drank some. Fact is, I took two or three little sips, which is how you're usually supposed to drink wine, no matter what color it is, instead of chugging it down, all at once, in one big gulp. That wine felt nice and smooth in my mouth and smooth going down the old pipes too, which is what Dad calls your throat. I'm telling you, my dad's got a different word for everything.

I had to pretend it was my first taste of wine, 'cause I didn't want my mom and dad to know that Mamie and Winnie and me used to sneak some from the fridge a few times when they weren't home. Old Winnie would fix us up a plate of those ritzy crackers with some hunks of Swiss cheese to have along with the wine.

I think wine is usually pretty good to drink now and then, even though I'm not all that crazy about the taste. I mean, wine is OK, but I'll take a good old Coke or a Pepsi with lots of ice any time. A creamy root beer in one of those frosty mugs is way delicious too, 'specially when you need something to wash down a hunk or two of Swiss cheese. By the way, when I was little, Winnie tried to fool me by telling me never to eat the holes in the Swiss cheese, 'cause they were poison. Old Winnie sure likes to kid around a lot, but she can't fool me; at least not anymore. I mean, there's no possible way you can eat the holes, when you think about it.

So anyway, I was about half way into my surf and turf when Mom said I was eating too fast. She told me to slow down and come up for some air. I put down my knife and fork to take a breather, and my eyes happened to take a look up toward the front of the restaurant. Don't you know, there was Penny, right up there at a table by the windows. You could of knocked me over with a feather.

Penny looked just like a famous movie star to me; that's how beautiful she was. She was with her mom and dad, just like me, but they didn't look like famous movie stars. I mean, they looked just fine, but nowhere near as beautiful as Penny. Sometimes the kid is prettier than the parents, and sometimes the parents are prettier than the kid. You can never tell how it's going to work out.

I figured Penny and her parents were out for a celebration dinner just like us. I was so excited to see her that I stood up from my chair and gave her thumbs up and a big wave. Penny saw me too, and she waved right back. It was sort of a little wave I thought, but I didn't mind too much, 'cause Penny is a bashful type of person that usually doesn't like to give too many big waves to friends she sees at Italian restaurants.

When I saw Penny, my heart started pounding away really fast under my shirt. I didn't say anything to my mom or dad about my heart, though. There are some things a high school graduate can keep to himself. You have to be cool is what I'm saying. It's not like I was still a little Dicky that had to tell my mom and dad everything I was thinking about, 'specially stuff that made my heart pound really fast under my shirt.

Mom thought it would be good manners if I went over to say hello to Penny and her parents. Dad said I should go over there too, but I was still sort of bashful when it came to meeting a girl's parents. And, it wasn't like Penny was going to talk to me or even smile or anything, anyway. I mean, she barely waved at me, so why would she talk to me?

I figured I would probably just be stuck up there with a red face from being embarrassed, 'cause I ran out of words to say to her mom and dad. I was thinking they might have a hard time understanding my speech too, 'cause I never talked to them before. So, instead of going up to where they were, I just finished my breather and went back to chowing down on my delicious dinner before it got too cold.

Then, the front of the restaurant caved in. It was like one of those explosions from an atomic bomb or something that you see in a war movie. Honest.

What happened was this bus crashed into a guy on a motorcycle cruising down the street. After that, the driver lost control of his bus, and he ran up on the sidewalk and plowed right through the front window of Bonofaccio's. Penny was very lucky all right, 'cause she got knocked out of the way and only got hurt in her ribs. Some of the broken glass that was flying around cut up her face, too. Her mom and dad weren't so lucky, though, 'cause they got caught under the tires of the bus and got crushed to death in a fatal accident that killed them.

Maybe some guys that are old enough to graduate from high school have already seen enough dead people so it doesn't bother them anymore. What I'm saying is maybe it's possible for a guy to get used to seeing dead people after a while. I can tell you for sure, though, that I'm not one of those guys. Fact is, being anywhere around dead people is a place I don't ever want to be. It still gives me the Willies.

I remember from when I was a little kid, maybe around eight or ten years old I would say, that one of my father's older brothers died. When your father or mother have a brother, that's your uncle. When they have a sister, that's your aunt. When your mother or father don't have any brothers or sisters, then you don't have any aunts or uncles. And, it doesn't matter if you like it or not. That's just how it works.

So anyway, my uncle was this fat, friendly guy that usually smiled like a lot of fat guys do. Jolly is a good word for how he was. He always wore a dark colored suit with a long sleeve shirt under it and a tie around his neck, even when he came with us one time to the village park for a picnic on the hottest day of the summer. I mean, you could of fried an egg or two on the sidewalk; that's how hot Dad said it was, but my uncle with the dark colored suit kept on smiling and being his jolly old self anyway.

Uncle had an extra Hershey Bar, the kind with the nuts inside of them, in his jacket pocket every time he came over for a visit. He would eat his own Hershey Bar and give the extra one to me. By the way, there are some skinny guys that smile a lot, too. What I'm saying is that a guy doesn't have to be as fat as my uncle to be jolly.

My poor old uncle died of a heart attack in the middle of the night. Dad said he just went to sleep and never woke up. A couple of days later Mom and Dad took me to the funeral chapel where my uncle was laid out on his back in this wooden coffin with gold handles and fancy carvings all over it. Everyone said how peaceful he looked, almost like he was sleeping. Well, maybe he looked peaceful to them, but seeing my uncle, all stretched out and stiff looking, with that makeup on his face and his arms folded over his chest, scared the heck out of me. I mean, what's the sense of pretending a guy is sleeping when you know darn well he isn't. Fact is, my uncle was dead then and he's just as dead now, and he won't be waking up forever and ever. That's the honest truth, all right.

I got 'specially scared when Dad asked me to lean over the coffin and give my uncle a kiss good-bye. I mean, I never even liked kissing him when he was jolly, so why would I want to kiss him when he was dead? And, when you think about it, my uncle probably didn't care too much whether I kissed him or not. I did it though, 'cause it's usually good to do what your dad asks you to do, 'specially when you're only eight or ten years old.

I had bad dreams about my dead uncle for months. He'd be handing me one of his Hershey Bars with the nuts inside of them, except his hand didn't have any skin left on it. It was all bony like he was already a skeleton. I looked at his eyes, but there was nothing there except black holes with worms crawling out of them. It got so bad that I wouldn't even go to sleep unless the light was on. If it wasn't on in my room, at least it had to be on in the hallway. By the way, I never found out who Willie was and exactly why he was such a scary guy. I been meaning to ask my dad.

Seeing what happened to Penny and her mom and dad, right there before my eyes, was like a bad dream too. And, if it was bad for me, can you imagine how terrible it was for Penny? I mean, one minute she was having a good old time celebrating something real special, and just a few minutes later, she was watching some strangers stuff her dead mom and dad into a couple of big rubber bags and carry them away.

It was so terrible for Penny that she started screaming and rolling around on the floor with her arms and legs flying all over the place and her head banging up and down and spit coming out of her mouth. Finally, she fainted and some ambulance guys took her to the emergency room at the hospital. I know, 'cause Mom and Dad and me went right along with her. It was a good thing for us to do, 'cause no one likes to go to the emergency room all alone if they can.

When real terrible stuff happens, you have to forget what you're doing and go along with your friend to help her in whatever way you can. So, I forgot about my surf and turf real quick. I didn't mind all that much, 'cause I've noticed that what you eat toward the end of your favorite dinner is never as delicious as what you eat at the beginning, anyway. I asked Dad about that once, and he said he noticed the same thing, and that's why he always started his favorite dinners from the end. 'Course, it didn't take me all that long to figure out that Dad was just kidding around with me. I mean, when you think about it, there's just no way of starting your dinner from the end, 'cause wherever you start from is always going to be the beginning. My dad sure likes to kid around with me, all right. I'm onto his tricks, though.

Mom and Dad found out that Penny didn't have any close relatives left. There was nobody around to visit her and take care of her at the hospital or make the arrangements for the funeral of her dead parents. So, my parents and me and some nice lady that worked at the hospital looked after Penny. I went to visit her every day like a good friend is supposed to do. I prayed for her and her parents every night and every day, too. We took her to the chapel when it was time for the funeral and to the cemetery to say some prayers and to watch her mom and dad get buried under the ground forever.

I kept on visiting Penny at the hospital until she was better enough to leave. Then, me and my mom and dad helped her move into her new place to live. It's called a group home, 'cause a large group of people live there; I would say exactly around 14 people all together.

After Penny moved in at the group home, Mom checked up on her to make sure she was doing OK and had all the stuff she needed. But, I didn't see Penny for a while, a couple of weeks, probably. You have to back off and give a friend some private time when she's still sad, 'cause her parents were killed in a fatal accident and she's trying to get used to living at her new home with a group of 13 other people she hardly knows yet.

'Course, after I graduated from high school, I had plenty of time for going to the workshop and earning more money. I went every day, Monday through Friday, from nine in the morning until five at night. Everyone that worked full time at the workshop got half an hour for lunch and two 15 minute coffee breaks each day. I didn't have to drink coffee during my breaks though; I could have a cola or a root beer if I wanted. Or, sometimes I just sat around in the lounge and had a nice talk with one of the counselors that was having a coffee break and not drinking any coffee, neither.

Well, I got to work one morning, and was I ever surprised. I mean, you could of knocked me over with a feather, 'cause two of the counselors told me that Penny was coming back to work. That very same day, not tomorrow and not next week, Penny was coming back to work that day, all right.

Boy oh boy; was I ever excited to see her again. A bunch of those goose bumps popped right out of my skin just like that. I been meaning to ask my dad why they're called goose bumps, 'specially 'cause I've never seen a bumpy goose in any kind of picture or even in real life. Dad will probably know the answer, like he usually does. And, if he doesn't know the answer, I've noticed he's pretty good at making stuff up.

After I went to the bathroom, the counselors hustled me outside real quick so we could all meet Penny in front and welcome her back to her first day on the job. A girl usually likes to be welcomed back to her first day on the job after being away from work for a while. That's how it works.

When I saw my friend Penny step out of the car, I had some feelings inside of me that I didn't know I had. At least, I never thought those kinds of feelings were in there just waiting for the right time to come out. First, I was so happy that I probably had the biggest smile in the history of the world. I know my slits were showing; that's how big my smile was. But then, I got this funny feeling in my throat, sort of like a glob of stuff was in there that made it hard for me to swallow, and I felt like I was going to cry. A guy usually laughs and smiles when he's happy, but not always. Sometimes a tear or two will come to his eyeballs. And, what happened next was even better. I'll tell you about it, 'cause you'll probably like it.

Penny got out of the car, and she walked right over to where I was waiting for her. I wanted more than anything in the whole world to put my arms around her; you know, like maybe around her shoulders or back, and give her a nice friendly hug. I wasn't exactly sure if hugging Penny was the right thing to do, though. I was thinking that maybe some girls just don't like to be hugged, just like they don't like to give big waves to somebody they know in an Italian restaurant, or maybe it's not good manners to hug a girl unless she asks you to first. That's the kind of guy I am.

So, I just went ahead and told Penny how happy I was to see her, and don't you know, even before I could finish what I was saying, she put her arms around me and gave me a big hug that felt so good a shiver went through me all the way down to my toes and back up again. When Penny was still hugging me, she pulled her face a little bit away from mine. Then she smiled at me and told me, and I mean out loud in her own voice if you can believe it, that I was her very best friend. I almost didn't believe it.

At last, one of my wishes came true. Penny finally smiled and talked to me. It's the best thing that ever happened to me in my whole life. At least, so far. Honest. And, I sure was right about her teeth. They're pure white as brand new snow and exactly even with no spaces between them.

Penny and me got to be even closer friends after that. Like I already told you, it's not like I've had a whole lot of close friends in my life; fact is, except for Billy, Penny is only the second close friend I ever had. And, the thing about being friends with Penny is that it's way different from being friends with Billy.

Penny is the first thing I think about when I get up in the morning and the last thing I think about when I go to sleep at night. Even when we aren't standing next to each other at work, I can still hear her talking and laughing and see her smiling. I think about what her long blonde hair feels like, and if I try real hard, I can even smell the perfume she usually puts on her skin. It's like my head is all filled up with her. It's a good thing, having a friend like Penny, 'cause if any bad or sad thoughts ever come into my mind, I just go ahead and think about her, and then I'm very happy again.

After me and Penny got to be close friends, we started to do a lot of things together. We went bowling and to the movies and out for pizza and burgers. We went for bike rides and walks in the park, too. No matter what we did though, at first, I was usually kind of nervous when I was with Penny. I got a little sweaty, my heart pounded away again, and sometimes I noticed my hands were shaky. I worried about what to say to her and if my speech would be OK. Sometimes, I went over stories and jokes in my mind, sort of like practicing like an actor does, I guess you could say. You can never tell when you might get to one of those quiet times when no one is talking and you're feeling tense, 'cause it's plum quiet and you don't know what to say to fill up the empty space.

But, one neat thing about Penny is that she always knew when I was nervous. She just reached over to me and gave me a nice squeeze on the arm and a smile. She told me how much fun she was having and before I knew it, I was all calm and relaxed, and I forgot that I was ever nervous in the first place. When that happened, I didn't have to practice anything anymore, 'cause it was real easy to talk to Penny, and even if neither one of us talked, like we got into one of those quiet times I was telling you about, that was OK, too. When you're real close friends with someone, you don't have to be saying stuff to each other every single second. You're just glad to be with your friend. That's how it works.

After a few movies and going bowling and bike riding a lot, I got to thinking that it would be nice for me and Penny to try out some new things. You never want to get into the habit of doing the same things over and over again, 'cause you don't want your friend to get bored with the same old stuff. It's like if you keep eating cheese pizza over and over, sooner or later you get bored of it, but if you suddenly try a slice or two with sausage and green pepper on top, you start liking pizza as much as you did the first time you ate some. Like Dad always says: "Variety is the spice of life."

Anyway, I got to wondering about some variety that me and Penny could do that would be spicy, except I was having a problem coming up with something. When you're having a problem coming up with something, it's usually a good idea to have a talk with your mom and dad. They're older so they have more experience in life. They been around the block a few more times you could say, so they can usually give you some pretty good ideas for things to do when you want to have new kinds of fun with your friend.

Well, Mom and Dad and me talked about it for a while; you know, what kind of new things me and Penny could do, and Dad came up with the real good idea of taking Penny to a baseball game. Mom said she would pack us up a nice picnic lunch that we could eat before the game or even while the game was going on. To me, it was a real good plan, and when I asked Penny about going to a baseball game, she liked it too. Fact is, she was real excited about it, 'cause she never went to a baseball game in her whole life, if you can believe it. Can you imagine never being to a baseball game in your whole life? It's almost as silly as never eating pizza.

The day of the baseball game finally came, and I was happy to see it was sunny and warm outside when I woke up in the morning. No one likes to go to a baseball game when it's cloudy and cold. I mean, you could still wear your warm clothes and go to watch the game if you wanted to, but usually going to a baseball game isn't as much fun when it's cloudy and cold. And, if there happens to be a rainstorm outside, the game is postponed, which is another word for called off, until another day. I never figured out why they play a football game in the rain but not a baseball game. I mean, if you're going to get wet anyway, why should it matter what kind of game you're watching?

Anyway, I had a shower, and after breakfast, I took the picnic basket Mom made for us and headed out to get Penny at her house.

Penny and me walked the rest of the way to the ballpark together. When the place you're going isn't too far away and the weather is nice and sunny outside, you should always walk, 'cause it's good, healthy exercise. A guy could even lose a pound or two maybe, depending on how far the place he's walking to is and how fast he might be walking to get there. The faster you walk, the more weight you're going to lose. That's how it works. You shouldn't walk too fast, though, 'cause you don't want to get all sweaty when you're with a girl that happens to be your best friend.

I was wearing one of my sailor hats, so I wouldn't get sun burnt at the ballpark, 'specially on the top of my head where a guy that doesn't have too much hair can get burnt real easy. You can never be too careful about getting sun burnt; if it happens too much you could even get cancer of your skin which you never want to get if you can.

'Course, I knew exactly what streets to walk on to get to the ballpark. Fact is, Penny and me got there early, about an hour before the game was supposed to start. It was good to be early, 'cause there was still plenty of good seats left, and I wanted her to see the batting practice and fielding practice and maybe even get some autographs from the players before the game started. I didn't want Penny to miss a single thing.

Well, it turned out that me and Penny had plenty to talk about at the baseball game. There wasn't even a single one of those quiet times I was worried about. The reason for all the talking was that Penny didn't know the first thing about baseball. I mean, not even one little thing. She didn't know any of the rules, the names of the bases, who the pitcher and catcher were, or what a foul ball or a bunt or a homer was. She didn't think it was nice when some people behind us got mad and started yelling to kill the umpire, and she was surprised when a guy in the stands caught a foul ball and didn't throw it back to the players.

The funniest thing was after I told Penny that one of our guys stole second base, she asked me if he would be punished for it. Honest. And, when one of their guys got a walk, she asked me how come he ran all the way to first base. Boy oh boy. What I'm saying is Penny knew a lot of things all right, but baseball sure wasn't one of them. When you think about it though, nobody usually knows everything, or even something, about everything.

I'm telling you, I couldn't stop talking for a second; that's how much explaining I had to do. I didn't mind though, 'cause I could tell Penny was having a good time at the baseball game and catching on to the rules with hardly no trouble at all. A smart girl like Penny catches on to the rules of the game real quick, except for a double play, which took her a while.

After the game was over and our team won, me and Penny walked across the street to a park that had tables so people could finish having their picnics. We were so busy during the game, me explaining stuff and Penny catching on to the rules, that we never got around to polishing off Mom's lunch, which turned out to be way delicious, all right.

Mom packed a lot of delicious food into the picnic basket, like she usually does. There was roast beef and chicken sandwiches, dill pickles, chips, fruit, soda pop, and bags of M and Ms, the kind with the peanuts in them, for dessert. Mom put in some of those little napkins too, the ones that are already cold and wet when you open up the package, so you can wipe off the ketchup or mustard or whatever else might of dripped onto your chin or your shirt. There sure was a lot of tasty food, but, except for part of one pickle that tasted a little too ripe, me and Penny emptied the basket. A guy and his best friend get plenty hungry at a baseball game all right, 'specially when they haven't had anything to eat since breakfast, and they been talking almost nonstop without a break.

So anyway, Penny and me were just sitting on those picnic benches which weren't all that comfortable, 'cause they were made out of wood. Half the time we were talking back and forth and half the time we were finishing our picnic lunch. The rest of the time we were just looking at all the other people that were having a good time at their picnics, too.

It was a nice relaxing chat we were having; mostly we talked about the ballgame and about work. Some people say that time sure

flies by real quick when you're having fun. I think those ⸺
must be right, 'cause it seemed like before Penny and me knew it,
the sun was going down, and it was time to walk home before it got
too dark out. I don't know if you knew it, but when the sun goes
down here, it comes up in China. That's why it's daytime and the
Chinese people are up and around when it's nighttime here and we're
sleeping. It works out real good, it seems to me, 'cause somebody,
either here or there, is always up and around to keep an eye on things.

The day after the ballgame and the picnic in the park, me and
Penny were in the lounge at work having our coffee break. Almost
out of the blue I would say, Penny asked me if I ever thought about
moving to a new house, a house where my mom and dad didn't live.
I didn't feel like answering that question, 'cause I usually don't like
to think about sad things. So, Penny said I should try to think about
her question another time, whenever I felt like it. Then, she asked
me to explain what a double play was again.

The next day Penny asked me the sad question again. I figured
that when a girl asks you the same question two days in a row, you
might as well try to answer her, 'cause she'll probably keep on asking
you on the third day and fourth day and many days after that until
you finally do. So, I told Penny the truth like I always did.

I told her I started worrying when I was a little kid about where I
would live after my parents were dead and up with the angels in
heaven above. I told her I'd been thinking about it almost every day
since her parents were killed from being run over by the bus in the
fatal accident. That's when Penny said I should move in to where
she lived at the group home. And the thing is, she thought I should
move in there right away, even though my mom and dad weren't
dead yet, or even close to it.

At first, I didn't think Penny had such a good idea. I told her I
didn't want to move away from my mom and dad, Winnie and Mamie,
and the nice house that I grew up in and was so used to living at. I
had my own room for privacy, and now, I even had my own color
television for the shows I wanted to see. I knew where everything
was at my house, and I had my own bathroom for that kind of stuff.

Winnie and Mom cooked up my favorite meals, and Mamie kept the whole house neat and clean, except for my room that I kept neat and clean all by myself. So, why would a guy move away from all of that good stuff when he didn't have to is what I was thinking?

So like I said, at first, I didn't think Penny had such a good idea. After I told her all of my reasons for not wanting to move yet, Penny said she understood how I was feeling. Even so, she asked me to please think about it some more and talk with my mom and dad about it. I promised her I would. Just because you talk about moving with your mom and dad doesn't mean you're going to do it. I mean, you could go ahead and move if that's what everyone decides is the best thing for you to do, but there's no rule saying that you have to do it.

Most nights I don't have too much to say at the dinner table, 'cause it's not good manners to talk when you have food in your mouth. Besides, Mom and Dad are usually talking about who's going to get a lot of money after somebody else dies or who gets to be with their children after a divorce or some other kind of lawyer stuff that's hard for me to understand. Fact is, even if I do understand a little bit of what they're talking about, lawyer stuff usually isn't all that interesting to me. By the way, I think moms and dads should both see their children after they get a divorce. They should still love their kids even if they don't love each other anymore is what I'm saying.

Anyway, this one night, I gobbled down my meat loaf, mashed potatoes, and broccoli with the cheese sauce without taking a single breather, and just as soon as Mom and Dad stopped talking for a couple of seconds, I said I had a question I wanted to ask them. 'Course, Mom and Dad, being as polite as they are, stopped eating, even though they weren't finished yet, and asked me what I had on my mind.

Dad always says that when a person has something on his mind, he should get right to the point and not beat around any bushes, not that I ever figured out yet exactly what bushes he was talking about. So that's just what I did. I spoke up real quick and asked them how long I should keep on living at our house with them. "Should I wait until after you die before I move, or should I move to a different house right away or at least pretty soon?" was my exact question.

I could tell that my exact question was a big surprise for Mom and Dad. They didn't say a single word to answer my question, and they got these real serious looks on their faces. Mom took off her glasses two or three times and breathed on them to make them wet. She wiped them off with a napkin each time and put them back on. Dad raised up one of his eyebrows, the left one I think, and rubbed his chin a few times. I've noticed that Mom and Dad usually do those things when they're thinking real hard about the answer to an exact question that catches them by surprise.

All the time that Mom and Dad weren't answering my question, Mom was looking at Dad, and Dad was looking at Mom. It was like each of them was waiting and hoping that the other one would start off with an answer. Finally, Dad said I asked a tough question, not a stumper, but still a tough question, that Mom and him needed some extra time to think about. He said they would sleep on it and kick it around for the rest of the next day. That was Dad's different way of saying Mom and him would talk it over. Then, we would have a family talk the next night after dinner. That was the deal.

Before I fell asleep that night and most of the next day up 'til dinnertime, I thought some more about moving to the group home where Penny lived. After all that thinking, I still didn't like the idea of leaving my house too much, even though, when you think about it, most grownup guys move away from their parents to live in their own place. So, I guess you could say I was a little confused, 'cause most of me wanted to keep on living with my mom and dad, but a little part of me was thinking that since I already graduated from high school and was grown up and all, that maybe it was a good time for me to move.

Don't you know, Winnie cooked up a delicious dinner that night. It was something she never made before, but from the name of it, jumbo laya, I had a hunch I was going to like it. When it comes to dinner, I like almost anything that's jumbo. It's got a lot of brown rice in it and some spicy tasting hot sauce that makes your nose run, a few vegetables I never heard of, and big chunks of sausage and chicken all mixed in with everything else. It was so tasty that I had a couple of big helpings and one smaller one. I'm telling you it was so delicious I almost forgot about the family talk for a while.

Winnie and Mamie cleared all the plates and glasses and brought some coffee, the kind that doesn't keep you up all night, to the table. Dad got a serious look on his face and cleared his throat. Whenever Dad cleared his throat and got a serious look on his face at the dinner table, I knew he was almost ready to start a family talk. Mom got ready for the family talk by scraping off some rice that got stuck to the tablecloth and pouring some coffee. She wiped off her glasses a few more times, too.

I figured Mom and Dad must of stayed up almost all night talking about where I should live. I even thought they probably didn't do much of their lawyer work that day, 'cause they needed all that time to figure out exactly what to say to me at the family talk. I mean, deciding where a guy should live, 'specially when the guy is your one and only son that's lovable, is pretty serious business, all right.

Fact is, I never found out exactly how long Mom and Dad kicked around my question about moving to a different house, but they sure had a lot of words to say when the family talk finally got going. Mom started by telling me they were feeling real healthy, 'specially for some people that were getting pretty old. They just had examinations from their doctor, and they did real good. Dad had a case of diabetes, which happens when your blood gets too sweet, and Mom had too much fat floating around in her blood. But, neither one of their blood problems was too serious as long as they remembered to take some medicine on time. 'Course, I was glad to hear that Mom and Dad were feeling good, but to tell you the truth, I still wasn't exactly sure what it had to do with our family talk.

Dad did some talking next, and I started to understand what they were getting at better. He said that even though Mom and him didn't have any bad sicknesses or anything like that, sooner or later, just like everyone else, they were going to die. He said there are at least two things that a person can count on for sure. First, nobody goes through this life without paying some taxes and second, nobody gets out of this life alive. Death and taxes happen to everyone. "You just can't get around them," Dad said. That's how it works.

Then, Dad said that both him and Mom didn't want me to wait until after they died to move to the group home where Penny lived. They thought I should do it right away, while they were still feeling good. I guess they could tell I was plenty surprised, 'cause the rest of our family talk was about the reasons for not waiting too much longer before I moved.

When I asked Mom and Dad what the big hurry to move was, they said it's real hard for somebody, even a grownup guy, to move out of his house, and it's also real hard for somebody when his parents die. So, if a guy has a choice, he doesn't want to have both of those hard things happen to him at the same time. If I went ahead and moved while they were still feeling good, alive and kicking, like Dad says, I could get used to the idea of living on my own and taking care of everything by myself so it wouldn't be so hard for me when they finally died and went to the angels in heaven above.

It was turning into a sad family talk all right, 'cause my parents' eyeballs got wet like they usually do just before a person starts crying. The more we talked about it, though, the more I had to admit to myself that moving pretty soon to the group home where Penny lived wasn't such a bad idea after all. It would be sort of like my old friend Billy growing up real fast and leaving his mom and dad's house when he went away to college. I got to thinking that every guy should have a chance to move away from his mom and dad when he finally grows up. It's one of the things that a guy does when his name finally changes from Dicky to Richard.

Even though it was sad, we kept on going with our family talk and some more reasons why moving pretty soon would be OK. The group home wasn't very far away, and Mom and Dad could visit me any time. They could help me set up my room, and I could come home for visits and for Winnie's delicious dinners maybe once or twice a week. We could visit each other on holidays and even go on trips together. I mean, it wasn't like I was going to a jail or some other terrible place where I would only get bread and water to eat and I would never see my parents again in my whole life.

And, another neat thing about moving I was thinking about, even though I didn't say it out loud to my mom and dad, is that I would be able to see my best friend Penny even more. I mean, her room would be right down the hall from mine, if you can believe it. We could eat breakfast together in the morning, go to work together, come back home, have supper, and even be together until it was bedtime. Me and Penny could be together all the time, like best friends are supposed to be. That would be way cool, you got to admit. Then, the family talk was over.

The next Sunday, when Mom and Dad had a day off from work, all of us went over to the group home. Penny already knew we were coming, so she was waiting for us at the front door. Carolyn and Tom Doherty were waiting there, too. Carolyn and Tom would be like my second mom and dad at the group home. A guy usually feels very welcome when people are waiting for him at their front door.

'Course, we had already been to the group home a few times, so nobody had to give us a tour of the place. Mom and Dad and me just went straight into the parlor, which is another word for living room, and sat down on a sofa. Tom and Carolyn sat across a table from us, and I helped myself to a chocolate chip cookie that was sitting there looking real delicious on one of those silver trays with the fancy lace napkins you put cookies on. I liked it when Penny sat next to me and had a cookie, too. It feels real comfortable when your best friend sits next to you for some cookies and a talk about where you're going to live next.

Well, Tom and Carolyn didn't believe in beating around any of those bushes, neither. Right after I polished off my chocolate chip cookie and picked off a couple of crumbs that were sticking to my shirt, they just came right out and asked me what I thought about moving to their house.

Tom and Carolyn were looking at me; Mom and Dad were looking at me, and Penny was looking at me, too. When somebody asks you a question and everyone else that's around just pipes down and sits there looking at you, it's real easy to figure out that they're waiting on you to answer the question. By the way, if you ever have any crumbs sticking to your shirt, like maybe from a cookie or a cracker, the easiest way to get them off is to lick your finger just before you start picking. That way the crumbs stick to your finger instead of your shirt. Then you just lick your finger and everything is clean as a tack.

So anyway, I went ahead and answered the question like I thought I should. In my best speech and talking slow so everyone would understand me without being confused, I told Carolyn and Tom how much I loved my mom and dad and how nice it was for me to live at our house. I told them that it would be OK with my parents if I kept on living with them, but in our family talk they thought it was a good time for me to be a grownup guy and start taking care of more things by myself. I told them that my mom and dad did such a good job of helping me get to be a grownup that I was finally ready to go out into the world on my own.

Carolyn and Tom smiled and shook their heads up and down when I told them it would be better for me to move while my mom and dad were still feeling fine, instead of waiting until they were very sick or even dead. When I said that last part, Mom and Dad and Penny shook their heads up and down and smiled, too. Then I was finished answering the question, so I didn't talk anymore. I think I did real good.

Well, things worked out pretty smooth, all right. One of the guys that was already living at the group home got terrible sick and had to move to what you call a nursing home. A nursing home is a home with nurses that have the job of taking care of guys that happen to be so sick alls they can do is lay around in bed all day and get some shots or take some pills. You go to a nursing home when the doctors can't help you in the hospital anymore, but you're still too sick to take care of yourself at your regular home.

'Course, you never want to be happy about some other guy being terrible sick, but fact is, if that other guy didn't have to move to the nursing home, there wouldn't of been any room for me where Penny lived. I mean, I might of been on some kind of waiting list for a very long time, months or even years maybe. You can never tell how long you're going to be on a waiting list of some kind.

Carolyn and Tom and all the rest of us decided a good time to move to their house would be in exactly one week, when the next Sunday rolled around. That would give me plenty of days to figure out which stuff I was going to take to my new house and some more days to pack it all up. First you decide what stuff you're taking, and then you pack it up, and then you move. One step at a time, steady as she goes, is how it works.

Boy oh boy. A guy just doesn't know how much stuff he has until he starts going through all of it when he's trying to decide which things to take to his new house and which things to leave behind at his old house. At first, I was having such a hard time deciding what to take that I figured the easiest thing to do would be to just take everything. Then, Mom reminded me that I wouldn't be having my own room anymore, and I would only have one closet and one dresser. It's a good thing she reminded me, 'cause I forgot all about that part.

Fact is, I got a little confused and even a little discouraged there for a while, maybe for around a day or two I would say. I got to wondering if maybe I made a bad mistake about moving. I mean, here I was packing up to move away from my good old house with my own private bathroom and my own bedroom in the attic that had plenty of closets and lots of dressers to a new house where I would only have one closet and one dresser in a room that I would have to share with some other guy. I'm telling you it was like I was getting homesick even before I moved away from home, not that I know if that's even possible.

'Course, it didn't take Mom and Dad very long to tell I was getting a little confused and discouraged. When you think about it, your mom and dad know you better than anyone else in the whole world, so it's easy for them to know what's going on inside your mind. Even if you don't come right out and say it, your parents can usually tell if you're feeling confused or discouraged or happy or homesick or however else you might be feeling.

I stopped being so confused when Mom said we should make a list in writing so we could check off the things that I would need for sure at my new house. That would be all my clothes that still fit me OK and things like my toothbrush, deodorant for under my armpits, my electric shaver, and other stuff that a guy uses in the bathroom every day.

Then, I could pack a few extra things like a deck of cards and some games and pictures of Mom and Dad and me. Dad said I should leave all of my other things at their house, at least until I could tell exactly how much room I had at my new house. I could always bring more of my stuff over later on. That was the plan that helped me stop being so confused and discouraged.

Well, the plan worked out pretty good. The next Sunday rolled around just on time like it always does, and Mom and Dad helped me move into my new house. 'Course, before we left, I said goodbye to Mamie and Winnie. Don't you know, they chipped in some of their own money, probably around ten bucks each I would say, and bought me a new radio with an alarm clock for my room. Both of them told me to behave myself real good at my new house and to make sure and come back and see them all the time. Then, I gave them each a big hug, and I left my good old house.

All the boxes we packed up fit into the car real easy, even the one with the new boxer shorts and socks I bought during the week. Dad said that anyone that moves to a new place to live should have some new boxer shorts and socks. And, as long as we were shopping for that kind of stuff, I got three of those checkered shirts in different colors with the button down collars, a couple of sweat shirts and tee shirts, a couple of pairs of new Levis jeans, some corduroy pants, and a new pair of sneakers, too. I kind of like having brand new clothes, 'specially after they're not so brand new anymore.

Right after we got to the group home, we met my new roommate. Ernie is a guy with Down syndrome too, except he's older than me, maybe about six or eight years older I would say. He wasn't bashful or nothing when Mom and Dad said hello; instead, he shook my dad's hand, and he gave Mom a hug. He said he spent some extra time cleaning up the room, so it would be nice and neat when I moved in. He even helped us carry up some of my boxes. Ernie was real nice and friendly right from the first. That was a very good thing, 'cause no one wants a roommate that isn't friendly or might even be grouchy. Nasty would be the worst.

I got all unpacked, and Mom and Dad helped me find a good place for everything and put everything in a good place. In hardly no time at all, my new room was neat and clean just like I like it. Carolyn and Tom invited Mom and Dad to stay for supper, but they had to get right home to get ready for their lawyer work the next morning.

'Course, Mom got to crying some tears like she does any time something sad happens. And, Dad looked pretty sad, too, even though I didn't see any tears dripping out of his eyeballs. I gave them each a big long hug and told them to be happy, 'cause I was perfect. I told them I was a grownup guy that was starting out on a new part of my life. Then, my parents went home, and me and Ernie washed up to get ready for dinner at my new house.

It was real nice, that first dinner at my new house. It's not that the food was so great; I mean, it was pretty good all right, but not nearly as good as Winnie's. The nicest part about dinner was how friendly everyone was to me. 'Course, I had dinner there once before so it wasn't like I was a perfect stranger or nothing, but still, except for Penny, nobody else in the dining room knew me very good.

Every person at the dinner table took a turn standing up, if they could, and they all introduced themselves to me. They told me their names and what they did for work if they had a job. A few of them told me how long they were living at the group home and what they liked to do for a hobby. Tom told me I better listen up real good, 'cause he was going to give me a quiz later on, but I knew in my head he was just kidding. I'm telling you; just like my dad, that Tom is a real kidder.

Then, it got to be my turn for an introduction. I was a little nervous about it, but I stood up just like you're supposed to do. I said I was happy to meet everyone, and I told them my name was Richard. I said I worked at the same place as Penny, and we always tried to work right next to each other. Then, I sat down, and everyone passed around some spaghetti and meatballs that was pretty good, I have to admit. I ate nice and slow, so I wouldn't drip too much. I had some seconds, but no more after that, except for dessert, which was cold ice cream on top of a piece of warm apple pie. The pie melts the ice cream into a puddle, and it's way delicious, all mixed up like that in your mouth.

After dinner, I helped to clear the table. Then, me and Penny were playing some games of Checkers. Penny's roommate Denyse and Ernie were playing too. The way it worked was that two of us played one game and two of us played another game. Then, the winners of each game played each other, and the losers of each game played each other. It was pretty much fun, even though I only won a few games. Everyone already knew the rule about never moving your men in the back row, so I couldn't fool them or nothing.

Fact is, I started getting pretty tired when we were playing Checkers. A guy gets pretty tired on moving day, all right, 'specially when he gets up early and he's carrying boxes around a lot of the time. It's not such good manners to yawn when you're playing Checkers with people you just met, so after one more game, I said goodnight like you're supposed to do, and I went up to my new room. Ernie was tired too, so he came with me.

After I washed and brushed to get ready for sleeping, I was sitting on the side of my bed thinking about everything that happened to me during the day. Ernie was taking his turn in the bathroom getting washed up, too. That's when I happened to look over to where Ernie's bed was, and I noticed his bookshelf for the first time. Sometimes when you're so busy putting your own stuff away, you don't see everything that's in your new room, 'specially stuff that doesn't belong to you.

Ernie's bookshelf must of been at least three or four feet long I would say, and it was filled up with all kinds of books. Some of those books were fat, and some of them were skinny. Some of them had hard covers, and some of them had soft covers. Some of them were laying flat, and some of them were standing up straight. But, what surprised me the most was when Ernie was finished getting washed up, he came over to his bed, picked out one of those books, and started to read. I mean, just like that, he started to read, if you can believe it. I could tell he was reading all right, 'cause he was pointing at the words, one after the other, and moving his lips a little bit as he was going along.

I guess Ernie must of noticed I was watching him read, 'cause after just a little while he looked up and told me he always read for a few minutes before going to sleep. He said reading made him feel nice and relaxed, and I should help myself to any book on his bookshelf any time I wanted.

When I told Ernie I didn't know how to read yet, he asked me if I still wanted to learn. 'Course, I told him I did want to learn, and right then and there, almost like out of the blue you could say, Ernie said he would teach me. I mean, here was another guy with the extra chromozones just like me, and he could read real good. So, I figured if Ernie learned how to read, he was probably the best person to teach me how to do it, too.

Well, like I said, it's about a month after I moved in at my new house. It took me a little while to learn where everything was and what kinds of chores, like vacuuming the rugs and drying dishes and doing my laundry, I was supposed to do. But now, you could say I'm pretty much settled in here. I got into a routine would be a good way to put it.

'Course, being able to have more time with Penny is the best thing about living here. Just like I was hoping, we eat breakfast, go to work, and eat dinner together. Then we're together before it's time to go to sleep. I sure can't wait to see her each morning. Penny's never grumpy in the morning like a lot of people can be; instead, she always has a smile and a good morning for me. When you have a best friend like Penny, there's nothing you wouldn't do for her. That's how I feel. Honest.

The next best thing about my new home is Ernie. Without beating around any bushes, he's teaching me to read, all right. We practice every night before turning the lights off, and I can tell it's getting easier and easier for me. Fact is, I'm getting better each time a day passes. Now, I'm not saying I can read the kinds of books that a professor at a college or university might give you for homework, but anyone could tell I'm coming along real good. And, even better, while I'm practicing my reading, I'm starting to do some printing, too. Alls you need to do is write down the letters, one at a time in the right order, until you spell the word that's in your mind.

You can never tell how good I'll get at reading and printing if I keep on practicing. The thing to do when you want something real bad is to keep on practicing instead of just sitting around and wishing. When the going gets tough, the tough get going, all right.

CHAPTER IV
Penelope

A strange little girl lived in your neighborhood. She looked like everyone else, but she didn't speak your language. Her senses distorted what she saw and heard. You shunned her, because her behavior was peculiar. She was unhappy most of the time. So, she moved away to live in her head. You called her autistic.

One gentlewoman and her dear husband nurtured the strange little girl. They made a home for her, and they taught her things. They cared for her no matter what. They loved her without reservation. They were humane, generous, and graceful people. The child loved them in return, and she will never forget them. They were my mother and father.

I'm feeling better now. I talk to people. I look into their eyes, and I smile. I don't spin my charms. My senses are still very acute, but I can concentrate longer without being distracted. I sleep soundly most nights, and I like a long, hot shower in the morning. I listen to music, and it doesn't smell or taste. I don't see colors, either. People come close, and the humming is softer. Usually, I can't hear what they're thinking, even if they touch me. I don't even mind when they touch me. I'm still autistic, but I'm feeling better now.

I'm better at mourning, too. Mourners go through stages. After the horror and shock, there was a time I refused to believe my mother and father were dead. None of it was happening. It was just a nightmare. I would wake up soon, they would be there, and things would be just like they used to be. "Denial" is the word psychologists use.

When my parents' deaths were no longer deniable, I felt desperate. I'd been deserted; often I was frightened, on the edge of panic. Those feelings went away and self-pity took over. "Why me?" I wondered. "What did I do to deserve this?" Next, I was angry. I was still new at venting my feelings, so I was sullen for a while. Then, the "What if?" questions began.

What if the graduation ceremony started an hour later? What if the principal gave a longer speech? What if Bonofaccio's Italian Kitchen closed because of a gas leak? What if we felt like Chinese food for dinner? What if we had a flat tire or got stuck in traffic? What if Dad took longer finding a place to park? What if we sat toward the back of the restaurant? What if the people sitting near the window had a second cup of coffee? What if the man on the motorcycle stopped to pick up his girl friend? What if the bus driver didn't panic? What if he didn't drink? The questions went on and on, each followed by the same fantastic answer: They would have lived happily ever after.

Carolyn and Tom never talk about my parents unless I start the conversation. And even then, I do almost all the talking. They don't try to analyze my feelings; they don't offer any advice; they don't try to cheer me up; they don't lecture me about acceptance. Instead, they just listen. I know I have their support, and they know I need to mourn at my own pace, in my own way. They're very smart people.

The truth is I'm still a long way from accepting the death of my parents. Perhaps I'll get to that point some day, but for now, I want them back. What I am able to accept is the fact that "What if?" questions are futile. Fantastic answers earn no points. There will be no happy endings, no miraculous resurrections. At least, I've come to terms with that.

My mother and father are never far from my thoughts. I was their only child. My birth was a momentous occasion, and, for a little while, they were joyful and excited. They looked forward to happy times and pride in my achievements as I grew and developed. Then, with no warning or preparation, everything changed. They ran smack into the truth. I was someone other than they anticipated. The fulfillment and happiness they expected weren't going to happen. Autism shattered their dreams.

My parents never stopped loving me. They prayed for me to get better, and they took me to lots of doctors. They went so far as to send me, painful as it was for all of us, to the professor's school far from home. But, during all the time they were loving me and searching for someone to help me, I believe my parents were mourning, too. Their grief wasn't for a child who died though; it was for the normal one who was never born.

Like me, I think my parents went through stages as they mourned. There had to be times when they asked each other: "Why us?" And, once in a while, perhaps late at night after a particularly bad day, they had to wonder: "What did we do to deserve this?" There might even have been times when my parents wished I didn't exist. I would have understood. Their lives would have been so much easier if peculiar Penny ceased to be and another child, a normal person like they were, came to take her place.

I'll bet they asked their share of "What if?" questions, too. What if I hadn't had that wine before I knew I was pregnant? What if I didn't catch the flu bug during my third month? What if I didn't take pain-killing drugs during delivery? What if I had breast-fed? What if we noticed her odd behavior earlier? What if we tried harder to find the right medical specialist? What if we tried one of those experimental dietary treatments or vitamin supplements? Ultimately, they saw the futility of those kinds of questions. Fantastic answers earn no points. There would be no happy ending, no normal child resurrection.

With that realization, my mother and father began learning about autism. It took them some time to understand the difference between having something and being something. I don't *have* autism; I *am* autistic. This isn't a surface disease that can be scraped away to expose a normal child underneath. There are no psychotherapies, antibiotics, special diets, vitamins, or brain surgeries that are effective remedies. That's because autism is at my core; it's not what I have; it's what I am. When my parents understood that, they started coming to terms with the problem.

It's true that I'm feeling better, but I haven't been cured. Autism still interferes with my life. It colors every experience, every thought, every sensation, every emotion, and every encounter I have. It remains at the center of me, as I suspect it will forever. It is, after all, the essence of Penny.

Living at the group home has been fine. It took a while, but Denyse helped me get used to the routine. We like being roommates. Each knows when the other doesn't feel like talking and wants to be left alone. My housemates are nice too, and I can usually be around them without feeling uncomfortable. Going from being alone to living with a large group of people is a pretty long leap. I'm still up in the air, but I'm going to make it.

Carolyn and Tom did provide some direction. They encouraged me to go back to the workshop. It was a good idea. I was happy to get out and see the counselors and my classmates again. I was especially happy to see Richard. I smiled at him, and we talked. We went to the movies, out to eat, bowling, for long walks, bike rides, and to a baseball game and picnic in the park. Richard moved here not long ago. He has grown up. His roommate is teaching him to read and write.

I went to the workshop every day and did my best to stay busy on the weekends. I tried not to mope around, and I didn't think I was depressed. But, I wasn't all that happy, either. In fact, there were times I felt edgy. I was just a little short with people. Carolyn and Tom noticed. Denyse noticed. So did Richard. Something was missing for me, something apart from my mother and father.

Carolyn and I were drying dinner dishes and stacking them in the kitchen cabinets. We were working silently, until Carolyn asked me what I did at the workshop that day. When I didn't answer, Carolyn asked me again. I didn't exactly boil over, but both of us knew I was pretty darn irritated.

Finally, I told her I did the same thing I did the day before and the same thing I would do the next day. I put piles of small metal screws into small plastic bags. I took a coffee break. Then, I put piles of bigger metal screws into bigger plastic bags. After lunch, I did the same things all over again. Carolyn and I looked at each other and began to laugh. We laughed so hard that tears came to our eyes and our stomachs hurt.

It wasn't hard to figure out what was missing. The workshop

wasn't the best place for me anymore. It was a comfortable place to be; it was an easy place to be, but so is being asleep in bed. It was time to move on. I wanted something more interesting to do. I needed to find work that would be more challenging. Like Richard, I had to grow up.

Even with help from Carolyn and Tom, finding a job wasn't easy. Really, it turned out to be so difficult and frustrating there were times I was tempted to give up and just keep going to the workshop. I kept searching though, and I learned a lot. People who say: "It's a jungle out there," are exactly right. So is Richard when he says: "When the going gets tough, the tough get going."

Like most people I guess, I started looking for a job by reading through the want ads in the daily newspaper. I wasn't certain what I was looking for, but there were a few jobs I knew I didn't want. Baby sitting, factory work, and flipping burgers were definitely out. So were door-to-door sales, selling anything over the telephone, and selling shoes. I wouldn't have minded selling clothes or cosmetics in a department store or being a file clerk in an office, but I couldn't find any advertisements for jobs like those.

Then, I saw an ad for a beautician trainee at the Foran Brothers Beauty Salon. No experience was necessary, and the salary was more than minimum wage. Health and life insurance benefits were included. According to the ad, the environment was quiet and the people were friendly.

Learning how to do women's hair, manicuring their nails, and helping with makeup were things I knew I could do. It seemed like a job I'd like. I called and made an appointment for an interview the following morning. The lady on the phone asked me to be there at exactly ten o'clock. I thought I heard a snapping noise over the phone.

Carolyn didn't go to beauty parlors, and Tom never heard of the Foran brothers. They agreed that it sounded like a good job for me though, and they gave me some pointers for my interview. I needed to wear nice clothes, nothing too flashy, they suggested. That would be easy, because I didn't own anything too flashy. It was important to be as natural and enthusiastic as I could. My answers to questions should be brief and to the point. Answering questions briefly would be easy too, because until a little while ago I didn't answer questions at all.

Of course, Carolyn and Tom stressed the importance of smiling and maintaining eye contact. It wasn't a good idea to talk about salary or vacation time unless the person who was interviewing me mentioned those things first, but it would be fine to ask about things like hours and job responsibilities. I was very excited and nervous. I'd never had a job interview. I was on my way to trying something new and challenging.

The next morning I left plenty of time to get ready. I gave my hair some extra attention, and I forced down some cereal and fruit. Then, I took the bus to my first job interview. After a short ride through the morning rush and fumes that hardly nauseated me at all, I got off and walked about a block to the address the lady on the phone had given me. I got there ten minutes early.

There it was on the second floor. The Foran Brothers' Beauty Salon. The Foran Brothers' Funeral Parlor and School of Mortuary Science was on the first floor. I paced back and forth on the sidewalk taking some deep breaths. Just at 10 o'clock, a girl with a frown on her face came down the steps and out of the building. She looked at me and shrugged. I gathered myself and walked up to take my turn.

My interview was with the beautician who would have been training me. She looked and smelled loud to me with all the makeup she had on, eyelashes so thick they had to be fake, the gum she snapped as she chewed, and the smell of perfume coming from her and hanging all over everything in the room. She was nice enough, though. We had a brief chat about the weather, and she offered me coffee. She liked my dress, and we talked about the price of women's clothes. We talked about hairstyles, too. She "just loved" mine. Then, we got down to business. She was looking for an assistant to do the hair and put makeup on the faces and hands of dead people so they would look presentable when they were waked downstairs.

I'm sure the beautician liked me and wanted to hire me. After no more than 15 minutes, she came right out and said I was just right for the job. She offered a dollar an hour over minimum wage with a guaranteed raise after three months. And, I'd be eligible for insurance after 60 days. Then, she asked if I had any questions. I suppose I should have come up with at least one just to be polite, but I really couldn't think of anything.

The beautician invited me to watch a demonstration of her work on a "poor old lady who croaked from a stroke or something." The lady needed some "finishing touches" for her two o'clock wake, she said.

I maintained eye contact and smiled. I was brief and to the point. "Thanks for your time, but I just don't want to be around dead people every day," I said.

"How about two dollars an hour over minimum?" she asked, ending her question with a particularly loud snap of her gum.

I thanked her again, showed myself to the door, and hurried down the stairs to the street. The next girl was waiting in front.

I told everyone about my job interview at dinner that night, and all of us had a good laugh. Tom thought I should have taken the job, because none of my customers would have ever complained. Then, everyone at the table tried thinking up more imaginative names for the Foran Brother's Beauty Salon. My favorite was "Hair Today, Gone Tomorrow," but I liked "Heavenly Hair Styling," and "Truly Permanent Waves," too.

It was back to the want ads for me. I found an opening for a veterinary technician at an animal hospital. They needed someone to bathe and groom the animals, make sure they were fed on time, and otherwise provide general care. Learning to spot signs of illness and infection after surgery was part of the job, too.

Two fish named Inky and Goldy and George the gerbil were the only pets I ever had, but I always liked animals. I gave the hospital a call. One of the doctors spoke with me, and it sounded like a good job. I was starting to get excited until he told me the hours. They were looking for a person to work from midnight through eight in the morning. I wouldn't have minded caring for sick animals, but not during the graveyard shift. I didn't think sleeping all day would be good for me, either.

Then, I saw an advertisement from a company that made products people use to clean their houses. There must be a person who works for the newspaper whose job is to think up professional sounding titles for jobs that aren't professional at all. So, a garbage collector becomes a "refuse engineer" and a junk man becomes a "reclamation specialist." For this job, a "cleaning products distributor" turned out to be a person who walks from door to door handing out trial size samples of Mr. Clean.

I was told I could hand out no more than one sample per household, and when the lady of the house answered the door, I was supposed to say, "Free sample madam." Among the 15 of us who showed up to apply for the job, I was the only one who asked what to say if the man of the house answered the door. The interviewer didn't answer; he just sort of snorted and turned away. For 12 dollars a day and no benefits, so did I.

A long, discouraging series of rejections came next. Richard called them "strike outs." I interviewed for jobs as a pharmacy technician, nurse's aid, dental hygienist, floral arranger, checker at the supermarket, meat wrapper at a butcher shop, data processor, telephone operator, receptionist at an optometrist's office, postal worker, counter person at a delicatessen, and ticket agent at the train station. I didn't get any of them.

Of course, most employers were looking for experienced people. I understood that, but how does a person get experience when nobody is willing to give her any, because she doesn't have any experience? Even a brain surgeon gets to operate on his first patient somewhere along the way. It happens, I guess, because the patient is unconscious.

I got most discouraged after I tried for a job at the local school district. Carolyn heard they were hiring teachers' assistants in two of their classrooms for children with special needs. More of these classrooms were located in public schools now, right next to classrooms for children without special needs; you know, the kids who aren't retards, crips or weirdos. There must be a lot of empty classrooms in church basements.

I called and arranged for an interview at the district office. A lady told me to bring a record of my education and a list of previous employment. Of course, my list was pretty short. Except for the workshop, I didn't have any previous employment. As for my schooling, at first I was going to leave out the dead professor's school. Then, I thought I'd better be honest, so I put it down along with the church basements. Prestigious prep schools and Ivy League colleges hadn't been all that interested in me.

I thought I had a good interview. A supervisor in the special education department spoke with me. She explained the responsibilities of a teacher's assistant and the usual things like benefits, salary, and hours. I asked about the type of students I'd be working with if I got the job and whether I'd get any training after being hired.

I was hoping the school district needed a teacher's assistant to help in a classroom for autistic children, but that wasn't the case. The students had behavior disorders or learning disabilities or both. The district required and would pay for a new person to take a course at the community college about children with special needs. And, after being hired, a teacher's assistant would have a series of six in-service training sessions to learn classroom and behavior management techniques.

When the supervisor looked at my materials, she had some things to say about the famous professor. She knew of him and his school, but she'd never visited the place. She asked me how long I was there and what I thought of it. She'd heard of his suicide. Then, she shuffled my papers and stood. It was clear the interview was just about over. I rose to leave and asked when I could expect to hear from her. She told me they still had many applicants coming in and that the district would be contacting me as soon as possible. It wasn't my first taste of "Don't call us; we'll call you."

I heard from them in a month. They didn't call me; instead, I got rejected through the mail. "The position for which you interviewed attracted a large group of experienced, highly qualified candidates from whom to choose. Therefore, we regret to inform you that the district is unable to offer you a position at this time. We shall keep your application materials on file for consideration should we need additional help at some future date. Please accept our best wishes for success in your employment endeavors," the letter said.

Another strike out. At least it wasn't a form letter, although they did manage to misspell my name.

With the way my job hunt was going, I felt defeated. Rejection isn't fun. I might have been feeling sorry for myself. Nevertheless, I couldn't help but think I might never be one of those "experienced, highly qualified candidates" so long as prospective employers knew I was autistic. I had been naive enough to think that a school district, so proud of offering services to children with special needs, might actually have been willing to give a graduate of that same special needs program an opportunity to show what she could do. Not on your life. I guess they were willing to teach weirdos, but hiring one was another matter. There was some good news, though. I was getting pretty darn capable at interviewing, and my non-flashy wardrobe had grown to three outfits.

Finally, I saw a job listing for an accountant's assistant. Like the position at the beauty salon for the recently dead, no previous experience was required. I didn't know anything about accounting, but I had always been pretty good with numbers. With nothing to lose, I decided to apply.

This time a man answered the phone. He said, "Max Eberhart here." I asked about the job opening, and he said he was a certified public accountant, in practice by himself. He needed someone to help him complete income tax forms, answer phone calls, make appointments, and do other office work like receiving clients, duplicating, and filing.

I told Mr. Eberhart I had no experience with accounting or income tax forms, but he assured me that as long as I was a high school graduate who was willing to work hard, he could teach me everything I needed to know. "Actually, I'm looking for a person with no experience, because they haven't learned any bad habits," he said. Then, he invited me to come to his office for an interview the following afternoon. This time I heard wheezing and heavy breathing over the phone.

I was appropriately dressed and on time the next day. The office was on the ground floor of a professional building. A directory in the lobby listed some physicians and dentists, along with two clinical psychologists, a chiropractor, an optometrist, two lawyers, and an insurance agency. At first, I had a good feeling about the place. At least, no dead people were around. I stopped feeling quite so good when I met Mr. Eberhart.

He was obese and damp. What used to be his chest had fallen to his stomach, and he had that kind of pouch below his belt that you see in people who are seriously overweight. He waddled rather than walked, I think because his thighs couldn't possibly get past each other. There were beads of sweat on his forehead, and, sure enough, he made wheezing noises when he breathed. His hair looked oily, scraggly and unkempt. He had a full-length beard that covered his jowls and made me think of a nest. His clothes were a mess, too. Sweat stained and too tight; they should have been thrown away, maybe even burned.

A stinking blue haze from the fat cigar he was smoking hung in the office. Mr. Eberhart chewed on it through the whole interview, and the end he kept in his mouth was soggy. Strings of dark green tobacco hung from it. Ashes kept falling on his beard, shirt and desk. The cigar went out a few times, and when he relit it, I couldn't miss his tobacco stained fingers, ragged nails, and what looked like a class ring digging into his flesh.

He spit a couple of times, quick, unconscious little spits somewhere off to the side. He used his fingers to pick more stubborn bits of tobacco from his tongue that was coated with some brownish yellow stuff. Stink from the cigar mingled with body odor and stale food I could smell but didn't see. I didn't gag or anything, but I had an unpleasant, queasy feeling. I really wanted a job, but I worried whether I could possibly put up with being close to this man for 40 hours a week.

The work sounded interesting enough. At first, I would be

checking to make sure all the necessary information was included and no errors in math had been made in preparing the tax forms. Mr. Eberhart told me he'd be willing to send me, two afternoons each week, to a tax preparation training course. Then, as I got more familiar with the forms and procedures, I would begin to prepare some of the simpler ones myself. The rest of the time I'd be doing general office work.

We talked about salary and benefits, both of which were generous. Mr. Eberhart was friendly, and he seemed like an OK sort of man, despite his sloppy appearance and disgusting habits. I kept telling myself they were surface things that didn't make him a bad person on the inside. As much as anyone, I knew how hurtful it could be to make quick judgments about people based upon their looks and behavior.

In fact, Mr. Max Eberhart seemed to be a nice, peculiar person. Just like me. So, when he offered me the job, I took it. I'd be working for a hairy, dangerously overweight, eccentric, poorly dressed, smelly old man who sucked on fat cigars, but I would start my new job, my first real job, clean and fresh, the following Monday morning.

I got to work that Monday, and my boss helped me feel comfortable from the start. The office was obviously cleaner, and the air seemed much less polluted. Someone had opened the windows and sprayed some pine scent around. Ashtrays were empty and magazines were neatly stacked. Floors were washed and rugs were vacuumed. Still, despite the weekend cleanup, I had a feeling that as the workweek wore on, the blue haze and the mess would reappear.

My desk was off to one side of the office. New pencils and pens, writing paper, a stapler, calendar, pencil sharpener, paper clips, and other office supplies were on top. A bouquet of fresh flowers was there, too. The card said, "Welcome Penny." A plate with six fresh donuts sat next to the vase. By 10 o'clock, Mr. Eberhart had eaten five of them, and he was eyeing the last one, even though I'd already taken two bites.

I spent most of that first morning learning where things were and how they worked. I got the hang of transferring phone calls and setting up conference calls pretty quickly. Working the duplicating machine, the calculators, and the coffee maker was easy, too. Mr. Eberhart was just beginning to convert to computer programs to complete tax forms, and he gave me a quick introduction to how all of that worked. I wasn't really surprised with the file cabinets. Like my employer, they were bulging, cluttered and messy. There were enough files to know that business was booming. This was a very busy office.

It was noon before I looked at the clock again. Mr. Eberhart was meeting for lunch with two men who had recently opened business establishments in town. He had already helped them write their business plans, arrange for some loans, and implement bookkeeping systems and billing procedures. At lunch, they would be talking about expansion and other long term plans. I was a little nervous when my boss invited me to come along. It felt good to be part of things, but I knew I wouldn't have anything to contribute at the meeting.

The plan was to walk over and meet the clients at a Chinese restaurant two blocks up the street. We had to stop three times for Mr. Eberhart to catch his breath. He went to the curb twice, made this loud hacking noise, and brought up some green stuff from who knows where. When he wasn't spitting, he asked me what I liked to read, and when we weren't talking, he hummed musical tunes I didn't recognize. A half dozen people greeted him. He introduced me as "my new, beautiful, and bright assistant who has already made my office a nicer place." It was when I started liking him.

At last, we got to the restaurant and sat at a table in a private area off to the side. The clients arrived on time, and I stood to meet them. Mr. Eberhart struggled to lift himself from his chair, and he said, "Penny, say hello to Roger and Robert Foran, the owners of the Foran Brothers' Beauty Salon and School of Mortuary Science."

Can you beat that? I gulped and smiled as best I could.

The Foran Brothers were young, nicely built men with huge appetites. Two waiters kept bringing heaping plates of food to our table, but my three luncheon companions had no problem cleaning them. While they were eating, they did their business. I was really impressed with Mr. Eberhart. There wasn't a single question he couldn't answer. He resolved every one of the business problems the Foran Brothers brought to the table. He outlined some plans for the future. He did all those things quickly in what seemed to be efficient and creative ways. I felt another flash of insecurity with my own lack of knowledge, until I reminded myself that it was only my first day.

After tea and almond cookies, Mr. Eberhart offered cigars to the Forans. They declined, but he lit one for himself. They spoke about yesterday's baseball game for a while. Then, my boss excused himself and waddled off to the men's room. Robert Foran, the younger brother, told me how lucky I was to have landed a job with Mr. Eberhart. "My brother and I think he's a genius, and he's a very nice man, too. If you can look past the surface stuff, he'll teach you more than anyone else in the business," he said.

Mr. Eberhart returned at the same time one of the waiters brought the check. After some bickering with the Forans, he paid for lunch. That's when I began to learn about expense accounts. We stood to leave, and everyone shook hands. I thought Robert Foran might have held my hand just a little too long. I didn't mind though. He was a very handsome young man. And, nice, too.

Each day was filled with new experiences. On Tuesday and Thursday afternoons, I went to my training course. I came back to the office, and Mr. Eberhart showed me how to apply what I'd learned. When I made mistakes, he was patient with me. He took the time to give me three or four similar examples until I got things right. Gradually, he gave me more and more responsibility, and soon I had learned enough to complete simpler tax returns on my own. I even began to make some small contributions at business lunches with clients.

I was loving my job, and, even though I didn't need it, earning some money on my own gave me a good feeling. It's true too, that as I learned more about tax forms and accounting, I learned more about my boss.

Max Eberhart was 55 years old. He finished college when he was

21, passed the CPA exam with honors the first time he took it, and practiced accounting ever since. He never married, and both of his parents died a few years ago. He lived alone, in an old Victorian house, not far from the office. He had an apartment in Paris, too. When he wasn't working at his practice, he had his books, music, painting, and gardening. The flowers on my desk the first day came from his back yard.

In May, when the tax season was over, Mr. Eberhart closed his office and took a long vacation. He was passionate about travel. He'd been all over the world, most of the time traveling by himself, but sometimes going with groups on organized tours. Of all the places he'd visited, he liked France the best. He told me all about Paris and the small towns and villages in Provence. Of course, he went on and on about the restaurants, but he loved the language as well. In fact, my boss was perfectly fluent in French, as he was in Spanish and German. His Italian, Russian, Japanese, Hungarian, and Greek were passable as well. "My Mandarin and Hebrew are a little weak," he confessed.

I couldn't help but think that the Foran brothers were right. Mr. Eberhart was a genius all right, not just in business and language, but across many different areas. In music, for example, he did more than just listen to it and hum it. He played it, and even better, he composed it. I was impressed, even envious.

"Yes, I can play six instruments fairly well, but I suppose guitar is my favorite," he told me. When I asked what style of music he liked best, he told me he was partial to anything that made the hair on his arms and the back of his neck stand up. "It doesn't matter if it's classical music, rhythm and blues, hard rock, or folk. I like it all, as long as it makes me feel good, and I write some, too. I try to write a new song every week," he said. How could you not like this man?

There was an art gallery between the office and some of the restaurants we went to for lunch. On the way to eat one day, Mr. Eberhart noticed a painting in the window. There was a sign under the painting that said it was an original Mondrian. Until that afternoon, I had never heard of Pieter Mondrian.

We stopped and looked at the painting through the window. Then, we went inside. Mr. Eberhart asked a hard looking saleslady if we could have a closer look at the Mondrian. A row of five trees, covered with green leaves beginning their turn to autumn colors, was receding into the distance. The painting looked very peaceful and beautiful to me.

Mr. Eberhart told the saleslady he was almost certain the painting was a fraud. She got very angry. "How could you possibly know that?" she asked. Worst of all, the saleslady, so skinny she probably stuck her fingers down her throat a lot, emphasized the word "you" in her question, as if anyone who was obese and sloppy looking couldn't possibly know anything about art.

My boss was a perfect gentleman. He didn't lose his temper; he didn't even raise his voice. He just smiled and told the lady that Mondrian had a "general revulsion" against green, growing things, and on those few occasions when he painted trees or flowers, it was always one tree or one flower, never a group. The skinny saleslady raised her plucked eyebrows and softened a little. She muttered something about checking her sources. Then we wished her a good day and left.

When we walked past the gallery two days later, the saleslady waved and smiled. The painting was still in the window, but the sign wasn't. Mr. Eberhart invited her to have lunch with us. They spoke about the impressionists. We had a new friend. How could anyone not like this man?

There was a television set in the office. Sometimes, when we weren't overwhelmed with work and sometimes when we were, Mr. Eberhart would turn it on to watch Jeopardy. The first time I saw him in action, I sat there with my mouth open. Of 60 possible items, my boss knew 59. He missed one that had to do with Civil War battle sites. "I knew that," he said; "it just slipped my mind for a moment."

Then, he went on to tell me how intellectually curious people who engage in stimulating mental activities demonstrate a significantly lower prevalence of dementia, clinical depression, and Alzheimer's disease than folks who are intellectually lazy. When I asked him if something like that couldn't also be said about the relationship between stimulating physical activities and heart disease in 55 year old men, he laughed, shook a finger at me, and called me "Mon belle jeune fille." I picked up a French-English dictionary and figured it out.

Mr. Eberhart was the most interesting man I'd ever known. It wasn't long before I was comfortable around him, even though I was amazed at how much he knew. Some people might be intimidated when they overhear their boss discuss the various types of subatomic particles with a client who is a Professor of Physics and just 15 minutes later discuss Italian renaissance cities with a client who is a travel agent. Actually, it wasn't intimidation I felt at all. Instead, it was a combination of admiration and affection.

Of course, Mr. Eberhart knew that being overweight was unhealthy and smoking was a dangerous, obnoxious habit. He knew, too, that his manner of dress, personal habits, and unkempt appearance could be unpleasant for people around him. He had an answer for all of that though. "People don't care what I look like, what I'm wearing, what I smoke, or how healthy I am so long as I save them a couple thousand big ones in taxes," he said.

I told him I cared, and he seemed surprised. For the first time since I met him, he had no answer.

Richard and I kept busy. We had our walks, bike rides, and movies, and after dinner, there was always time for a board game or a game of cards. Lately, though, he wanted to read aloud to me. He was improving very quickly. His reading was still slow, but he was able to sound out more words, he was getting more fluent, and he had even begun to use proper inflection. He was very proud of himself. I was proud of him, too.

On one of our Sunday walks, Richard talked about the workshop. "I don't like it there so much these days," he said.

"Is it because we don't work next to each other anymore?" I asked.

"I sure do miss you like crazy during the daytime," he said, "but it's the jobs we have to do that are making me crazy."

It turns out that Richard had become just as bored packaging screws and stuffing envelopes as I had been.

I remembered hearing the director and some of the counselors talk about the kinds of jobs they brought to the workshop. "People who were mentally retarded actually preferred doing very simple work. Richard wouldn't get bored, because he liked low level, repetitive kinds of jobs. Doing the same thing all day long helped Richard feel secure. Richard would get confused if he were given a variety of tasks. Richard would feel overwhelmed and frustrated. Richard would fail."

The director and counselors thought all those things, but nobody ever bothered to ask Richard what he thought. If they had, they might have learned there is no separate set of rules for people who are mentally retarded.

It's true that Richard is the only mentally retarded person I've known very well. What he's taught me, though, is that except for not scoring so high on intelligence tests and being slow to learn some subjects in school, he's no different than anyone else. He feels happy or sad, safe or afraid, calm or nervous, angry or pleased, confident or insecure, just like the rest of us. He also gets bored, just like the rest of us, when he's asked to do the same dumb things every day at work. Over and over and over again. There is no separate set of rules for people who are mentally retarded.

A workshop isn't for prisoners serving life sentences without parole. After a time, at least some of the workers should leave. When they can take direction from a supervisor, relate well to fellow workers, and be prompt, reliable and clean, the next step should be a real job in the community. Richard was ready for that step, and I was going to help him take it.

The next day, I told Mr. Eberhart about Richard.

Of course, "the encyclopedia man" knew all about Down syndrome. He knew it "resulted from a trisomy of chromosome 21 instead of a pair, and the probability of its occurrence had a positive correlation with maternal age at the time of conception." He knew that people with Down syndrome were usually moderately mentally retarded, and they often had some physical problems as well. He knew they usually weren't capable of much academic learning or holding down a job in the community.

Mr. Eberhart knew all that book stuff all right, but he didn't know Richard. So, he was surprised when I asked him to help me find a job for Richard. My dear boss was less surprised after he met my friend.

Richard had been anxious to see where I worked. I invited him to come to the office to see what I did at my job and meet my boss. He got permission to leave the workshop a little early on a Friday afternoon, and he showed up right on time, as he always did. I was on the phone when he came in, so I motioned for him to have a seat. He was neat and clean looking with one of his new button down shirts, a pair of dark slacks, and a shine on his shoes. Richard looked really fine to me, maybe not drop dead handsome, but surely nice looking enough.

Mr. Eberhart returned from a meeting just as I was beginning to show Richard around the office. He didn't wait for an introduction. He just smiled, pumped Richard's hand, and said, "You must be Penny's friend Richard. What a firm handshake. I'm so pleased you could visit our office. Call me Max. Take your time, look at anything you like, and when you're finished, we'll all polish off these leftover bagels together." Then, he lit his cigar, excused himself, and started returning phone messages.

I took Richard on a tour of the building. We went into some of the offices, and I introduced him to the receptionists. We met one of the clinical psychologists leaving for the day and the chiropractor on his way out of the men's room. We met John, the building's chief custodian. He was washing the floors with some detergent that smelled like pine. Everyone was very friendly to Richard. On the way back to my office, Richard asked me what a chiropractor did. I wasn't sure.

Back in my office, Mr. Eberhart was already munching a bagel thick with peanut butter and jelly. Richard had one too, while I was showing him the duplicating machine, computers, and files. I explained that each file was for a different person or company that came to us for help with their income taxes or business matters. Richard looked into every drawer. My boss grinned when he overheard Richard telling me the files could sure use some "straightening up."

When it was time to leave, Richard shook Mr. Eberhart's hand again. He told him he was happy to meet him, and he thanked him for the bagel. Then, my good friend surprised the heck out of me. He said, "Max, how about coming over for supper with Penny and me at our house. I'll give you a tour of the place, and you can meet our roommates and our substitute parents. You can see my room too, where I keep everything neat and clean and in the right place."

Max was delighted with Richard and the invitation. We made a date for Sunday supper. In just two days, my boss would come over and have dinner with Richard, me, and the rest of the people at our group home. It's not that I hadn't thought of inviting him; I guess I just wasn't quite ready to answer the questions I knew would come up.

We waited for Mr. Eberhart on the front porch. He parked and got out of his car, and like Richard always says, "You could have knocked me over with a feather," when I saw him walking up the sidewalk toward the porch. He must have spent Saturday afternoon at the barbershop and a clothing store. Except for a neat moustache and goatee, his beard was gone and his hair was styled. He was wearing a blue sport jacket, white shirt and tan vest, khaki slacks with a neat crease, and a pair of well-shined loafers. He had a big grin on his face. He turned completely around so we could admire his outfit, and he said, "How do you like the new me? I'm one of those fat guys who's light on his feet." I smelled after-shave lotion.

Supper was just fine. Mr. Eberhart was so charming and so much fun I could tell everyone liked him right from the start. Somehow, he knew exactly when to be quiet and listen and exactly when to ask a question or make a comment. He talked with Ernie about his books and Denyse about her artwork. He told Tom about a new tool, some type of power drill I think it was, that he wanted him to try. He thanked Carolyn for the delicious dinner, even though it wasn't, and he shared some gardening tips with her.

During dessert, Carolyn rose to put some records on the stereo. That's when Mr. Eberhart asked if we'd like to hear some live music. Then, he went back to the trunk of his car and got his guitar. Everyone sat outside on the front porch, and Mr. Eberhart played for us. He played classical music, popular music, rock and roll, and folk music. He sang new songs he had written himself and old songs everybody knew. Carolyn and Denyse joined in and made it a trio. Tom brought out his harmonica. Ernie played a comb wrapped in tissue paper. About 20 neighbors walked over for the free concert. Mr. Eberhart took requests and everyone sang along. It was a terrific time, and Carolyn and Tom wouldn't let him leave until he promised to come back and "sing for his supper" again. Before Mr. Eberhart walked back to his car, he hugged Richard and me. His cheeks were soft and smooth.

The next afternoon at lunch, we had a long talk. As I suspected, Mr. Eberhart was very curious. He asked if I would mind telling him how I came to live at the group home. By this time I was willing to talk, and I decided to tell it all. As our food got cold, I told Mr. Eberhart about being autistic. I told him about my parents. He listened carefully to what I was saying, all the while holding my hand. When I stopped talking, my boss asked the waiter to reheat our lunches. While we were waiting, he thanked me for telling him about my life, and he told me the thing he admired most about people was courage.

Mr. Eberhart had already spoken to John, the custodian, and some people who managed the office building. If Richard wanted a job, he could come to work as John's assistant three days a week. The other two days he could help out around our office. I would teach Richard how to run the duplicating machine and do some filing, and Richard would help us keep everything neat and organized. A place for everything and everything in its place. That's the kind of guy Richard is.

Now, Richard and I work at the same place again. John is teaching him all sorts of things besides washing and waxing the floors. He's learned how to do some electrical repairs. He's learned how to start up and keep the heating and air conditioning units going. He helps John with cleaning offices, painting, keeping the grass cut, and fixing problems with the plumbing. John says it sometimes takes Richard a little longer to learn things, but once he catches on, it's there forever. Richard never misses a day of work. He insists we leave our house 15 minutes earlier than I used to, so we will always be on time.

Richard started slowly in our office. At first, he vacuumed the rugs, washed the floors, emptied wastebaskets, and picked up after Mr. Eberhart. Soon after that, he learned how to use the copy machine, and I've been able to turn most of the duplicating over to him. Next, he started to help me clean out and rearrange the files. The file cabinets became Richard's responsibility, and he whipped them into perfect order in three days.

Mr. Eberhart had built a very successful practice in a disorganized, messy office. I had a hunch he liked it that way. Not only had he tolerated the disarray for a long time; he seemed to prefer it. Maybe, my boss, eccentric as he was, needed a place to work that looked like he did in order to feel comfortable. So, I was a little worried as the office turned into a clean, well-organized place.

How wrong I was. It turned out that Mr. Eberhart enjoyed a cleaner and neater office as much as he enjoyed a cleaner and neater Mr. Eberhart. He got a sensible diet and some medicine from his physician, and he joined a fitness center at the YMCA. After work, he took Richard and me to exercise three afternoons a week, and together we lost a total of 102 pounds. Mr. Eberhart lost 88, Richard lost 15, and I gained one. It was as if doughnuts and bagels disappeared from the planet.

Our boss entered a 10-kilometer run, and he promised he would quit smoking if he came in last. He also promised to quit smoking if he didn't come in last. Richard and I were waiting for him at the finish line. Max finished toward the back of the pack. He crossed the finish line exhausted but smiling. He clasped his hands over his head in victory. Everyone who participated got a T-shirt, and everyone who finished got a certificate. Max wore his shirt to work the next day, and the certificate hangs on the wall behind his desk. I'm positive there are still stinking blue hazes hanging in offices throughout the country, but not in ours.

Dozens of letters came and left our office each day. Most of them were in regular size business envelopes, correspondence to and from clients. Sometimes, though, larger packages of mail had to be taken to the Post Office or delivered by messenger. Fees paid for postage and to private messenger services added up to a fair amount of money each month, I'd say at least several hundred dollars.

Richard told Mr. Eberhart he could make the deliveries himself. He was sure he could do it faster and better and that he would save a lot of money. Max gave him a trial. He was amazed, as he should have been. Richard was the first person he'd ever known who had a perfectly accurate map of the city permanently fixed in his head and knew exactly which streets to take to get to places in the shortest amount of time.

Now, Richard zips around town on his delivery bike. Clients are pleased with the quick service. Mr. Eberhart is pleased with the money he's saving. Richard is pleased with his raise in salary and the tips. He's also pleased with the shirts Max had made for him. They have "Rapid Richard's Delivery Service" sewn on the back.

Two of our clients have already asked Richard to make deliveries for their firms on Saturday. Max is helping Richard get some business cards printed. Not bad for a guy who, until recently, was putting screws into plastic bags all day long. In fact, Richard has become an important person at our office. I can tell he knows it, too. He stands up straight, and he keeps his tongue in his mouth. All the time.

The Foran brothers got it just right. I was very lucky to have landed a job with Mr. Eberhart. I didn't have to tell our boss how I felt about him, either. He knew very well, and a good thing was happening. It seemed to me that our boss felt the same way about us. Richard, Penny, and Max Eberhart had become the best of friends. Almost like family.

CHAPTER V
Max

I lay in a bountiful supply of winter storage. I have an inordinate amount of adipose tissue. I'm a tale of horror told by the bathroom scale. I'm portly, paunchy, pudgy, blimpy, big-boned, rotund, stocky, thickset, wide-bodied, full-figured, a lard ass, or a load and a half. Whatever the euphemism, I'm fat. Ask me why and initially I'll implicate my metabolism. If that isn't convincing, I'll blame it on a genetic predisposition. During rare and reluctant moments of candor, I may admit that I eat too much and exercise too little.

I've learned a good deal about obesity, a problem that has become epidemic. Indeed, current surveys indicate one out of three people is overweight. Our sizable minority may be sub-classified as fat, obese, or morbidly obese. As we swell ever upward through these subcategories of surfeit, there is an increasingly negative correlation with life span, a statistical way of saying the fatter we grow, the fewer winters we'll have available to store adipose tissue.

Legendary examples of morbid obesity have been documented. One Robert Earl Hughes was the heaviest human being whose weight has been verified. He weighed 1,069 pounds; thus, when he died, it was necessary for his relatives to bury him in a piano case. They lowered Robert Earl's abundant remains into the ground with a crane. Arthur Knorr, also one of the world's 10 heaviest people, was 6 feet tall and weighed 900 pounds. During the last 6 months of his life, big Art gained 300 pounds. He truly gorged himself to death, not an altogether unpleasant way to succumb, I would submit. Another interesting case is Miles Darden who tipped the scale at a gargantuan 1,020 pounds. His wife weighed 98 pounds and bore him three children. She died before he did. Without witnessing her passing, one is left with all manner of unpleasant conjecture regarding the precise nature of her demise.

I've learned a lot about the brain, as well. Fat people don't necessarily have bigger ones. Indeed, whether it's perched atop the neck of an obese person or an emaciated one, on average, the brain weighs only three to four pounds, a very small percentage of total body weight. Yet, it is clearly the most important organ in the body. It has evolved to the extent that our species is unique in intellectual and creative potential. Thus, we are able to think in abstract terms, contemplate the future, reflect upon the past, and develop a sense of self. We attend to what is happening around us, respond appropriately to danger, and remember the faces of old friends we haven't seen in years. We speak with others, record the literature of our society, and read the histories of others. We are stirred at the sight of a painting or the sound of music.

We store everything we have ever learned, long after that learning has left our consciousness. We are capable of imagination out of which a range of exquisite expression has issued, from primitive drawings on the walls of caves to the Mona Lisa, from tribal drums to the great symphonies, and from the wheel to vehicles that will eventually take us to other planets. And, this magnificent brain of ours is all crammed up there between our ears, efficiently protected by the hardest bone in the body.

The brain is never at rest, even when we sleep, and it seldom breaks down, although the probability of such a dire outcome increases to the extent that we abuse it with toxins like alcohol and narcotics. Breathing environmental pollutants doesn't help much, either. Eventually, the passage of time, strokes, and senility do their devastation, but until then the brain serves us eminently. When that service ends, so do we.

Neuroscientists readily admit they are far from unraveling the brain's complexities. They have made some significant discoveries in the last decade, however. They tell us that neurons develop at the astonishing rate of 20,000 per second throughout the entire prenatal period. Thus, by birth, we have approximately one hundred billion brain cells, a quantity equal to about half the number of stars in our galaxy. Each of these cells is connected to thousands of others. These connections, or synapses, form an elaborate chemical and electrical network that never rests in a lifelong search for stimulation. Indeed, the brain is implacably hungry for input, and, with proper nourishment, it grows ever more powerful. It seems that mine was well-fed.

Children who are intellectually gifted often have parents who are similarly endowed. Mine had advanced degrees and were talented artists, musicians, and linguists. From the moment of birth and throughout my early years, Mom and Dad served up a wholesome and varied diet of brain food. Along with art and literature of all sorts, it included music and whopping portions of language. If I heard baby talk at all, it was in four different vernaculars. More often, I heard adult talk, typically news of the day, discussions of significant developments in the arts, and debate on controversial issues. Day trips to museums, children's concerts, art exhibits, and other cultural events were routine.

I read *The Adventures of Huckleberry Finn* and *The Hardy Boys* when I was a young child. Such an accomplishment wouldn't be particularly noteworthy, except for the fact that I was still a toddler, barely three years old. I don't remember precisely how I learned to read, perhaps because it was as easy and natural as learning to speak. My parents simply read to me every night at bedtime, and soon I was reading to them.

French, Spanish, and German were natural and easy for me as well. With English, my parents spoke them at home, so I did too. Indeed, I was a preschool polyglot, a young child who attained fluency in languages as effortlessly as my age mates built towers with blocks. Now, as an adult, I don't think in English and subsequently translate my thoughts into these other languages. On the contrary, I think in all four with equal ease such that each could be considered my native tongue. It may be that early and simultaneous exposure to four languages made it easier for me to learn others as I got older.

Music came to me with similar facility. I listened to it; then I did it myself. To my parents' delight, I had perfect pitch. Mother would hum a series of musical tones, and I'd play them back on the piano. I did this quickly and without error. I played simple melodies when

I was four and soon began composing tunes of my own.

Motivated by their desire to maximize my musical talent, and I suspect some parental ego as well, Mom and Dad arranged for private piano lessons. My teacher was the formidable Hildegarde Weissmuhler, an arid spinster with a lot of blue in her hair and blood. Her teaching technique was precisely equidistant between rigid and inflexible. Lessons were only slightly less painful than getting poked in the eye with a sharp stick. If I ventured a demonstration of even a glimmer of originality, the result was a stern verbal admonition. In German, of course. My punishment for attempting anything truly creative was a rap on the knuckles and half an hour of scales.

Notwithstanding her best efforts, Fraulein Weissmuhler was unable to suppress my urge to experiment. I progressed to the point where I was fascinated with the possibility of rejuvenating Bach fugues. I had the notion of transforming them to jazz. Predictably, Hildegarde the Teuton thought my idea was profane. Normally phlegmatic, she came all unglued one day when, with a gust of pent up defiance, I offered up Chopin's Minute Waltz in a boogie beat. "Nicht gut," she hissed as she stormed out of the house. I wouldn't have been surprised had she proffered a shrill "Sieg Heil," while simultaneously stretching her arm heavenward and clicking her heels. Happily, she never came back. In their wisdom, my parents recognized the stultifying effect of her tutelage and retained a less anal teacher.

With school, music, and reading everything I could get my hands on, I didn't have much time to do anything else. Except eat. I managed to find enough time each day to consume about 10,000 calories, mostly in the form of bovine or porcine flesh, potatoes of any variety so long as they were drenched in butter or sour cream, and all things chocolate, especially milk shakes and eclairs. It was the beginning of my enduring love affair with saturated fat. Thus, I became at least as prodigious in girth as I was in music and language.

After only three weeks in kindergarten, the teacher pinned a note to the blouse of my sailor suit. My parents were obliged to attend a conference at school. They heard that teacher was puzzled by their "cherubic" five year old child who preferred silent reading, alone in class, to group games and healthy exercise in the gymnasium. Also, teacher complained that my questions in class were a rather constant disruption to her lesson plans. I suspect those questions she had the most trouble answering were the ones she found the most disruptive. I must have been one insufferable cherub.

My deportment was different enough to require an evaluation by the school psychologist. While probing my as yet unripe psyche, he administered a widely used intelligence test, one that continues to be used to this day for the purpose of determining which children are sufficiently fast or slow at learning to require special attention in school. Early in the test, the psychologist asked what I would do if I cut my finger. I knew I was supposed to refer to some treatment, perhaps dispensing an antiseptic or applying a bandage. However, in a flash of creativity and rebellion, and with a wide grin, I told him I would bleed. I'm not sure I got any points for that one.

In fact, that was the first of a series of intelligence tests I was given throughout grade school and high school. The results were consistent. Such tests weren't difficult for me, and I always scored in the superior range.

Given my accelerated rate of development and obnoxious tendency to flaunt it, other children my age didn't exactly line up to seek my friendship. The preschool polyglot rounded into the primary grades pariah, for then, as now, scholarly and musical achievements weren't valued nearly as much as prowess on the diamond, gridiron, or hard court. This is particularly true when the scholastically and musically gifted individual is a fat boy.

My classmates were ruthless with their verbal taunts and physical abuse until I discovered that my heft was matched by a good deal of strength. Hesitantly at first, but with growing enthusiasm and vigor, I began to defend myself. In the process, I gained revenge by punching the stuffing out of a number of erstwhile bullies. Once they were down, I sat on them; end of story, as it were.

Dad spoke with fond and no doubt exaggerated recollection regarding the substantial amount of athletic prowess he'd demonstrated during his youth. Indeed, one might have surmised I was sired by none other than the great Jim Thorpe. He was certain I'd inherited some jock genes and had thus been endowed with athletic ability on a par with my linguistic and musical talents. So together, we searched for my sport. It wasn't a fruitful quest.

Contrary to the notion that fat people are buoyant, I sunk like a slab of granite in the swimming pool. Basketball and football, which require agility and running speed, were equally frustrating. I could whack a baseball a pretty good distance, but fielding, particularly catching balls necessitating a bend at the waist, was beyond me. Throwing a ball was difficult too, since I was never certain which arm to use. Finally, I found my niche in ice hockey, not that I ever developed any real proficiency at skating, stick handling, or other fundamental skills essential to any level of competence at the sport.

With a brilliant flash of strategic wisdom, the hockey coach suggested I play goalie, a position where my physique, inert though it was, constituted a very wide and thus relatively effective barrier to all but the most accurately propelled pucks. Only the low hard ones aimed at the corners eluded me. My athletic career came to a premature and painful cessation after a practice session when I tripped on a step leading to the locker room, fell face first to the floor, and fractured my mandible. The worst part was having my jaw wired shut for two months, although I managed rather nicely on milkshakes. One makes whatever sacrifice is necessary to stave off malnutrition.

The Quiz Kids became a popular radio show while I languished in grade school. A panel of young people, chosen for their vast knowledge of essentially useless information, answered questions with facility sufficient enough to amaze the listening audience, most of whom thought we were freaks. I made regular appearances on the show for three years. I pored over the entire Encyclopedia Britannica and other fact-laden tomes and committed most of their content to memory. Thus, I was the star of the show, the youngest freak on the panel.

Strangely, most of the Quiz Kids, even with their tremendous fund of information, seldom demonstrated much in the way of imaginative or creative thinking. I began to understand there are many different kinds of intelligence; that is, different ways to be smart. Rote memory of isolated facts is but one kind. And, absent the ability to put those facts together, manipulate them, and subsequently formulate something unique or at least divergent, it is relatively worthless. This is true unless one aspires for a career as a Quiz Kid, of course. Incidentally, I have come to understand there are many different ways to be stupid, too.

High school went much better for me than grade school. This is not to suggest that puberty was all that benevolent. Instead of the vertical growth spurt I would have preferred, I sunk into adolescent obesity with a plop. The only positive result was my voice sunk as well, and the director of the mixed chorus was sorely in need of resonant baritones. The school orchestra and jazz band were happy to have me too, and these were activities that brought me some healthy recognition and status among my peers.

I'm not implying that hordes of svelte female classmates, or even one or two of the more corpulent ones, wanted to socialize with me; however, at least they tolerated my presence in the hallways and cafeteria without the banal attempts at witticism I had come to know so well. "If they painted him yellow, 40 school children would jump on board," is representative. So too is "Pull up a couple of chairs and sit down."

Three musically inclined friends and I formed a band in high school. We called ourselves "The Critical Enigma," a name without a scintilla of significance to any of us but which we knew sounded profound, or at least puzzling, to our less semantically precocious classmates. We performed fairly decent renditions of folk music and soft rock, and we got regular gigs at private parties and school social events. Even some of the jocks admired our efforts.

One former band member chose orthopedic surgery as a career. He practices in Aspen, thus assuring a constant flow of broken bones, ruptured tendons, and income. Another owns a deli in Manhattan along with a half million shares of IBM he bought low. Pastrami and chopped liver sandwiches are his treat whenever I venture to the Big Apple. The three of us have remained friends over the years and visit often.

The fourth member of the group, a taciturn and cadaverous looking marathon runner with a facial tic, who actually swallowed organically grown spinach and broccoli, brussel and bean sprouts, alfalfa, granola, wheat germ, and megadoses of vitamins, died young from a heart attack. Logic forces one to conclude that pastrami and chopped liver on rye have substantial life sustaining properties, but health food will kill you right quick.

I did have one date in high school. She was Jeanne Jacobowski, a nubile specimen of adolescent pulchritude, who distinguished herself as a member of the National Honor Society, girls' gymnastics and tennis teams, debate team, drama club, psychology club, community service club, and cheer leading squad. At least as distinguishing were her perky breasts, long, shapely legs, cantilevered buttocks, and complexion with nary an adolescent zit. To my utter amazement, she leaned against me at my locker one afternoon, licked her lips, caressed my face with baby's breath, and asked if I'd like to accompany her to the semi-monthly sock hop at school. I figured it was my mind that captivated her.

I thought our date went reasonably well. Jeannie, as she preferred, was easy to talk to and didn't seem to mind dancing from afar, way out there at the periphery of my abdomen. I made a conscious effort to moderate both my pace and quantity of pizza consumption later on. On our way home after eating, she told me I was the most intelligent boy she'd ever known. She held my hand and taught me a few Polish words. I got that delicious feeling in my stomach that marks the beginning of an intense adolescent crush, the kind one remembers forever.

On her front stoop five minutes later, Jeannie kissed my cheek and abruptly left me in a moderate state of oxygen deprivation. She probably assumed it was animal lust when in fact it was mostly the walk home plus climbing eight steps leading to her door that left me panting. Before summoning a taxi to drive me home, I trudged back to the pizzeria. Refueling, posthaste this time and to maximum capacity, helped ease the pain. Subsequently, I called Jeannie twice for dates, but she was busy. She went to our senior prom with the much-acclaimed captain of the varsity basketball team, a classmate with a lot of muscles, mostly between his ears. I went with my guitar. So much for my intellect and learning to speak Polish.

With my grades, rank in class, superior performance on college aptitude tests, and musical ability, applying to colleges was a process I managed with assurance. It turned out that Yale was happy to have me. In fact, I arrived on campus with enough advanced placement credits to begin matriculating as a sophomore. I planned a dual major in Art History and Business. On my own, I audited as many foreign language classes as I could.

It was an eclectic course of study that concurrently satisfied my artistic, linguistic, and pragmatic appetites. A half dozen ethnic restaurants near campus and one basement hovel of a joint that served up succulent charcoal broiled Polish sausage on steamed poppy seed buns, typically six at a time and slathered with mustard, pickle relish, grilled onions, tomatoes, a mess of cheese fries, and grease of unknown origin, satisfied my gastronomic appetite.

A fraternity which did not automatically shun the quadruple extra large invited me to pledge. It was known as the "melody house" on campus, since students who demonstrated musical aptitude were recruited. I fit right in; in fact, for the first time in my life I actually flourished in a social situation. I played saxophone in a jazz band, piano in a chamber music quintet, and guitar in a pop and folk music trio. I sang in the university glee club and in a barbershop quartet, as well.

My coursework was more than challenging at Yale; at times, it was downright difficult. I had to put forth unusual effort to make the Dean's List. Most of my classes were small, and many of the professors were fascinating scholars, demanding, yet willing to work with students individually. I was in the company of extremely bright, highly driven classmates who were liberal enough to look past my bulk and get to know me. And, most inconceivably, I even had my 15 minutes of fame on the athletic field. It was the gridiron, to be specific.

One of my pledge brothers, at once a high school All-America football player, chess master, published poet, piccolo virtuoso, and straight A student, prevailed upon me to function as something called a "blocking back" on the fraternity football team. After some stubborn reluctance, I finally relented. It turned out to be one of my more enjoyable gigs. The concept was a simple one. My responsibility was to remain in an upright position and function as an impenetrable barrier to members of the opposition bent upon molesting our quarterback. I was a tad clumsy at first. When I stumbled and fell to the ground, alarmed observers on the sidelines would rank the resulting tremor on the Richter Scale.

After a lot of encouragement and a little practice, a surprising degree of latent athleticism emerged. I began knocking down two opponents at a time. I did this with such consistency and panache that my fraternity brothers agreed upon a nickname. They called me "The Tree." What d'ya know about that? I became something of a jock, of all things. In the sports section of the university newspaper, I was named to the fraternity all-star team. I sent the article to Dad. He couldn't help responding with one of his favorite aphorisms: "When the going gets tough, the tough get going."

Given that the sexual revolution was still some time in the future, the coeds in New Haven and nearby environs were adamant about keeping their legs crossed. Hence, a nearby cathouse was frequented by a large and representative sample of the male population on campus, even some of the more handsome mesomorphs. The first time I went was my first time. Three fraternity brothers who accompanied me were aware of my status. So was almost everyone else back at the house. Word got around that The Tree was "losing his cherry." Damned clever with words, those Elis.

The ladies slouched against a pink wall. One applied lipstick, and another plucked some errant hairs from her eyebrows. A couple of them, perhaps fearful of being pulverized, actually had frightened looks on their faces as I waddled by, and I suspect some who had managed to maintain any sort of relationship with the Almighty were beseeching Him with: "Please Lord; let him pass me by, and I promise to go home and finish school."

I surveyed the lot, trying my best to feign nonchalance, at the same time that my heart was nearing fibrillation, until I found one who didn't look disgusted. Things worked out just fine, thanks to Shirley, who had to be the prototype for the harlot with a heart of gold. She was highly skilled, too, really quite imaginative in her ability to position large objects in three-dimensional space. I showed up one evening with some gyros and my guitar, hoping to barter for a free ride. Shirley compromised by offering a substantial discount and tossing in a few extras. In the afterglow, I played Malagueña for her, and we polished off the sandwiches. I liked her a lot.

During the summer between my junior and senior years, the university glee club toured France, Germany, and Italy for seven weeks. We had two or three performances each week, so there was plenty of free time to explore the wonders. It was my first trip abroad, and it blew me away. I returned to campus with a firm resolve to go back on my own, as often as I could. I love all of Europe, but I am particularly fond of Paris and the south of France.

Fall semester, I took a course entitled: "Advanced Entrepreneurial Practice." Students were required to devise and implement a detailed business plan. We had to choose a product, locate suppliers, describe methods for buying goods and tracking inventory, develop marketing and advertising techniques, and formulate record keeping systems. All this had to be done during the first three weeks of the course. The duration of the term was devoted to implementation; that is, getting our businesses off the ground. The challenge was to translate our book learning into reality. The entire experience was a hoot.

Choosing a product was simple. I considered the female population on campus and wondered what they needed and liked well enough to spend a bunch of money on, either their own or daddy's. Cold weather was coming. Sleet and snow would surely follow. Bingo! Cashmere sweaters. Fashion trends in New Haven at the time required the well-dressed coed to own at least a dozen, in varying styles and colors, of course.

The rest of the plan followed easily. I arranged an appointment with a representative of the largest women's clothing store in town. When I assured her of an exclusive sales contract, she consented to stake me to a sample kit of eight sweaters without requiring capital investment on my part. Should my plan fail, my only obligation was to return the sweaters. It was a no-lose arrangement.

I enlisted a sales representative, a "sweater girl," I called her, at each of the sororities and women's residence halls on campus. For announcing the date and purpose of my impending visit, posting a sales brochure and a list of discounted prices, and distributing the sweaters when they arrived, sweater girls got a freebie for every dozen sweaters sold and a 10 percent commission on total sales.

I showed up on the designated evening with my sample kit and took orders after study hours. I got my money up front, doled out my commissions, paid my supplier, and pocketed the rest. A week later, my sales reps delivered soft and durable two ply v-necks, crew necks, turtlenecks, and cardigan cashmeres to their housemates, now sufficiently stylish and warm.

I earned $15,000 my senior year, and I got an A in the course.

In retrospect, my college years were productive and happy. Living with about 50 others helped me hone my people skills. Studying with fellow students, many of whom were at least as bright, talented, and highly motivated as I, taught me some sorely needed humility. Interesting coursework and brilliant professors motivated me to focus and further develop my intellectual and academic skills. Success in the rag trade made me confident in business. In fact, things went so well for me at Yale that for a while, I pondered the idea of extending my stay in academia by enrolling in graduate school. Or, at least hanging around a while to sell sweaters. Not for long, though.

Wanderlust set in the summer after graduation, and the urge to explore prevailed over graduate school. I desperately wanted to get back to Europe, and, thanks to the cashmere caper, I had more than enough cash to finance the trip. I spent most of my time in Hungary, Austria, and Czechoslovakia. I had no rigid schedule to maintain, so I poked around Budapest, Vienna, and Prague, sometimes hooking up with a tour, but most of the time preferring to head out on my own. It was really quite simple to barter a "Night of Music and Song with Max" for a free room. Board, of course, was another matter. After a 10-day layover in France on my way home, I was firmer than ever in my commitment to make travel a priority in my life.

At home, I ran into one of Jeannie's cheerleading friends from high school. Now a second grade teacher with what looked like a terminal case of anorexia, she told me my one time date and everlasting crush graduated with high honors and a degree in Psychology from Vassar. Jeannie lives in Poughkeepsie, plans working toward a doctorate, and is engaged to a veterinarian. I don't know; maybe I should have called her a third time.

I spent what remained of my profits on a car. Thus, I was mobile but essentially broke. Further excursions abroad or anywhere else would require that I enter the work force to earn and save some money. Also, I was justifiably concerned about satisfying more basic needs like food and shelter. So, armed with my sheepskin, I took the review course for aspiring public accountants. I pulled up a couple of chairs, sat for the CPA examination, and passed on my first attempt.

I had to decide whether to seek employment in an established accounting firm or start out on my own. I had a hunch I'd have a difficult time working for anyone else, so I chose the latter. Dad loaned me three months rent for office space, and I took out a bank loan for equipment and materials. With totally unwarranted confidence, I had 500 business cards printed. I ran a couple of ads and waited for clients. These would be taxpayers seeking my advice and counsel to help them deprive the Internal Revenue Service of all but the absolute minimum to which it was legally entitled. None came.

It took about a month for the panic to set in. Except for the building custodian, the city fire inspector, and the mailman, I was the only homo sapien who set foot in the office. What does one do with a surplus of 497 business cards, I wondered? I put them in my desk drawer and alternated between reading the complete works of Isaac Asimov and playing some soulful blues on my harmonica.

Bills came from the utility companies, and phone calls came from my parents. I experienced night sweats, anxiety attacks, and other symptoms of depression. I fantasized about Jeannie, Shirley, and how easy it would have been to earn a comfortable living selling cashmere sweaters. I had something in my mouth every moment of the day, either foodstuff or Havanas. Perhaps sucking on cigars satisfied some primitive, oral fixation. Whatever the motivation, Freudian or otherwise, smoking had a calming effect, it elevated my mood, and I felt it was a relatively benign addiction.

I bought my cigars at a kiosk around the corner from my office building. It was run by Hector and Socorro Contreras, an ambitious couple from Juarez, who had recently become citizens and entrepreneurs. My fluency in Spanish paid off quite nicely. We became close friends. They invited me to restaurants where the food and diners were authentically Mexican. They were my first clients.

I shall never forget Hector and Socorro. They introduced me to some of their countrymen, and many of them welcomed assistance with tax matters and business affairs. It wasn't long before I had a couple dozen files in the cabinet. People were coming to my office; I was meeting my expenses, paying off my loans, and earning a nice living. My clients called me "El gringo gordo," but they said it with affection.

I was so euphoric with this initial success that it took me a while to realize what should have come to me more immediately. If I could function as El CPA to the Spanish speaking, why not go after the Greeks, Russians, French, German, Japanese, Italian, and Chinese as well? I figured there had to be people who would prefer to do business with an accountant who was native to this country but happened to speak their language.

I took out ads in foreign language newspapers, distributed business cards and flyers to groups in their communities, and made bilingual presentations about small business operations and accounting practices to the Sons of Italy and similar organizations in China Town, Japan Town, and Greek Town. Soon, I had all the business I could handle. Life was good.

I'm confident I would have done well in graduate school; however,

I really didn't feel the need to have more letters after my name. Also, I liked the idea of learning without the constrictions imposed by a set curriculum. So, I embarked upon an ambitious program of self-study during which I became more fluent in languages and read a lot more about contemporary art. I learned a good deal about gardening, too. It might have been less erudite than my other areas of interest, but seeing tangible results of the fruits of my labor was very satisfying. I would have enjoyed a scrimmage or two at blocking back, but no one sought me out. Gridiron all-stars tend to have short careers, y'know.

Some might say I should have embarked upon an equally ambitious program of weight loss. In fact, I have done just that. Many times. During the last 20 years, I have lost 1200 pounds, give or take a few. Thus, somewhere out there, perhaps mingling in a pool with lost socks, pocket combs, and ballpoint pens, more than a half-ton of my lipids are floating around. Hey, everything has to be somewhere.

Obviously, since I'm still wheezing in and out, I have subsequently gained 1200 pounds, give or take a few. My weight has been as volatile as the Dow-Jones average during uncertain economic times. As a result, my closet is crammed with clothes of so many sizes, I'm thinking of implementing a system that will separate them by color-coded markers. Red will stand for elephantine.

I have tried every diet there is and, for me, none works very long. As an example, there was my brief, albeit intense, relationship with Jenny Craig. I would come home no less than famished after working hard all day. What I had to look forward to in the form of culinary reward was a frozen dinner made by some of Jenny's skinny and sadistic associates. The box said "Sirloin Steak," and indeed the contents were tasty. However, that particular cut of beef could only have come from a mutant, miniature cow. Before I devoured my entree in one lupine chomp, I would appraise it from all angles. It could have easily fit into my navel, with room for all four sprigs of broccoli and the fake cheese sauce as well.

I have also tried hypnosis and diet pills along the slippery way to slender. The former was effective only to the extent that I managed a brunch engagement with the hypnotist. It was our first and last date. I have the feeling she took my fourth trip to the buffet as a rather less than subtle denunciation of her therapy. The pills resulted in heart palpitations, tremors, anxiety, and persistent insomnia spanning a period of two months. And, given six to eight more hours of frenzied consciousness, I had a lot more time to raid the refrigerator. Calories don't count after two A.M., y' know. You could ask anybody.

My most bizarre attempt at weight loss called for the consumption of cabbage soup. I was encouraged to have as much of it as I liked. The catch was I couldn't have anything else. I lasted eight days on this preposterous regimen, during which time I shed 12 pounds and generated enough gas to warm Irkutsk and the surrounding rural areas through the dead of winter. The hyperbole is only mild. Of course, I gained everything back, plus three pounds to boot, no more than a few days after I returned, with a vengeance, to my 18 ounce marbled sirloins, twice baked au gratin potatoes, and chocolate eclairs. Sluggish metabolism and genetic predispositions can be potent adversaries indeed.

I contemplated marriage once. Claudette worked at Weight Watchers where one of her responsibilities was to lead pep talks. Claudette called them "inspirational group discussions." Groups consisted mostly of middle aged women who had dutifully shlepped their cellulite pocked thighs and sundry edemas to another weekly meeting. Claudette was also required to weigh everyone at the start of the meeting. She sat behind a desk while I took my turn on the scale. The result was a digital readout visible only to the two of us.

One reward for progress was a bell I got to ring if I lost two or more pounds during the preceding seven days of deprivation. Claudette watched the scale in anticipation and cheered me on every time I rang that ridiculous bell. I did it 49 consecutive weeks and lost 108 pounds. That's when Claudette suggested I take her to dinner. By the way, the bell rang in F, although it sounded a little flat on humid days.

Claudette is a pretty French woman, born in Saint-Remy de Provence, who came to this country with her parents when she was twelve. These were people of means who were able to provide a fine education for their daughter. But, beyond the French language and Weight Watchers, my first inclination was that we had little in common. Her primary concerns were exercise physiology, women's health issues, and philately, of all things, areas of interest that had never caused my juices to flow, as it were.

Soon, however, I learned that Claudette was taking harp lessons and had a lovely, if somewhat nasal, singing voice. We hit it off; indeed, one might say we pulled each other's strings. We began having dinner together, sans alcohol and fat, several evenings each week, and it wasn't long before we were seeing each other almost every day.

When a person sheds triple digit poundage, the equivalent of a grown woman's body weight, what remains is not a muscular, v-shaped torso, rippling with well-chiseled abdominals and sturdy pectorals. Nor, do his biceps bulge with renewed vigor. Rather, the flesh continues to sag; the only difference is there's less of it. Alas, ringing the bell each week didn't herald burgeoning sex appeal, only that I was growing thinner.

Thus, when the appropriate moment for lovemaking arrived, I felt conflicted and insecure. On the one hand, Claudette was someone I cared about and with whom I craved a lasting, intimate relationship; on the other hand, my body image was such that I was not all that eager to rip off my skivvies, so to speak. Some things one just can't hide, no matter what. I would have been pleased if Claudette had a secret blindfold fetish she was eagerly waiting to indulge.

It turned out that Claudette was a woman with considerable intuition. She was sensitive to my dilemma and solved it by closing the door to her boudoir, pulling the drapes, and turning off every light in the house. Think of coal. It was only after several episodes of alternatively raucous and tender lovemaking by braille that she opened the door and turned on a five-watt nightlight in the hall. It was the dimmest she could find.

Illumination progressed through a series of gradual stages beginning with a light in the distant foyer and one in the hallway.

Next, the lights in the adjacent bathroom and on the nightstands next to the bed came on. Finally, whatever murkiness remained was purged by the ceiling fixture in the bedroom and flourescents around the mirror above her dresser. Substitute sound for light, and we went from the faintest pianissimo to the most blatant fortissimo.

Our lovemaking got to the point where I felt like we were coupling on the pitcher's mound at Candlestick Park during a night game with 50,000 rabid fans cheering, or more likely booing, in the background. I should mention that with all her intuition and sensitivity, Claudette had a considerable amount of loose flesh herself. In any case, our combined sag stopped being an issue, and we began talking of marriage.

Claudette and I never made it to the altar. Our story would be better, or at least more sensational, were I able to say she was really an undercover agent working for the CIA. While engaged in covert operations designed to sabotage the development of biological warfare and equally heinous weapons of mass destruction by certain Middle Eastern despots, she mysteriously disappeared on the eve of our nuptials. Notwithstanding ceaseless and heroic efforts on my part, she was never heard from again. Or, if that's too much of a stretch, how about Claudette contracting some rare and debilitating disease and forcing me to leave her despite my stalwart protestations and selfless promises to care for her in her invalid state for the rest of our married but barren lives?

What happened, in fact, is nowhere near as melodramatic. Quite simply, as the time for posting invitations grew near, I realized that while we were certainly compatible and enjoyed each other's company, I didn't love Claudette, didn't care to have a family with her, and didn't want to spend the rest of my life with her.

Claudette hardly suffered the anguish of a jilted lover; in fact, it was a sense of relief she felt, given that her frame of mind regarding marriage was much the same as mine. Happily, we have remained good friends, even to the extent of sharing an occasional weekend tryst during which time any display of rare stamps remains verboten. Instead, both lust and fortissimo abound.

I'm certain the outcome of my affair with Claudette was a good one. I suspect a psychiatrist would gladly accept thousands of my dollars to probe my psyche and unveil the "subconscious motives" underlying my reticence to marry; however, I'm not all that interested. The truth is I'm happy, despite the fact that I've regained all 108 pounds, once again necessitating daily visits to the red section of the closet. In light of my regression from after to before, neither Weight Watchers nor Jenny Craig have solicited photographs for their brochures. Perhaps they're lacking a wide-angle lens.

My dear parents died 11 months apart, Mother after a prolonged battle with breast cancer and Father quickly, from a cerebral hemorrhage. Their real estate, investment portfolio, life insurance, and savings had a value of more than 15 million dollars. This inheritance, along with their art collection, extraordinary musical instruments, library of rare and first edition books, and other personal property made me an extremely wealthy man. It wasn't until I met Penny and Richard, however, that I became rich.

"Don't stare; it isn't polite." Such was the parental edict whenever I chanced upon a physically handicapped or visibly retarded person near my childhood home. I assumed if I weren't supposed to stare, talking might be equally taboo, so I had no friends with disabilities. This was consistent with the fact that I didn't have many friends without disabilities, either.

Of course, I've read some of the literature, both professional and lay, on Down syndrome and autism, but Richard and Penny are the first people with those kinds of problems I've known. Penny came to me when I advertised for an assistant in the newspaper. A stunning young woman came into my life that Friday.

The adage that beauty is in the eye of the beholder seems valid enough; after all, the person judged beautiful by one observer may not be so judged by another. But, the adage does not apply in all cases, and Penny is one clear example of an exception. It doesn't matter whose eye is doing the beholding; in fact, she is an incredibly beautiful young woman. Assuming it is a chance alignment of genes that ultimately determines physical attractiveness, Penny hit the genetic jackpot. Or, for those with a more spiritual bent, He took more time with her blueprint. Again, one tries not to stare.

Penny learned her job with no trouble whatever. She's bright, inquisitive, entirely capable of self-direction, and anxious to master new skills. At the office and her training course, she is a "quick study" one might say. Her professional interactions with clients and social contacts with others in the building are reserved and appropriate. Her oral and written communication are excellent. These proficiencies surely belie her autism; indeed, it wasn't until she felt comfortable enough to speak with me about her past that I became aware of the problem as well as the dreadful details of her parents' deaths.

It was Penny who introduced me to Richard. Whereas Penny's autism is invisible, Richard's Down syndrome is obvious. There are the distinctive facial characteristics. The epicanthic folds in the corners of the eyes give them an Asian appearance. This, along with a broad, flat nose, ears set low on the face, and tongue appearing too large for the mouth make individuals with Down syndrome look very much alike, as if they were all siblings within the same large family. As a result of this striking similarity, one notices Down syndrome almost as quickly as morbid obesity.

Incidentally, it was an English physician, Dr. Langdon Down, who, in 1865, first described the problem in a medical journal. He coined the term "Mongolism," reasoning that the slanted configuration of the eyes must somehow be indicative of Mongolian ancestry. Despite his fuzzy thinking and unfortunate terminology, Dr. Down was given the distinction of having the condition named after him. Such information is likely to be totally useless to anyone, save hopeless Jeopardy addicts or budding quiz kids.

Pinning labels on people can be misleading, even hurtful, for it often leads to the acceptance of false truths. When an entire class of individuals is clumped under the same umbrella, the likelihood that every member of the class will be seen as identical to each of the others increases. That's why *all* men labeled "black" have good rhythm, have a predilection for fried chicken and watermelon, can run fast, rebound above the rim, and have generous genitalia. These are maxims, gospel, emmis, as it were.

Similarly, it is quite tempting to assume that *all people* with Down syndrome are identical. They are all moderately or severely mentally retarded, none has the ability to read or write, they all require custodial care in an institution, and none can succeed at anything but the simplest, most repetitive type of job. Everyone accepts those truths too, at least until someone like Richard comes along who breaks the rules.

It's true that Richard doesn't do well on standardized tests of intelligence. Whatever the genetic, neurological, or environmental reasons, his ability to quickly manipulate verbal and quantitative concepts is limited to the extent that about 98 out of every 100 people do better on such measures than he does. This limitation, however, hasn't precluded his learning to read, write, and do basic arithmetic operations.

Socially, Richard is well above average; thus, he is very skilled at relating to his family and friends. Furthermore, he has proven his ability to function quite effectively on a complicated job requiring relatively advanced organizational and mobility skills. Given his combined social and vocational capabilities, institutionalization would be a totally inappropriate option. And, to complicate matters, he happens to like fried chicken and watermelon.

There are many different kinds of intelligence indeed, most of which are not measured by standardized tests. However, consider a different type of test. Consider one that measures map skills like the ability to visualize and recall direct routes between geographic locations, and Richard will score at the very top of the scale. Consider one that measures awareness and sensitivity to the feelings and needs of others, and Richard will be deemed gifted. Or, consider one that measures loyalty and compassion to friends and Richard will be a genius.

Thus, despite his label, Richard has some highly developed strengths, capacities that are not merely worthwhile but are indeed vitally important traits in the routine course of human interaction.

But, he has earned no academic honors and he looks "funny," so he will never matriculate at Yale or any other college. He's a mongoloid, don't you know?

As we dipped into each other's lives, Richard, Penny, and I became a tightly knit threesome. Beyond our time together at work, I have visited their home, and they have visited mine. I have met their roommates, substitute parents, and Richard's mother and father. We have had dinner together and gone to movies and live theater. We have become a close and improbable trio, the three of us bound together by excess. One has excessive beauty, another has excessive chromosomes, and the third has excessive appetites. The three of us are having an abundantly good time.

Penny was tenacious in urging Richard and me to begin a physical fitness program. Despite our fervent wishes for medical advice to the contrary, our physicians concurred in the wisdom of such a regimen. At first, activating our musculature for the sole purpose of moving our heft around was agonizing. The pain should have been anticipated I suppose, given that the most demanding physical activity in which Richard and I had recently partaken was chewing on hard salami sandwiches.

We suffered mightily those first days after workouts, without much sympathy but a plethora of encouragement and liniment from Penny. Ever so slowly, the pounds came off once again, muscles acclimated, and arteries opened. I began feeling better, even energetic, I thought. In a moment of weakness, I actually entered a 10-kilometer running race. It was probably premature and foolhardy, because just as I passed the nine-kilometer mark, I hallucinated. I saw a bright white light at the end of a long tunnel and felt the presence and comforting love of my long-dead maternal grandparents. Honest.

Six people, out of the nearly three hundred who participated in the contest, struggled to the finish line after I did. I am certainly aware of my time; however, I shall be no more specific than to report that the streetlights were aglow toward the end. Like Rocky Balboa, however, I was elated to have gone the distance. While my dead relatives are waiting, I've given up cigars. Perhaps such a sacrifice will delay their ultimate welcome.

Moving three colors down in the closet and my heightened energy level sparked some other changes. I shaved my facial hair, except for a neat moustache and goatee, and took to visiting a "hair stylist" who, so far as I can tell, charges a lot more money for precisely the same services as my barber once provided. I had a complete physical examination, and I began eating broiled fish, steamed vegetables, and large quantities of fruit as part of a weight loss maintenance program. Of course, I avoid cabbage as if it were hemlock. I turned my den into a workout room I used on days I didn't go to the YMCA. I bought a new wardrobe at a "regular" clothing store rather than the big and tall shops I had frequented most of my life. From fatty to fop, it was a veritable metamorphosis.

My habit has been to take a major trip when the tax season ends. This year, I was anticipating two weeks in France. I wanted to take long weekends in Paris at the beginning and end of the trip. For the eight days in between, I would headquarter in Avignon, rent a car, and take day trips to some of the nearby hill towns and villages in Provence.

My young friends hadn't done much traveling; certainly, neither had been out of the country. Richard had spoken with some enthusiasm and a lot of curiosity about his parents' trips abroad, and from conversations describing my own trips, I could tell that Penny longed to travel as well. So, without as much as a thought about complicating factors like parental permission, I invited them to come with me. Penny's responded with a delightful squeal, and Richard said, "Count me in."

It wasn't the first time I'd met Richard's parents. They had come to the office to thank me for giving their son a job and helping him adjust to his work. Indeed, they were effusive in their display of gratitude, and I remember being somewhat uncomfortable during our meeting. They made me feel as if I were some saintly sort of chap whose primary purpose in life was to provide succor and sustenance to unfortunate handicapped people in our midst.

It was difficult to convince Richard's parents that I'm neither a saint nor an employer who had given their son anything other than a chance to show what he could do. In fact, Richard has worked hard and well for me, and by the same standards applied to any other worker, irrespective of IQ, he has done an excellent job. For that, I told his parents, I wanted to display my own gratitude.

They were thrilled to give Richard permission to make the trip. We spent the next half hour or so talking about Paris. These were some devoted gastronomes who had somehow discovered a few Parisian restaurants before I had. Some of their art was French, and we discussed their collection for a time as well. Before I left, Richard's parents inquired as to whether I'd be interested in consulting with them on a case involving tax fraud. Hey, even a saint does business once in a while.

At the group home, Carolyn and Tom referred me to an agency that provided the paper work and ultimately granted permission for Penny to travel with me. These necessities behind us, I planned the details of our itinerary and went over them with Penny and Richard. It was a good thing they needed passports, because it reminded me it was time to renew my own. Then, together, we counted the days until departure, packed our bags, and took a limousine to the airport.

It was an extraordinary journey.

CHAPTER VI
Richard

So many things are going on since I moved to my new house that my head feels like it's spinning around on a yo-yo or even a merry-go-round. *Vrroom*. Stuff is happening to me so fast I get dizzy if I don't slow down once in a while to give my poor brains a rest. What's way cool, though, is that all the things that are happening to me are good things. It's always much better to get dizzy from good things instead of bad things. Then, you'll have a happy life. That's what I think, all right.

One good thing is that I'm a much better reader than I used to be. I wouldn't say I'm an expert at reading that can read the kind of books you get for homework at college or nothing that hard yet, but with Ernie teaching me every night and me working as hard as I can to improve myself, I'm good enough at it to read some of the pages in the newspaper. Not just the funny pages neither, but the grownup stuff too; you know, like some of the stories on the front page under the headlines, and which teams won the baseball games, and the list of everybody that died since yesterday's newspaper came out.

Obituaries is another name for the list of dead people. Dad once told me he reads the list of dead people before he gets out of bed every morning just to make sure his name isn't on it. 'Course, I went ahead and told him that if he just got out of bed quick as a flash, he would know he wasn't on the list without even having to read it. Then I figured out that Dad was just fooling around again like he does all the time.

Ernie has some books which are for guys only. He calls them his secret books. I've been spending some of my free time reading those books lately. Not too much of my free time, more like a short to a medium amount, I would say. Except for the cover, Ernie's secret books don't have even a single picture in them. So, alls you have to do is concentrate on reading the words, and while you're reading the words, you can make up some of your own pictures in your imagination if you want to. I would say I've got a pretty good imagination, all right.

Another good thing that happened is I took a trip over to the office building where Penny works at her new job. I was sort of half way between scared and nervous that first time I went to Penny's office. It's not that I was afraid I might get lost on the way over there or nothing, 'cause like I said, I'm usually very excellent at knowing my directions and all the streets and avenues and boulevards in town. Fact is, I was a little scared, 'cause I was going to the business office of a grownup man that I never met before. I mean, the only other business office I ever went to was Mom and Dad's, and 'course, there was no reason for me to be scared about going to their office, 'cause I already knew everyone real good by the time I got there, except for the receptionist, and she's the type of person that keeps a bunch of Snickers Bars in her desk drawer, so nobody would be scared or nervous about her anyway. Snickers Bars are even better to eat if you keep them in a freezer instead of a desk drawer. They're real hard, so you bite them with your boulders.

When I took my trip to the office where Penny worked, I got to meet Mr. Eberhart, and right after I met him, I wasn't nervous anymore. Boy oh boy, the first thing I noticed about Mr. Eberhart is what a nice, friendly guy he was. The second thing I noticed was that everything about him was pretty big. He had this great big stomach hanging way down over his belt, although, now that I think about it some more, he might of been wearing suspenders instead of a belt. But, whatever he was wearing to hold his pants up at the time, his stomach was so big I got to thinking right off how hard it must be for him to tie his shoes. I figured he was one of us guys that didn't like to go to the beach too much, neither.

He had this great big beard that was turning gray on his face, too. It was the kind of beard that would of covered up all of his pimples, if he had any. 'Course, with all that fuzz on his face, nobody could tell for sure if he had any pimples or even some scars from old ones that fell off when he was a teenager. He smoked these big thick cigars that stank up his office from all the smoke he blew out. I'd say about half of the smoke came out of his of his mouth and another half came out of his nose. I'm not exactly sure, but he could of swallowed the rest.

Mr. Eberhart gave me this big friendly handshake, with just the right amount of squeeze to my knuckles, not too soft and not too hard, along with a friendly smile, and a pat on the back. Then, he asked me to help myself to some big bagels with peanut butter and jelly on them if I wanted to join him. Those bagels were plenty good to eat all right, although I usually like them even better after they've been toasted.

Boy oh boy. That was a ton of stuff to remember from the first time you meet someone, 'specially if you're the type of guy like me that has trouble remembering things once in a while. And, there's way more, too.

Mr. Eberhart asked me to please call him by his first name, which is Max. That was another friendly thing to do, 'specially for a grownup guy that's older than me and smart enough to be the boss of his own business. I mean, it would of been OK with me to call him Mr. Eberhart or even sir, but I must admit that calling people by their first name makes me feel more at ease, which is another word for comfortable or not scared.

I had such a good time at Penny's work that just as it was getting to be time to say goodbye, I thought it would be nice of me to invite Max to come and have supper with us at our house. I had a hunch he was the type of guy that liked his suppers all right, and when someone is polite and friendly to you, it's always a good idea to be the same way to them. It's called the golden rule, which is one of my favorite rules, not that I ever figured out the exact reason for the gold.

Well, it turns out that Max was very happy I invited him to our house. You should of seen him when he got out of his car, right on time, which is the polite thing to do when you tell someone you're coming over to their house for supper. People should always try their best never to be late, 'cause you can never tell if maybe they got hurt real bad in a fatal car crash or something.

Max looked like a new person, at least on the outside of himself. He looked so different that if you had two feathers, one for me and one for Penny, you could of knocked both of us over. Max was all dressed up, neat as a tack, with a sports jacket, slacks, a nice shirt that didn't fit him too tight, and shiny looking shoes, the loafer kind with no laces to tie. He went to the barbershop for a shave and a haircut since we saw him last, too. "Spiffy" is what Penny called him. I never heard that word before, but I figured out what she meant pretty quick.

All of us at the group home had a real fun time that night Max came to eat supper with us. When he got done eating and talking in a nice, friendly way to everyone and was finished having some desserts, he got his guitar out from his car and played some pretty good tunes. I usually don't like to sing along too much, 'cause my voice is kind of crummy, but most everyone else did, even some neighbors that came over to listen and sing and have a real fun time right along with the rest of us on the front porch. No one wanted Max to leave for his own house after he started playing his music and singing his tunes.

The next good thing that happened was I got a new job at Max's office building, the same place where Penny works. Fact is, I was getting plum bored with the jobs I was doing at the workshop. I mean, you don't mind doing the same stuff each day over and over again when someone like Penny is standing next to you doing the same stuff over and over again that you're doing. But when she leaves and you miss her at your job every day, and there's nothing much to do except put the same screws into the same plastic bags, then it's real easy to get bored and even a little sad, discouraged you could say, some of the time.

So that's why it was such a good thing when Max said I could come over to his office building and start a new job that wouldn't be so boring. 'Course, I had a talk with my mom and dad about changing to a new job, and just like I thought, they were sure happy for me, too. Parents are like that, you know. They usually don't like it too much when their son is bored at his job most of the time. And, if you're going to be bored, it's even worse when you're not making much money for it.

Now I have the kind of job where I do different things every day, instead of just screwing around all the time. Hah! That's sort of a joke I made up. Y'know, screwing around, 'cause alls I did on my old job was put the screws into the plastic bags. Anyway, even if my joke isn't all that funny, when you have that kind of boring job, the time doesn't go by so fast. Seems like the day will never end, that's how draggy it is, almost as long as it takes for the whole year to pass by 'til your next birthday rolls around.

Well, at my new job, it's like zip and it's lunchtime. Then there's another zip and the day is all over, almost as fast as a blink of your eye. Just like that, it's Friday again, and I'm heading over to the First National Bank, whistling a happy tune, 'cause I'm about to sign my paycheck on the back of it and give it to the teller lady for a deposit. Then, I just sit back over the weekend while my money is earning some more of that good old interest.

At first, when I went to the new job that Max gave me, I worked mostly with John. He's the chief custodian, which means the same as the head janitor, at the office building. He taught me how to do most of the things a janitor does; you know, like keeping the building clean inside and outside and making sure the boiler and the air conditioner keep working like they're supposed to when the weather is too cold or too hot outside. A few times I didn't exactly get what I was supposed to do, so John showed it to me all over again. He didn't mind.

I help him cut the grass and water the flowers too, and when it gets to be winter, he's going to show me how to work the snowblower machine. If he shows me how to do it once or twice, I bet I'll be real good at driving it. It's one of those big ones that you sit on and steer, almost like a tractor, 'cause we have to get the snow out of this real big parking lot in the back of the building. John says it's about the size of half a football field, which is a pretty big parking lot all right, 'specially when it's all covered up with snow past your knees, or even higher, that you got to move out of everyone's way so they have a place to park.

The rest of the days I worked in the office with Penny and Max. They needed some help cleaning up the file cabinets and getting everything organized into the right places. There's hardly anyone that can find the right places for things better than me. I think Max sort of liked it when I fixed it so he could find things quicker in the files and on his desk. There's a place for everything and everything in its place, like Dad always says.

Penny taught me how to work the copier machine, which you use when you need to make exact copies of letters and other kinds of papers that the boss of a business usually needs. You can never tell when you might lose an important letter or something, so it's a good idea to have one or two extras, just in case you do. It's just about the same thing as having an extra sailor hat for a spare.

The copier machine was easy to work once I got the hang of it. Alls you have to do is push certain buttons, and you can tell it how many copies you want to make and how big you want the letters to be and even if you want your copies to be in black and white or in Technicolor. I learned how to put in more paper when the last stack runs out and how to put in a new ink holder when the old one dries up, too. Once I practiced up a few times, working the copier machine got pretty easy to do, all right. Like I say, alls you have to do is push the right buttons. You don't even have to wait around until it's done making the exact copies, but I usually do just in case any paper gets jammed up like it does once in a while.

After I got perfect at the parts of my job like keeping the files neat and working the copier machine, I started being the chief messenger for the office. What happened is I saw the delivery guy picking up letters and packages just about every day, so one day I just spoke right up and asked Max if he would give me a chance to make some deliveries instead. I figured it would be a snap to get on my bike and whiz around town a whole lot faster than the delivery guy in his truck that probably gets stuck in traffic a lot and maybe has to stop every now and then to look at his map, 'cause he might not always be exactly sure of what streets and avenues to drive on all the time. And, with me whizzing around making the deliveries, Max wouldn't have to pay any more money to the delivery guy. He could save even more money on postage too, which is another word for stamps.

So now, besides helping John with the janitor stuff and keeping the files organized in the office and working the copier machine, I'm the head guy in charge of deliveries for our office. Some of the other bosses that have their own offices on my delivery route are asking me to make deliveries for them, too. I guess they could tell right away that I was very good at making deliveries. One of those other bosses even called up Max on the phone and told him I was reliable, which was his way of saying he could count on me. It's a good thing to have people count on you.

One day at work, Max surprised me with a present. He got me three dark blue shirts that have "Rapid Richard's Delivery Service" in white letters printed on to the back of them. Even though I wear them all the time, I always have at least one clean shirt when the other two are in the wash. Sometimes, I have two clean ones when only one is in the wash.

Boy oh boy; I'm making a pile of dough. First of all, I get my regular paycheck from Max every single week. It's way more than the paycheck I used to get at the workshop, and I only got a paycheck at the workshop every two weeks. Then, added on to that, the other bosses pay me cash money for making their deliveries on time. And, most of the time, I get tips, too, 'specially when I drop off a package or a letter a little early. Like I say, it's a pile of dough I'm making, all right. Pretty soon I'm going to treat Max and Penny to a nice lunch at the Chinese restaurant. Max usually pays for lunch, so when I come up with some clams it will be a big surprise.

Max showed me how to keep a record in a little black book of all the cash money I get. I call it my little black income tax book. If you're a good citizen that's honest, you have to send a piece of paper called a form to the United States Internal Revenue Service every year when it comes time to pay your income taxes. On that form, you tell them exactly how much money you make every year, even tips, and you better tell the truth, too.

Max warned me that those guys at the IRS, which stands for Internal Revenue Service, if you take a look at the first letters of each word, can get pretty picky, even nasty sometimes, with folks that try to be greedy and keep all of the money they earned for themself. I didn't believe they were nasty at first, but now I know it's true, 'cause Mom and Dad told me the same thing. You can even go to jail if you cheat on your income taxes.

'Course, I was going to be pure honest when it came to paying my income taxes anyway. I figure the IRS must be pretty good at catching all the people that are already cheating, and besides, ever since I was a little kid, I always wanted to grow up to be a good citizen that doesn't have to go to jail. But, there was something I wasn't too clear about. I had a question buzzing around in my brains that I didn't know the answer to, so after thinking about it for a while and still not coming up with any kind of answer that made a lot of sense to me, I just came right out and asked Max about it.

What I asked Max was to tell me exactly what happened to the dinero that me and all the other good citizens were forking over to the IRS. Like I say, I always want to be pure honest and all that, but I think when you give someone some of your money to spend, even a little of it, you should get to know exactly what they're going to use it for. That's only common sense, seems like to me.

Max told me he liked my question, and he took some of his busy time to answer me. That's another thing I like so much about Max. No matter how busy he is, he's always patient and never makes me feel like he doesn't want to talk to me or that I'm asking dumb questions. So, Max told me my income tax money would be spent on a lot of very important things like paying scientists, that are like doctors, to find ways for people with bad diseases to get better, paying for soldiers and sailors to protect us if we have to fight against some foreign country that wants to have a war with us, paying for food and medicine and places to live for homeless people, and building nice and smooth new highways so people that might be afraid of flying in airplanes could still travel around our country pretty quick and easy.

After hearing about all those things that my income tax money would be used for, I felt a lot better about forking it over, except for the part about paying soldiers and sailors to fight in wars that people get killed in, no matter how careful they are. What happened is I got to thinking that if the IRS in this country stopped spending any money for wars, maybe the IRS in other countries could do the same thing. Pretty soon there would be no more money to fight wars. Soldiers and sailors from all over the world would stop getting killed, and they could come back to their nice homes in time for the holidays and get busy taking care of their families.

After a whole bunch of parades to welcome the soldiers and sailors home, folks could just go about their business and live in peace. They could spend the money they don't need to spend on fighting wars anymore on something better, maybe like a new refrigerator or a used car or some new shoes for their kids, at least. Or, if folks already had those things, maybe they would want to give some of their extra cash to some doctors that are trying to fix Down syndrome.

I told Max that when I get a little better at letter writing, I'm going to write a good one to the IRS and explain my new way of using our income tax money to those guys, which you have to admit is a pretty good grownup idea. Max sure liked my idea; he even said he would go over my letter and check it to make sure I didn't spell any words wrong and I put all those marks in the right places you're supposed to put them in.

Another good thing is that everyone I know is telling me how proud they are of me. My mom and dad, Carolyn and Tom, Max, Ernie, and my best friend Penny; they just come right out and tell me they're proud of me all the time nowadays. I get a happy feeling about myself when I think about how good I'm doing. And, one of the things that makes me happiest is that I'm doing good in the same place as everyone else, right here with Max and Penny in the grownup business world, where regular people work, not just in some special school, that really isn't special at all, for mongoloids in the basement of a church with no swings or slides outside. By the way, rapid is another word for fast.

The latest good thing that happened is Max invited Penny and me to come with him on a vacation trip all the way across the Big Pond, which, like I said, is what Dad calls the Atlantic Ocean. He wants to take us to Paris, France, if you can believe it. Now that's a doozy of a good thing you have to admit, which is why I saved it for last. There must be some excellent words in the Webster's Dictionary that would tell exactly how excited I was when Max asked Penny and me to come with him on his trip, but I sure don't know them. I mean, the best I can think of is it was like I used to feel coming down the steps to look under the tree on Christmas morning back in the days when I was a kid named Dicky, except better. That guy Webster had to be a real smart guy to know all those words, and in the right order, too.

'Course, I'm still a minor, which is what a guy is called until he becomes a major on his 21st birthday, so Max came over to my old house to ask my parents for permission to take me along on his vacation trip. Mom and Dad had a nice talk with Max about my vacation trip to Paris, France, and after a little while, my parents were very happy to say I could go. They were happy to know that Max invited Penny to come along, too. You probably remember how much my mom and dad love Penny, which is a lot, in case you didn't remember.

I'll sure be glad when I finally get to be a major, 'cause that's when you're an official grownup with no more doubt about it. Then, in case anyone ever asks you, 'cause maybe they're not exactly sure if you're a very young major or a very old minor, alls you have to do to prove it is whip out your wallet where you keep your identification, or ID for short, and there it is in black and white, all legal and everything.

Mom and Dad and Max had some good suggestions about what kind of stuff I should pack in my suitcase. They knew all about the right kind of clothes and other things to take on a vacation trip to France, 'cause of all their own trips that they already took there. At work, Max had the good idea of making an extra copy of our day-by-day schedule for the trip, an itinerary you call it. I made one to give to my parents so they would know exactly where I was every day. Max even put all the telephone numbers on it, just in case there might be an emergency of some type. Or, who knows, Mom and Dad might miss me so much they would just feel like giving me a call, even if there was no emergency. That's the way it works when you're lovable to someone.

It's a good idea for your parents to know exactly where you are every day, 'specially when where you are happens to be all the way across the Big Pond. That's so far away that it's going to take us about eight hours to get there on a super fast jet airplane, and I'm plenty excited about it, 'cause this will be the first time I've ever been on an airplane of any type, even a slower one. I told Max it was my first time, and he said he would try to get me a seat by a window so I could see everything real good.

If there's only one seat left by a window though, I decided to let Penny sit next to it, 'cause it's her first time going anywhere in an airplane, too. Or, maybe Penny could sit next to the window when we're going up, and I could sit next to the window when we're coming down. The other way around would be fine with me, too. Either way would be sharing, and that's always a fair way to do things, whether you're talking about windows on a super fast airplane, or a pizza, or anything else.

Me and Penny went to this place where they take pictures of your face for your passport, which is a little blue book you have to take with you any time you go to a far away country. For once, I took a pretty good picture, 'course not as good as Penny's, but at least good enough so I don't mind showing it to anyone. After that, me and Penny just counted off the days until it was time for us to pack up our suitcases and go with Max on our vacation trip.

Before you know it, there we were, with our suitcases all packed up and good old Max, driving off to the airport in one of those long black cars, limousines you call them, that we could see out of but no one could see in to. It was just like we were some very important people, maybe senators or even famous movie stars. It's a good thing

I went to the bathroom a couple of times before we left; that's how excited I was.

We got to the airport with time to spare, just like you're supposed to do. It's real important to get to the airport with time to spare, even as much as a couple of hours before your plane leaves, 'cause there's a lot of things to take care of. I mean, you just don't stroll right onto the airplane, whistling a happy tune, and fly away to Paris, France, just like that.

Some people dressed up in their work uniforms ask you a few questions about your suitcase, and you have to show them your passport picture. Another guy makes sure you have a ticket and gives you what's called a boarding pass that you use when it's time to get on board the plane. You give your suitcase to the same guy that gave you the boarding pass, and he puts a white tag with some letters on it to make sure it goes on the same plane that you're going on. Max checked to make sure of that, all right. I mean, nobody wants to go to a different place than their suitcase.

Then, you have to walk through this special doorway where a lady is watching some machine that looks almost like a TV and listening for a noise that can tell her if you have any dangerous things in your pockets. Max told me that once in a while they catch some crazy people that are trying to take a knife or a gun or some other dangerous thing like a fatal bomb of some type onto an airplane.

Max and Penny walked through the doorway with no trouble at all, but when I walked through, here comes this sort of loud sound, like a beeping noise, that told me in a flash I must of done something wrong. 'Course, I knew I wasn't the type of guy that carries a knife or gun or a bomb in his pants, so I couldn't figure out why the beeping sound happened. I felt sort of funny, embarrassed would be a good word for it, when everyone started looking at me, and I got even more embarrassed when the lady told me to take everything out of my pockets and go around and walk through the doorway all over again. At least I didn't have to take any of my clothes off, 'specially my shoes and socks.

The second time I went through the doorway I walked a little faster. I was real happy, 'cause there was no beeping sound. Max said it was probably the new money clip made out of silver metal of some type that Mom and Dad gave me to keep my money straight that made the beeper go off the first time.

Was I ever glad, relieved you might say, 'cause nobody likes to get on an airplane with a crazy guy that makes beeping sounds happen 'cause he might be a mad bomber on the loose. I was wondering too, why they don't get a better machine at the airport that can tell the difference between a knife and a money clip, so regular guys like me that are minding their own business and just going on a nice vacation trip to Paris, France with a couple of his friends won't get so embarrassed all the time.

As long as I got on the subject of money clips, the last thing we did before we finally got on the airplane was walk over to a special kind of bank they have at the airport where you change some of your United States money into French money, if you happen to be going to France, of course. Max said I should give the teller lady 50 dollars of my spending money, and she would change it into French money and give it back to me.

People that live in France call their money franks instead of dollars, which can be a little tricky until you figure out exactly what's going on. The first thing that was tricky to me was why the bills came in all different sizes instead of being all the same size like at home. Then, I noticed real quick that the more a bill was worth the bigger it was, so a bill of 100 franks gets a bigger size than a bill of 50 franks which gets a bigger size than one of 20 franks and so on down the road. The more they're worth, the bigger they are. That part was pretty easy and made good sense to me.

What was more tricky to me and took me a longer time to figure out is why the teller gave me so much money back in trade for my 50 dollars. I mean, when I counted it all up, it came out to 250 franks. I even counted it all up a second time to make sure I didn't make a mistake. Fact is, I thought it was the teller lady that made the mistake, 'cause 50 dollars should be 50 dollars, no matter if you're spending it in the United States of America and you call it dollars or you're spending it in France and you call it franks.

Then Max told me it takes five of those French franks to make one of our United States dollars, so even though it seemed like I was getting more money from the teller lady than I should of, those 250 franks were worth exactly the same amount as the 50 dollars I gave her in the first place. 'Course, I caught on in a snap after that, even though I never found out who Frank was. He must of been a famous guy, at least in France.

After I understood what Max was explaining to me, it still seemed to me like there must be an easier way to handle this money business, some way that wouldn't be so tricky. Maybe everyone, no matter what country they live in, could use money with the same name that would be worth the same amount. People could kick it around some and come up with a name for money that everyone liked, let's say clams, just for an example. Then, nobody would get mixed up anymore, 'cause 50 clams would be worth 50 clams, no matter what country they were in. I mean, if a French guy or a German guy or an Italian guy or a guy from any country at all was poor and homeless and came up to you on the street wondering if you could spare a few clams, you'd know exactly how much he had in mind with no trouble at all. I'm not sure who I should write a letter to yet with my idea about fixing the money problem, but it's probably not the IRS.

Finally, Max and Penny and me finished all our business and we were just sitting around on these hard chairs with a big crowd of other folks that were all ready to go on the same airplane with us to Paris, France. A lady's voice came over this machine, a loud speaker I think it's called, and she said we could begin to get on board the airplane in about five minutes. Then she said some French words that I didn't understand. 'Course Max did, 'cause he's an expert on just about every language there is, or at least most of them. I mean, he even talks Chinese, if you can believe it.

'Course, I've seen a ton of airplanes in my time, starting way back there in the days when I was still a little kid. Most days, you look up to the sky two or three times, and there they are, sometimes making a noise and sometimes leaving a trail of smoke behind them.

But, those airplanes I saw in the sky when I was a kid were always way up there looking real small, almost tiny, 'cause they were so far away. The farther away something is, the smaller it looks, until it gets so far away you don't see it at all. 'Course, whatever you been looking at is still there; it's just so small that you can't see it anymore. That's how it works.

This time, though, I could see the airplane we would be flying on through the window, just sitting there on the ground right up close to my eyeballs, looking so big I couldn't believe it and neither could Penny. That's when I first started to get a little nervous, 'cause I couldn't figure out how anything as big as that, with all these people getting on board and all their suitcases weighing it down, could possibly lift off the ground and stay up there, flying through the sky, steady as she goes.

I asked Max about it, 'cause he knows just about everything there is to know about everything in the world, not just stuff about different languages and money. I got a little more nervous, not panicky or nothing but real nervous, after Max told me he wasn't sure he knew exactly how it lifted off the ground and stayed up, neither. Even a smart guy like Max doesn't know everything about everything I guess, or even something about everything.

Next, it was time for us to walk through this long tunnel until we got to the door of the airplane. Waiting right there at the door, there were a couple of very pretty ladies, flight attendants you call them nowadays instead of stewardesses, Max told me. They gave us a nice howdy do and welcome aboard and showed us to our seats. The seats were real easy to find, 'cause they were up front in the first class part of the airplane. Me and Penny got to sit right next to our own windows, and Max sat next to me.

I wasn't all that sure, but it seemed to me that we were already getting some special kind of treatment, 'cause most of the other passengers went straight on back to other parts of the airplane that didn't look quite as classy as the first part we were in. I mean, we had some big seats to sit on, the kind that are way soft, almost cushy you could say, and give you enough room to be comfortable on if you ever want to spread yourself out and have a nice nap or two while you're flying all the way across the Big Pond. The bathroom was pretty small though, with a lock on it that's hard to work.

Max told me we'd be flying way up there at more than 35,000 feet. A person that's good at figuring out arithmetic problems knows that's about seven miles up in the air. If you ever had to walk seven miles, 'cause maybe your car or bike broke down, then you know how far that is, except this is seven miles up in the sky instead of seven miles down some road. Max told me some more things, too. We were heading so high up in the sky there's hardly any air outside of the plane to breathe. And, not only that, it's usually freezing cold up there, too. It's a good thing that jet airplanes come with their own supply of hot air.

Fact is, I was wondering about many things just before my first airplane ride. Not just about how such a heavy airplane takes off from the ground and stays up in the sky, but other things like how the pilot knows exactly which direction to go, 'specially when it's total dark outside the plane. And, if the wind up there happens to be blowing right at the airplane at a faster speed than the airplane can fly, almost like if there was a hurricane or something, would we get blown back to where we started? And, what would it feel like on my body to be zipping along at about 500 miles an hour, which is faster than a speeding bullet goes through the air when someone shoots it? I was wondering, too, what it would feel like to go right through the middle of a cloud and what clouds look like from the inside of them and how it would be to see some clouds from the top instead of from the bottom? Like I said, I was wondering about a lot of things that were just popping into my head all at the same time, seemed like.

Well, that was some ride on that airplane, all right. After we hooked up our seat belts and we were ready for the take off, the airplane started to roll down the runway pretty slow. Right away it got to going faster and faster, until I opened my eyes and saw some buildings and cars down there below us that looked small as toys. Then I heard some loud noises coming from under the plane, and the wing on my side started to tip over enough for me to notice the tip. That's when

I closed my eyes again, only tighter.

I could feel my heart pounding away under my shirt, and my forehead was starting to sweat up a little. Max told me not to worry, 'cause the noise was from the wheels coming up and the wing was tipping like it always does when an airplane makes a turn, so I could calm down and not squeeze his arm so tight. That's when I was the most nervous, and I sure was glad I was sitting next to Max instead of Penny, 'cause I would never want to hurt her arm or any other part of her.

The same pretty ladies that welcomed us aboard started bringing us good things to eat and some nice cold drinks too, and after that, I wasn't hardly nervous anymore. We got to see two Technicolor movies for free when we weren't eating and drinking. You hear the people talking in the movies through these earphones you plug in to some holes on the side of your seat. Max took some snoozes a few times, but me and Penny were so excited we could hardly sleep a wink. When Max was sleeping away, we just whispered back and forth some of the time, so we wouldn't wake him up.

Sometimes, when there were no clouds below us and it was still daytime outside, we could look out of our windows and see the Atlantic Ocean way below us. It looked real flat with no waves at all. Penny and me saw a boat, probably what you call an ocean liner, way down there, looking very tiny and making the water white behind it. I got to thinking that maybe there was a guy on that boat looking up at us and thinking how tiny we were way up in the sky. Then, before you know it, we couldn't see the boat anymore.

It was so smooth flying through the air and so quiet up there that if you didn't know any better, you would think you were standing still instead of zipping along like Superman, even faster than a speeding bullet. I mean, it's pretty hard to know how fast you're going unless there's something else up there to pass by.

'Course, when nighttime came, there wasn't much to see outside the airplane except for the moon and a few stars and some lights blinking on and off at the end of the wings. The strangest thing was the night didn't last very long at all. I mean, almost before me and

Penny knew what was happening, here comes the sun and it's a new morning again. When Max woke up, I asked him if the nights are always so much shorter when you're way up in a plane whizzing through the air.

Max explained the reason to me, but I must admit that all that stuff about the earth spinning around and the different time zones was pretty hard for me to understand. Fact is, I really didn't know what Max was talking about, except for the part when he told me that on the airplane ride back home, the night would be very long so things would come out even. That's how it works. You pay for the extra daytime in the beginning with extra nighttime at the end. Seemed fair enough to me, all right.

I must of dozed off myself for a while, 'cause the next thing I remember was the pilot's voice coming over his microphone and waking me up. He said we'd be landing pretty soon, and sure enough, when I looked out my window, there was no more ocean down there. It was solid ground, just like at home, and I could tell in just a few minutes that we were getting closer and closer to landing on it.

I heard the noise from under the plane again, and just like I thought, the next thing that happened was a little bump when the wheels touched down in a smooth landing on the runway. The pilot slammed on the brakes pretty quick, and we finally came to a stop right there in Paris, France to have some more of our vacation trip. Boy oh boy. First you go up and then you come down, and before you know it, there you are all the way across the Big Pond. You're exactly where you're supposed to be, and you didn't get lost even for a minute.

We made it off the airplane with no trouble at all, 'cause when you sit in the first class part, you don't have to wait very long to walk out through the tunnel the other way. When we first got off the plane, it was like it used to be when I couldn't read any words at all. I mean, I could see all the signs in the lobby of the airport easy enough, and the letters were the same as the ones we use back home, but I sure couldn't make any sense out of the words. Neither could Penny. 'Course, we figured out real quick the problem was that the words were printed in the French language, and that was why they didn't mean anything to us. It's pretty fair, when you think about it, 'cause French people that come to America usually can't read our words, neither.

Me and Penny learned some French words real quick, 'specially like hommes and femmes. I mean, it was a good thing they had pictures of a homme and a femme high up on the wall, 'cause that's how we figured out where to go to the bathroom. It was a whole lot bigger than the skinny bathroom on the airplane. There must of been 20 of us in there doing our business at the same time.

'Course, I don't know about Penny's femmes room, but the hommes room was a lot different than what I was used to back home. First of all, it didn't even have a flusher. It took me a while to figure it out, but you just back right up and away she goes. Then, when you wash your hands, alls you have to do is stick them under the faucet, and the water knows when to come on and go off all by itself. It did have the same kind of hot air blower to dry your hands that I already knew about. I don't like those hot air blowers too much, 'cause you usually have to finish the job of drying your hands on your pants anyway.

After that, we walked over to this place where your suitcase comes around and around in a circle. While we were waiting for our suitcases to come around to us, here comes this guy with a hat on his head that looks sort of like my sailor hat, except it's black instead of white and it's flatter. He's smoking the longest cigarette I ever saw, and it's sticking out of this long thing he's holding between his choppers. He gives Max a great big hug and some kisses on both cheeks. After they're done with their hugs and kisses, Max introduced me and Penny to his good friend Pierre, which is the French name for Peter.

Pierre came to meet us at the airport and drive us to the place where Max lives in Paris, France. Max goes to Paris so many times that he stays in his own apartment instead of staying in a hotel, which is where my mom and dad and most other people usually stay when they go on a vacation trip. Max and Penny and me will be staying in a hotel too, but not until we leave Paris in a few days to have some more of our vacation trip in a different part of France. It's a big country all right, but not as big as the United States of America, which is one of the biggest in the whole world except for China, maybe.

While Pierre was driving us over to Max's place, I found a map of Paris, France sitting in one of those pouches in the back seat. 'Course I didn't know the names of any of the streets or avenues where most of the people lived yet, so I gave it a quick look see. Truth is, I got a little worried about remembering most of the streets and avenues in Paris, 'cause so many of them started with Rue. I mean, how's a guy supposed to figure out where he is and where he's going when all the streets and avenues start with the same word?

It sure seemed to me like the neighborhood around Max's apartment was real spiffy. There were all kinds of fancy looking stores with men's and women's suits and dresses in the windows. More stores had watches and rings and other kinds of jewels in the windows, and a few other stores had fur coats, not just for women but for men, too. I figured out from looking at the price tags that most everything cost a ton of franks around Max's house.

There were a lot of places to eat in Max's neighborhood, too, and they sure had a few different names. Some of them were restaurants or cafes just like at home, but some were brasseries and bistros, which I never heard of before. Max explained the difference between them to me and Penny, and he told us we'd try all of them, or at least the ones that had tables and chairs set up right on the sidewalk underneath some umbrellas where some guys came around every once in a while to play music and sing a few tunes while you were eating something that tasted way delicious.

Way down at the end of the avenue, there was this beautiful building called an arc of something or other that hundreds, maybe even thousands, of people were always walking around and taking pictures of. Seemed to me like almost everyone in Max's neighborhood owned a camera of some type or another, 'specially the Chinese people that were really clicking away, almost one right after the next. They might of been Japanese people, now that I think about it some more. Or, there could of been some of each, like maybe half.

One polite thing that Pierre did was pick us up every morning just in time for a big breakfast. Max made sure everyone had a big breakfast, 'cause of all the energy we would need for sightseeing the rest of the day, or at least until lunch. The first morning I was real hungry for some delicious French toast with some butter and syrup and maybe a side order of bacon or sausage, I wasn't sure which. While I was deciding on the bacon or sausage, I got to wondering what the people call French toast in France. I mean, if we call it French toast in America, shouldn't they call it American toast in France? Max and Penny, and 'specially Pierre, thought that was really funny and made perfect sense.

Another part of Pierre's job was to drive us around to see some sights like a ton of bridges and towers and churches and museums. We took an elevator to the top of the most famous tower in the world, which is the Eiffel Tower. I recognized it right away from the picture books Mom and Dad brought me.

Lucky for us, it was a nice clear day with no fog floating by, so we could see all around the city and even some of the country. After a little while, that funny feeling in my knees that you get when you're way up high someplace went away, and I could stand right up close to the edge of the tower without being scared in the least. I'm not saying I leaned over or nothing, but at least I got closer to the edge than Penny. She stayed back a little and held on tight to my arm. I didn't mind.

We stayed at the Eiffel Tower for supper at the fanciest restaurant me and Penny ever ate at. It was inside of the tower, way up over 400 feet above the ground. If you take the time to think about it, that's higher than a football field is long. When we weren't eating, we could still look out these huge windows and see the sights. Max pointed out the world famous Notre Dame Church where this poor guy with a hunchback used to ring the bell. There's a Notre Dame in America too. It's a college though, instead of a church, and it's very famous for winning a lot of football games.

We must of had six or seven waiters at least and so many forks and spoons you could never run out. Max gave me some snails to eat, which I never ate before, and a few sips of wine, "bubbly," he called it, before I polished off my surf and turf.

One of the different things about having dinner in Paris, France is that some of the things are out of order, you could say. I mean, the waiter brings you a bunch of different kinds of cheese and crackers after your main course instead of before. Penny had some wine too and a delicious supper of some kind of fish I never heard of. It was easy for me and Max to tell what a good time Penny was having, and did she ever look beautiful in Paris, France. A lot of people, mostly young guys like me, but some older ones too, were looking at her all the time.

We had to hurry up and have our desserts real quick, 'cause Max was taking us to a ballet dance. I remember seeing ballet dancers once or twice on TV, but this was the first time I got to go to a real live ballet dance. Max took us to this big hall, not too far from the tower. We walked in, and a very nice lady showed us where to sit in some seats close up to the stage and right in the middle of things. Seemed like Max always got good seats, and it didn't matter if we were going on an airplane or to a ballet dance.

When I first got to thinking about watching a ballet dance, I wasn't too sure if I was going to like it. I mean, I always liked a circus or a baseball game, but fact is, I wasn't sure I was the type of guy that would like a ballet. Well, what I learned at the ballet dance that night is that you should never decide you might not like something until you try it out first. You have to keep your mind opened up is what I'm saying.

It was really something, all right. First of all, the lady ballet dancers were real beautiful. I mean, I didn't see what you might call an ugly duck in the whole bunch. They spin around and around in perfect time to the music without getting dizzy. Sometimes they run across the whole stage and take a few jumps now and then. A lot of times they're taking these real tiny steps, and the amazing thing about it is they're dancing around up there on the very tips of their toes. Now, that's got to hurt some it seems to me, least 'til you get used to it.

Then some men ballet dancers come out, and they're all dressed up in some costumes that are so tight you don't want to look, at least at first. They look so naked with their privates showing through their pants I was embarrassed to even look at Penny. They do these jumps so high in the air you don't believe it's possible, and then they take the lady dancers and lift them straight up above their heads while spinning them around some more. At the end, a man and a lady dancer hold each other in their arms and slowly sink to the floor, 'cause they're dead. The curtain comes down and everyone in the audience stands up and claps and yells until the curtain comes back up and all the dancers, even the ones that died, stand up and take a bow. You leave the hall right after that, and Pierre is waiting outside to drive you back to the apartment to hit the hay. I'd go to another ballet dance any time.

All the time Pierre was driving us around, him and Max were mostly talking French to each other. Penny and me thought it sounded real pretty, even though we couldn't understand any of the words. Fact is, most of the time, we couldn't even tell where one word stopped and the next one started up again. It was OK though, 'cause any time something important came up, Max would say it in English for us.

Max took us on some walks in Paris too, which were real fun. It's plenty nice to have your own chauffeur, which is the French word for driver, to take you all around though, 'specially, when you get tuckered out from all the walking. You can get almost exhausted you could say, after a long walk of about seven miles through some gardens or a museum or just through some neighborhood that's filled with different kinds of shops for Penny to go into and look at all kinds of stuff and even buy some of it with her franks.

Me and Max don't like to shop around at stores too much, so we usually waited outside for Penny. We just took it easy and looked at all the old buildings and all the people walking by and talking French to their friends. I was amazed when Max told me some of those buildings were already standing a long time before the Pilgrims had their turkey dinner with the Indians and Columbus came over to

173

America with his three boats. That's one of the things I won't ever forget about France and the other countries across the ocean. They were built a long time before the United States of America. By the way, even the little kids that were walking by us while Penny was shopping were talking French.

I don't think I ever saw Penny so happy. I mean, she was smiling and laughing all the time and never getting tired of seeing the sights and shopping in the stores and taking pictures seemed like every second and eating so much of that delicious French food that anyone could tell she was having the time of her life. When your best friend is happy, chances are you will be too. You get that good feeling all over is what I'm saying.

Once, Max saw me looking at Penny when she wasn't looking at me. I must of been smiling, so he asked me what I was thinking about. I tried to explain to Max how happy I was that Penny didn't need to put her tongue on the cold metal anymore and she didn't get all bothered at loud noises or bad smells, but he probably didn't understand exactly what I was saying. Maybe he did, but he probably didn't.

Pierre dropped us off one afternoon at Max's apartment so we could get a little rest before supper. Max told us a short nap would be a good thing to have, 'cause we might be staying out late that night. That's how Max is. He likes to give you little hints about what might be happening next on your vacation trip, but he doesn't really tell you exactly where you're going, 'cause part of the fun of it is being surprised.

So, we said oh revore to Pierre until later, and Max, Penny and me were standing in the lobby waiting for the elevator to take us up to the apartment for our short nap. The elevator doors finally opened, and boy oh boy was I ever surprised. Now, I'm not saying it was the surprise of a lifetime or nothing like that, but it was at least a medium to a big type of surprise, closer to the big type, I would say.

Three people were standing in the elevator when the doors opened. It looked to me like it was a mom and a dad and their daughter. I mean, I couldn't be sure, but that was my guess when I first saw the three of them standing there, and they were all holding hands, like people usually do when they're all in the same family coming downstairs on an elevator.

At first I didn't take too close of a look, at least at their faces, 'cause why would anyone look too close at the faces of three strangers riding in an elevator? You just stand back in a polite way and let them get off the elevator first. Then you go in, and that's usually the end of it until you get off at whatever floor you happen to be living on. I mean, chances are you're never going to see them again in your whole life anyway.

What happened this time that was different is that Max knew the people. Turns out they had an apartment in the building too, so they stopped for a friendly talk. That's when I looked at their faces, and that's when I got my medium to big surprise. The daughter, that was still a minor I was sure, was a girl that looked a lot like me. Very much like me, I would say. What I'm saying is that I could tell right off that she had some of the extra chromozones, too.

'Course, Max introduced everybody around, so I found out the girl's name was Ashley just before she found out my name was Richard. I shook her hand and told her it was nice to meet her, but after that I sort of ran out of stuff to say like happens to me once in a while. Finally, just as I was feeling my face getting red, I told her that Ashley was a nice name that I always liked the sound of. She said thanks and said she liked Richard, too. Then, she sort of looked down at the floor in a bashful kind of way. I think her face might of got a little red too, but I couldn't be sure of it. It's called blushing.

Now, I'm not going to fib and say that Ashley is as pretty as Penny, 'cause like everyone knows, there is no one as pretty as Penny. But, when I first took a better look at Ashley, I have to admit that even though she wasn't a knockout or even a girl you might call a doozy, she was sure someone a guy wouldn't be ashamed to have a date with, not that I was going to ask her for one or nothing.

After our nap, Max told me and Penny to get dressed up in our fancy clothes, 'cause we were going to a nightclub. A nightclub isn't a place I've ever been to, and I wasn't positive, but I was almost sure that Penny never went to one, neither. Max must of known by looking at our faces that we weren't exactly sure what happens at a night club, so he told us it was a place where you go to eat supper. After supper, some men and women sing some songs and do some dancing up on the stage, and after that the orchestra keeps on playing some tunes just in case anyone like us would like to get up and have a dance or two of our own. Max never told us, until we were riding back down in the elevator, that he invited Ashley and her mom and dad to come with us.

I'm telling you that a person can never know what the future will bring. I mean, it's easy to know what happened yesterday or even last week, 'cause that's the past, which means it already passed you by, but you can't tell what's going to happen next, 'cause that's the future, which means it hasn't happened yet, so how would you know about it? And, sometimes the things that happen right now, which is the present time, turn out to be the kind of things that aren't so pleasant, so you wish they were still in the future when you didn't know about them, at least for a while.

Anyway, we walked into the nightclub, and I could tell right off that this guy in a tuxedo, greeting us in a friendly way up near the front door, knows Max real good. He gives him another hug and those same two kisses on each cheek and calls him Mishooer Max. Then the same guy in the tuxedo takes all of us to this big table, which is kind of set off from all the other tables. It's the only table in the nightclub that's a couple of steps up and right in front of some big windows looking out at the street. I'm thinking right away that here we go again with the same kind of special treatment that we got in the first class part of the airplane and at the hall where the ballet dance happened.

Well, everyone sits down at our special table, and I'm feeling real happy, 'cause I'm sitting between Penny on one side of me and my new friend Ashley on the other. So far, I like this nightclub place real good, until I happen to look over at Penny to make sure everything is OK with her. I always like to check up on my friends to make sure everything is OK with them. That's the kind of guy I am.

Fact is, I can tell right off that something real bad is going on. Penny's hands are holding tight onto a napkin, and she's twisting it over and over again. Her hands are shaking real bad, and even though she's trying not to cry, the tears are just about pouring out of her eyeballs and running down her cheeks. By this time, Max is looking at Penny, too, and then he looks at me. From the look around Max's face, which is the kind of look you see when a person is surprised or maybe can't figure out exactly what's going on, I can tell he doesn't know why Penny is feeling so bad and that he's getting real worried, too.

Then it came to me, almost out of the blue it seemed like. I just knew in my mind what was bothering Penny so much and why she was crying so much. I mean, here she was, sitting at a table in a nice place with some people she liked to sit with, 'cause we were all her good friends. Only thing was, the table we were all sitting at was right there in front of some windows again, and right outside there were cars and motorcycles and busses going by in a steady line. So, like I say, I knew in a flash all the terrible bad memories Penny was having, all right. Her past was happening all over again in her present, and her future was very scary for her.

I got up from my chair real quick and walked around to Max to tell him what I was thinking. 'Course, Max understood what was happening in a flash. He shook hands and asked his good friend in the tuxedo to please hurry up and get a different table for us, maybe facing the stage instead of looking out the windows. After that, we all walked over to our new table by the stage, and by the time we got there, Penny was calmed down and smiling again, and she gave me one of her delicious hugs. She whispered soft in my ear, telling me that I was still her very best friend. When you're someone's very best friend, you almost always know what they're thinking most of the time, all right.

I'm telling you that once you get the right table, a nightclub can sure be a lot of fun. Before you know it, here comes a waiter. He's wearing a tuxedo too, and just like that, he pours out six glasses of the bubbly, which works out real nice, 'cause there's exactly one for each of us. 'Course, I'm thinking maybe I should tell the waiter that three of us aren't majors yet, but then I decide not to say anything. I mean, who knows? It's possible that the age for being a major in Paris, France is younger than it is in the United States of America. And, even if it's exactly the same, we're almost majors anyway, so it's not the same as the serious kind of cheating that greedy folks do on their income taxes.

Anyway, after drinking our bubbly one sip after the next and eating our supper and everybody having some friendly talk at the table, the lights in the nightclub suddenly go off, except for some spotlights in different colors that are lighting up the stage. At least 20 ladies come prancing out from behind the curtain. They're all lined up in a straight row, and they're wearing shiny pants that are so short you can almost see their butts, not that I was really looking at that part of them too much.

The ladies do this dance that's called the "Can Can." Fast music is playing, and they're all holding on to each other and smiling and standing in one place kicking their legs up at the ceiling one at a time. They got those kind of legs that you mostly see on younger ladies, smooth and skinny ones I'm talking about, not the fatter ones with all the wrinkles and bumps and those blue veins that you see on a lot of older ladies.

After the show, which had some other singers and dancers too, the friendly guy with the tuxedo that met us at the front door and that gave us the table away from the windows when we needed it so bad, came up on the stage and invited everybody at his nightclub, first in French and then in English, to hang around for as long as we liked and to come out on the floor for a dance or two.

The other waiter that first brought us the bubbly kept bringing us more of it and asking if anybody needed a refill. Right after that is when I did something that was way cool, all right, even though I'm not sure I would of done it so quick if I didn't drink all that bubbly, which must have something in it that makes you less nervous than you usually might be, I think.

What happened was that the guys that were in charge of playing the music started up playing some tunes that were softer and slower than the Can Can. Ashley's mom and dad went out on the floor for a dance. Then Max asked Penny if she would like to have a spin around, which they did. 'Course, with everybody else up there dancing, the only people left at the table were me and Ashley.

Fact is, I was having some trouble figuring out what to say to her now that we were all alone. I already told her I liked the sound of her name, so that one was used up. I thought about asking her how she liked the weather in Paris, France, but that sounded kind of dumb in my head. Then, just when I was going to ask her how many more days before she was going home, which wasn't a bad question I was thinking, she asked me the very same thing. 'Course, I answered her real quick, and then it got quiet again, except for the music playing.

Finally, I came up with the idea of asking Ashley if she would like to have a spin around the dance floor, too. With everyone else dancing around up there, I couldn't think of any good reason why me and Ashley shouldn't have a dance, too. Nobody likes to sit around like they're some kind of a flower painted on the wallpaper.

It's not like I was an expert at dancing or nothing, so it's a good thing that Ashley wasn't, neither. At least we knew where to put our hands when you hold onto the other person while you're dancing, and except for a few times, we hardly tripped or stepped on the other person's toes. Ashley smelled good from some kind of perfume that girls usually wear to make themselves smell like flowers. I always liked a girl that smells like flowers instead of onions or garlic.

I looked over to Penny and Max to check out how they were dancing, and it seemed like Ashley and me were doing just about the same kind of moves that they were. So, after the first tune, I just stopped worrying about how I was doing so much and had a good time dancing with Ashley and holding her in my arms, but not too close to the rest of me, while the music was playing.

Me and Ashley did some talking to each other at the same time that we were dancing, too. I told her what I did for work, and she told me what she did, which was working at her father's doctor office. She told me she likes to go bowling, too, and that she likes the movies more than anything. It's nice to talk with your partner while you're dancing, so you have something to do besides just holding on to each other.

I think Penny and Max were proud of me, 'cause Max gave me this big wink with one eye and Penny shook her head up and down and smiled at me when I was dancing with Ashley. Then, the guys that were playing the music stopped for a rest, and we all went back to the table at the same time. It worked out real good, and that's when I knew I would go dancing with a girl again, even if I didn't drink some bubbly first. Sometimes the things you think you're going to be nervous about turn out to be some of the best things you ever do.

When Ashley wasn't listening, 'cause she went to the femmes room with her mom, her dad told me I was a real nice guy and asked me to please make sure and call her up on the phone when we got back home from our vacation trip. That was a pretty good idea, I thought, 'cause the second time you have a date with a girl is probably much easier than the first time. I mean, at least you already know each other a little, like what you do for work and what your habits of good grooming are.

I almost forgot to say that before we left the nightclub, Max ordered us up some fancy dessert. I can't remember what it was called except the waiter lit the whole thing on fire right next to the table, if you can believe it, and when the fire went out, it sure was delicious to eat. I'm not sure, but the sauce tasted like it might of had some other kind of booze in it. Then, everyone started saying good night to everyone else, and it was almost time to go back to the apartment building.

Turns out that back home in the United States, Ashley and her mom and dad lived in a different suburb from the one we lived in, but it wasn't all that far away, and I already knew where it was from the map. I was glad her dad gave me her address and telephone number, 'cause I was just about positive I would call her up at some time in the future. When she picked up the telephone, I would say, "Hi, it's me, Richard, the guy that asked you for a dance or two at the nightclub in Paris, France." She'll probably remember me. I mean, I'm sure she will, 'cause it's not like anyone else asked her for a dance or two.

The next morning Max woke us up bright and early. Right off, I knew I wanted to sleep some more, mostly 'cause of the terrible bad headache I got just as soon as I opened my eyes, but Max wouldn't let me. A car that he rented for us was already waiting downstairs. Max would be the chauffeur on this part of our vacation trip to the southern part of France. If you look at a map, it's down toward the bottom and to the right from Paris.

Me and Penny got dressed quick as a snap, and to top things off, you could say, I decided to wear the hat that Pierre gave me for a souvenir. It was an exact copy of the one he always wears. 'Course, I gave him a polite mercy bow coo when he gave it to me and kissed him on both of his cheeks.

Chapter VII
Penelope

A family usually consists of a man and woman and their children. They live in the same house, and the children grow up together. Everyone has the same last name and the same ancestors. Ours wasn't like that, but Richard, Max and I were like a family in many other ways. If one of us needed help, the others gave it. If one of us got sick, the others took care. When one of us was happy or sad, so were the others. We shared a lot of time and fun activities. We shared some traveling, too. Our family went to France for a vacation.

Max wasn't sure how much we knew about France, so he went over a few basics before we left. It was as if Richard and I were in geography class, and Max was the teacher. He told us Europe is made up of many small countries, and France is the second largest. Only Russia is larger. It's a crowded place, too. Almost 60 million people live there. That's about a fifth as many people as in the United States, even though it's only twice as large as the state of Colorado. Paris is the capital, the largest city, and a very popular place to visit. We would be three out of around 40 million tourists who go there every year. When Max was done, I asked him if we were going to have a quiz.

It was a fantastic trip, even better than what I thought it would be. Richard and I couldn't wait to get up in the morning for more adventures. Every time we thought the next day couldn't possibly be better than the last, it was. Max planned things down to the smallest detail. The only bad part was how quickly the days went by. The person who first said, "Time flies when you're having fun," must have been on vacation in France.

I know there are dozens of beautiful cities in the world, but I can't imagine any as glorious as Paris. The architecture, the river, parks and gardens, boulevards, museums, restaurants, the people, the department stores and boutiques, the whole atmosphere of the place--everything is interesting because it's so different from home. Richard said it was like we were in a foreign country. He's become a real comedian since meeting up with Max. He gets some of it from his father, too.

Max was a perfect host. His apartment on the Champs Elysees is spacious, sunny, and filled with beautiful art. Original oil paintings hang on almost every wall. Bronze and glass sculptures grace the tables. Overstuffed leather chairs and sofas make for easy sitting and delicious naps. A grand piano takes up a corner in the living room. A bar takes up another. A balcony overlooking the boulevard is large enough for a table and chairs, and sometimes we had snacks and drinks while we watched the excitement below. A housekeeper came in every day, so we didn't even have to make up our beds.

Max had a strict rule about money. He didn't mind if Richard and I spent some of ours for souvenirs and presents for people back home, but that was it. He wouldn't let us pay for anything else, not even a breakfast. "You are my honored guests," he said. "You must save your money to care for me when I am old and frail."

We explored the city from early morning until about five in the evening. Then we'd come back to the apartment to relax or nap and freshen up for dinner. Except for one day, when Max wanted us to see what riding the Metro was like, Pierre was our driver. With his beret, cigarette holder, ascot, and kisses on both cheeks routine, he was just about as French as a person could be. It seemed as if every policeman in Paris was a close relative of Pierre's. They were happy to let him park and leave his car wherever he liked.

The Louvre, Rodin, Orsay and Picasso Museums, Notre Dame Cathedral, Eiffel Tower, Arc de Triomphe, Montmartre, Palace at Versailles, Sainte Chappelle, Luxembourg Gardens, Pompidou Center, a boat trip on the Seine--we did it all. We went to some out of the way places, too, places other tourists didn't seem to know about. With Max spurring us on and acting as our private tour guide, Richard and I learned a ton of new things. And, at the same time, we had a tremendous amount of fun.

Of course, we ate at some very fancy restaurants in Paris. Some of the waiters were a little snooty until they heard Max's French. Suddenly, they became our best buddies. Caviar, escargot, pate, scrambled eggs with truffles, roast duck with orange sauce, chateaubriand, coq au vin, and creme brulee (not exactly Big Macs with fries) were new to Richard and me, but Max insisted that we try everything. French people begin eating dinner late in the evening, and they're surely in no hurry to finish. Sometimes we sat down at nine or nine-thirty and didn't finish dessert until midnight.

Max got tickets for a ballet and took us to several nightclubs as well. I don't think I've ever seen anything as exciting as the ballet. The women are gorgeous and impossibly graceful up on their toes doing their spins and leaps, and the men, well the men are only magnificent. I guess I never realized how strong and athletic a ballet dancer needs to be. They lift the women and whirl around the stage holding them over their heads. When they leap, it's as if they're somehow able to stay up in the air longer than possible. And, all of this is happening while the most beautiful music is playing. Richard was amazed too, but I think he liked the nightclub with the Can Can dancers even more.

Max knew someone everywhere we went, so our treatment was extra special. We were always taken to a table or to our seats without having to wait in line. Waiters brought us appetizers and desserts even when we didn't order them. At first, it was a little embarrassing, but I got used to it really quick.

From our talks at home, I knew Max always had a wonderful time in Paris. This time, though, I had the feeling he enjoyed his trip even more than usual. He seemed to get great pleasure from planning surprises and watching Richard and me enjoy everything as much as we did.

Provence was lovely as well. We stayed in Avignon and took day trips from there. Our hotel had been a castle ("un chateau," Max called it) for several hundred years. Then, the family who owned the place moved away or died, Max wasn't sure which, and no one lived there for maybe 50 years. After the war, some wealthy Frenchmen renovated it, and now it's a luxurious resort. They even saved the moat and draw bridge. I'd seen pictures of places like it in travel magazines, but actually staying there was like a dream.

My suite had a bathroom bigger than most bedrooms, and it had a whirlpool tub with enough room for four people. The shower was marble, and it had a bench in case I needed to sit a spell. There was even a heater to warm my bath towels. There was a telephone in the bathroom, too; I guess it was for extremely busy people who had to take care of two kinds of business at once. It was the first time I'd ever seen a bidet. Richard had one in his bathroom as well, and he didn't hesitate to ask Max to explain what it was for. I pretended I wasn't listening.

Thick carpeting covered the floor in my bedroom. There were beautiful paintings on the walls, and mirrors everywhere, even on the ceiling over my bed. The bed was king sized and had posters in each corner. When we got home at night, it was made up with a down comforter and silky linen. A fluffy white bathrobe had been spread out for me. Chocolate chip cookies were on the nightstand. I could see the gardens from my balcony, and I slept with the windows open so the morning breeze and the birds would waken me early. It would be a shame to waste time sleeping in such a beautiful place.

Every day after breakfast we hopped in the car, and Max drove us through the countryside to visit some of the small towns and villages nearby. The rides weren't very long, usually no more than an hour or so. Along the way, we stopped and saw Roman amphitheaters and aqueducts, cathedrals and caves, waterfalls crashing down from the mountains, vineyards and olive groves, and ancient villages where the houses were built with stone slabs. While Max was driving, he gave Richard and me French lessons or sang some folk songs to us. Even Richard, who hardly ever sings, joined in.

Many of the villages were high in the hills, and some were having market days when we visited. Village people set up stalls in the town square and offered everything from fruits, vegetables and cheeses to fine clothing and jewelry. Often, there were street musicians playing their instruments and singing. Max didn't hesitate to harmonize, which only added to the fun. Of course, I bought presents for Carolyn, Tom, and Denyse, and I helped Richard pick out some things for his mom, dad and Ernie.

Cafes in the town squares served delicious lunches. We ate outside and watched the people stroll by. Max knew how much I enjoyed people watching. He smiled when he saw some young townsmen watching me, too. One of them even walked over and handed me a bouquet of yellow roses. "Je suis Jean Claude," he said. "Vous etes tres jolie, mon cherie." Jean Claude was quite jolie himself.

Everyone was very friendly in Provence. Max always invited folks to sit with us at lunch. Like our waiters in Paris, perhaps the people were so nice because Max was able to speak their language as well as he does. Or, it might have been because Max was just being Max, a kind and true gentleman, the sort of man people enjoy being with. "Charisma" is the word, I guess. Whatever it is exactly, Max had a lot of it. We feel blessed to know him. Richard and I love him a lot.

The first signs of trouble began on the flight home. Richard and I had our window seats, and Max was sitting next to me on the aisle. We were sipping on soft drinks and waiting for the flight attendants to serve dinner. Max was returning a glass to his tray table when I saw his hand trembling. He saw it too, and he joked about it. "Curious," he said. "It's a good thing I'm not doing brain surgery tomorrow, or I'd likely excise some poor guy's music lessons." It was typical of Max's sense of humor.

Dinner on the airplane was fine, even though we had been terribly spoiled by all those French restaurants. After eating, Richard and I fell asleep, and Max read a book. I opened my eyes once and saw Max had stopped reading for a nap. His book lay open across his chest, moving up and down with his breathing.

I fell back asleep and dreamed about my mother and father. I was a ballet dancer, and they had come to watch me dance. Father had a sad face, and Mother cried when they saw my partner was the dead professor. I woke from my dream when he dropped me. Max was awake too and in some pain. The same hand that had been trembling had curled up like a claw. He was rubbing it and pulling at his fingers, trying to ease what he called "the prototype for all cramps."

On the rest of the flight home, Max's hand looked fine. He didn't tremble or have any more cramps. He was his usual clever and jovial self, and the three of us had a good time talking about all we'd seen and done. But after landing, while we were waiting for our luggage, I saw him clench and open his fist a few times. He shook his hand as if it had fallen asleep. When our luggage finally came around, Max strained to lift his. "How could it possibly be so much heavier than it was when we left?" he asked. Richard carried it to the limousine.

Just as we were loading our luggage into the car, Richard's mom and dad arrived at the airport. They came to welcome us home, and, of course, they were especially happy to see Richard. "My mere and my pere," he yelled, and everyone had a good laugh. They were delighted with his beret and kisses on both cheeks, as well. Richard's parents drove him home, and I went in the limousine with Max.

Before he said good night, I asked Max to please see the doctor about his hand. He laughed it off and told me not to worry. "There are more old men with cramps than there are old doctors," were his words. Then, he held Richard and me close and thanked us for coming with him to France. How could it be? This dear man who had shown us the time of our lives actually thanked us for joining him.

Carolyn, Tom, and a few of our housemates were waiting at the front door, anxious to hear about our trip. Richard was still a little bashful about talking in front of a group of people, but once he got going, he really got into it. He told everyone about the highlights of our trip and most of the smaller details, too. From his description of our vacation, it was obvious that Max had become a very important person in Richard's life. He spoke about him with the same kind of affection he had for his father.

Richard and I got back to our routines very quickly. We couldn't help but reminisce about our vacation every time something happened to remind us of France. We'd see a man who looked like Pierre, a neon sign on a French restaurant, a travel advertisement in the Sunday newspaper for a trip to Paris, or have French toast for breakfast in the morning. Anything like that got us talking about our trip again.

Max encouraged us to keep working at our French. Three new words a day was his rule, and he went so far as to put a reward and punishment system into effect. For each word less than three, he deducted a dollar from our paycheck. For each word over three, we got a dollar cash bonus. Speaking sentences of five or more words got us two dollars. A two way conversation lasting at least three minutes would get us five dollars each.

Richard and I practiced every night. We learned the days of the week, the numbers, and how to tell time. Those were the easy things. Then, we started to work on the kind of every day things a traveler needs--asking for directions, where to find a bus or taxi, where to change money, and where to find a good hotel or restaurant. Remembering the words isn't so hard, but saying them with the right accent sure is.

When we accumulated 50 dollars, Richard and I opened a joint savings account at the bank. We were going to use it and any more bonus money for Max's Christmas present and dinner at a fancy French restaurant. Richard and I were determined to speak to the waiters in our new language, for three minutes at least.

About two weeks passed, and I had forgotten about Max's hand and any visit to the doctor. It was a Monday afternoon. Max and I had gone down the street for lunch. Richard couldn't come with, because he was wheeling around town making deliveries. On the walk back to the office, Max had an unusual amount of trouble catching his breath. He was huffing and wheezing so much we had to stop to rest every few steps. We finally got to the front of the building, but right at the entrance doors he stumbled and fell. He couldn't get his arms up in time to cushion his fall, so he banged his head on the sidewalk.

Max had some bruises on his nose and forehead, and his lower lip was puffy, too. Nothing seemed really serious, though. At least, no blood was gushing from anywhere. Always the jokester, Max said, "And now for my second act." I helped him to his feet and saw he was dripping perspiration. For a moment or two, I was afraid he was having a heart attack. I felt a little better when he told me there were no pains in his chest.

We made it to the office, but Max had a hard time unlocking the door. His hand cramped again, and he struggled to insert his key in the lock. After he got it in, he couldn't turn it. Later that afternoon I saw him trying to lift a paper clip from his desktop. He needed at least four tries before he was able to grasp it between his fingertips. He looked puzzled at first, then angry, then sad.

Trying to play his guitar and piano made him sad, too. His fingers were so stiff and clumsy he couldn't move them quickly enough. "I'm not sure what's happening to me, but I don't like it." he said. "My mind knows where my fingers should go, but my muscles just don't want to take them there." Then, his eyes filled up. There were no jokes this time. It may be that Max was beginning to worry about act three.

There were other worrisome things. Max complained of twitching in his arms and legs. It wasn't painful as much as it was annoying. He said it felt like something was crawling under his skin, and if he looked closely, he could see his muscles rippling. He felt twitching in his tongue too, and sometimes his teeth would chatter, even though he was warm. Buttoning his shirts and zipping his trousers took him a while. His feet swelled and hurt so much he took to wearing house slippers at the office. He walked very slowly and dragged his feet some. Spasms in his throat made him feel panicky at times. "I feel like I'm hungry for air," he said. With all these changes, Max finally made an appointment with his doctor.

The doctor didn't know exactly what the problem was, so he sent Max to a specialist. This was a neurologist who must have been very busy, because he couldn't see Max for 10 days. During that time, things only got worse. Max's shortness of breath made him gasp for air, sometimes when he was just sitting at his desk. He got very little rest at night. Painful cramps in his legs and severe indigestion kept him from sleeping. Phlegm in his throat, clogged ears, and nasal congestion aggravated the problem. Some nights, the only way he could get relief was to sleep propped up with pillows or sitting up in a chair. He was so tired during the day he fell asleep right at his desk.

Swallowing was another new problem and very distressing. Max had to cut his food into tiny pieces, or he choked on it and coughed everything up. But, handling a knife and fork wasn't all that easy for him anymore. Eating had always one of the great joys of Max's life, but now, it was an unpleasant chore. "From gourmand to garbage man," he joked. None of us thought it was very funny. Some days he sipped on a chocolate milkshake or had some soup for lunch. Other days he didn't eat at all.

Of course, Richard saw these changes just as I did. He pulled me aside one morning and asked if I knew what was wrong with Max. I told him everything I knew for sure. I told him Max was sick, and the doctors were trying to figure out exactly what was wrong. "Don't worry Richard," I said. "Max will be fine." That was foolish of me.

"I'm not worried Penny," Richard said. "When the going gets tough, the tough get going. Max is the kind of guy that gets better from bad stuff real quick, all right. You'll see; nothing can hurt good old Max." That was foolish of Richard.

After his examination by the neurologist, Max took a taxi back to the office. From my window, I watched the driver help him from the cab. It was painful, not just for Max, but for me as well. Not long ago, he was leading us up narrow footpaths, anxious to look down at the views from hill towns in Provence. Now, he was dragging himself into an office building, leaning on a walker, inching along, and looking down at the sidewalk. I had a black feeling, an omen of frightening things to come.

The doctors still weren't sure what the problem was, so they did more testing. Of course, I knew what urine tests, blood tests, and X-rays were, but some of the other procedures Max described were new to me. Even their names sounded scary, names like Electromyography and Magnetic Resonance Imaging.

Richard and I tried as best we could to go about our business. It wasn't easy, because Max wasn't getting any better. In fact, all his symptoms got worse, and some new ones started up. Max began drooling a lot. His problem swallowing caused saliva to accumulate in his mouth. With no place to go, out it came. He carried several handkerchiefs with him; "spit rags," he called them.

As Max lost control of his muscles, he lost control of his emotions, too. He took to quietly weeping at his desk. But then, no more than a few seconds later, he would burst out laughing, out of control and loudly, almost like a wild man. Anyone could understand his being depressed, but why the laughter, I wondered?

His mood swings made no sense to Max either, but he couldn't do anything about them. Here was a man who had always been totally rational and in complete control of himself. That's what made it so difficult for him. To be out of control and irrational were alien and only added to his anxiety and misery.

While waiting for the test results, I began feeling more of the old sensations I used to have. When I moved closer to Max, I heard the humming and felt his vibrations. I sensed what was in his head, too. His thoughts were dark blue. He was thinking about Richard and me. He smelled like ammonia, afraid and anxious. He had brain tumors on his mind. Had he known what his problem was at the time and what was in store for him in the future, I'm certain he would have been happy to settle for a tumor. "Fix up my brain, doc. I've got a lot of neurons to spare, but take care to watch out for the music lessons."

Lou Gehrig was a baseball player who played for the New York Yankees. I've never been much of a fan, but Richard told me all about him. Many people believe he was the equal of Babe Ruth. He was such an excellent player he was elected to the Baseball Hall of Fame. Less than one percent of all the men who have ever played baseball are in the Hall of Fame, so being elected is quite an honor.

While Mr. Gehrig was still playing baseball, he noticed his skills slipping away. He couldn't run nearly as fast as he once could, and hitting and catching the baseball got very hard for him, too. As the weeks went by, he began to shuffle when he walked. He grew so weak he had to retire from the game he loved so much.

Finally, after dozens of medical tests, his doctors figured out what was wrong with Mr. Gehrig. He had a disease called Amyotrophic

Lateral Sclerosis. Because the medical name for it is almost impossible to say, most people just call it Lou Gehrig's Disease. Actors, athletes, musicians, senators, and plain old regular folks from all backgrounds and walks of life--they have all had this disease. So did Max.

The neurologist told Max, and Max told me. He wouldn't talk about it, but I was relieved. At least the waiting was over. Finally, the doctors knew what the problem was. They even had a name for it. Now, they could get down to business and make Max well. Doctors diagnose diseases, prescribe appropriate treatments, and sick people get better. Then, everyone goes back to France. That's how it worked, I thought. From my own experience, I should have known better. Funny, how quickly we forget.

I walked to the library and sat down with an armful of material on Amyotrophic Lateral Sclerosis. One skinny pamphlet would have been enough. After reading for maybe 20 minutes, I closed my book. I'd learned everything I needed to know. The cause of Lou Gehrig's Disease is unknown, although doctors are beginning to suspect it's genetic. They think Max might have some abnormal chromosomes, just like Richard and me. Underneath our skin, way down at the very core of us, we're all the same.

Doctors haven't been able to discover a cure or even a treatment to stop the progress of the disease. Max's muscles will keep getting weaker until he is helpless. For a while, he will be totally dependent upon other people. Then, he will die. He might die quickly, within a year or so. Or, he might live 10 years or even longer. That's the ugly truth about Lou Gehrig's Disease. So much for feeling relieved.

Of course, Max didn't have to go to the library to read any books or pamphlets. He already knew all about Lou Gehrig's Disease. And, with that knowledge, he got down to the business of dying.

It's not that Max didn't try to get better, at least for a while. He took the medicines the doctors prescribed and suffered the side effects. He dragged himself to a physical therapist and did exercises instead of napping on his couch. He got stuck by an acupuncturist, stroked by a massage therapist, and manipulated by a chiropractor.

None of it worked.

A nutritionist put him on a special diet. Max stayed with it, all the while dreaming of pastrami sandwiches and contending, "people who eat health foods look like they died two weeks ago." He tried visualization and meditation techniques, hopeful that his incredible mind might be powerful enough to heal his weakened body. None of it worked. Mr. Gehrig's disease was a strong and relentless enemy.

Max was stubborn about coming to work. He came to the office as long as he could. At first, he would leave for home in the early afternoon. For a while, he made it until lunchtime. Then, he'd come in for about an hour in the morning. Finally, he couldn't come to work at all, because just getting out of bed left him exhausted.

Lou Gehrig's Disease is a master thief. It stole the things Max loved--gourmet dinners with friends, charming and winning over complete strangers, business lunches with clients, matching wits with the Internal Revenue Service, playing and composing beautiful music, and walking through art museums and gardens. In fact, the disease stole his essence; it robbed Max of everything he was. And, with all that Max had lost, it wasn't long before his will to live was exhausted, too.

Richard and I went to Max's house every day. Early one evening, he asked for a steak dinner. It wasn't on his diet, but so what? It would give him a little pleasure, so I was happy to cook it for him. When dinner was ready, Richard cut Max's meat and potatoes so he could swallow them easily enough. It took a long time to eat, because Max had to swallow three or four times after each mouthful to make sure everything had gone down. Still, I could tell he savored every bit of it.

After dinner, we talked for a while until Max said he was tired and wanted to sleep. Richard and I did the dishes, put them away, and tidied up the kitchen. Then, we kissed Max goodbye. "Au revoir, mon amis," he said. "Vous etes tres magnifique." He looked very handsome in his robe and pajamas. I saw his aura and his thoughts.

After we left, Max downed a bottle of sleeping pills for dessert. Off to bed he went, hoping to sleep forever. The only problem was he woke up the next day. Sometimes it's strange how things work out. Eating too much had always been bad for Max's health, but this time the food in his stomach weakened the effect of the pills and kept him alive. "Irony" is the word, I guess.

I know Max thought about suicide again, but he never tried it, maybe because he had waited a little too long and felt he was too weak to pull it off. Instead, while he still could, he wrote me a note. He sealed it in a brown manila envelope and told me where to find it at his home. "You will know when to read it," he said.

The day came when we had to close the office. It had been Max's place of business since he graduated from college. It was where he flourished and grew into a man. It was where, in the midst of the clutter and stinking blue haze, he helped people. It was where he said, "Max Eberhart here" the first time I talked with him on the telephone. It was a place that had been filled with doughnuts, bagels, and laughter. It was where he met Richard and me and where we came to learn what a rare and beautiful man he was.

On that rainy day, Richard and I cleaned out the office, packed up the files, went home, and wept.

Max's body continued to waste away in a slow, inevitable progression to paralysis. The muscles in his arms, legs, and trunk shriveled like dead plants. The only food he could swallow had to be pureed. A strapping hulk of a man had withered to a wheelchair bound invalid. Still, with all he was facing, he worried about Richard and me. He tried his best to lighten our load. "Come and look at my round rubber legs," he whispered, as the muscles of his face contorted into what was supposed to be a smile.

We don't think much about itches until we can't scratch them. Speaking is sort of like that too; it's something most people don't think about until they can't do it anymore. They just go ahead, flapping their gums with ease, fluently communicating their thoughts to others. But, when Max started having a problem speaking, I started thinking about speech a lot. I took another walk to the library. As easy and natural as speaking may seem, I learned it's actually a very complicated thing to do.

A person speaking at an average speed says about 12 to 14 speech sounds every second. In order for a speaker to combine those speech sounds and form words, dozens of muscles in the face, tongue, lips, and throat must move very quickly and in coordination with each other. If those muscles aren't working as they should, a person's speech will be difficult, even impossible, for others to understand. So speaking is complicated, all right. That's why human beings are the only ones who can do it.

At first, Max's voice grew hoarse, as if he had a bad case of laryngitis. He started to slur his words, as if he were drunk. Then, he began omitting certain sounds, mostly the endings of words. Finally, he couldn't say any words at all. Max couldn't talk at all, despite the fact that he had spoken ten languages not very long ago. He had gone from multilingual fluency to grunting in a matter of months.

Now, Max was quadriplegic and mute. Unable to move or speak, he was locked in a prison from which he could never escape. It was a maximum security prison where Max lived in solitary confinement without a chance of parole. It was the worst kind of prison imaginable, because his mind was just as sharp as ever. Lou Gehrig's Disease is more than strong and relentless. It is evil.

Carolyn and Tom helped us find caretakers for Max. These kind people came to Max's house every day and night. They bathed him, fed him, lifted him into his chair, turned on the television or played some music. They took care of his needs in the bathroom, gave him his medicine, and put him to bed. They checked him during the night, suctioned out his phlegm, and changed his position to make him comfortable.

No longer able to care for himself, Max was like an infant, except for the fact that infants have not yet developed any level of dignity. They cannot lose what they've never had. They are expected to wear diapers, drool, drip mucous from their noses, and be dependent upon their caretakers. Infants are easy to carry around, too. Max had lost many pounds, but moving him still took two strong helpers. It's that thing about dead weight, I guess.

Max's caretakers worked out a system for using a communication board. All the letters of the alphabet are printed on a sturdy piece of cardboard. A caretaker pointed to each of the letters in turn until Max grunted. In this way, he was able to spell out what he was thinking, letter-by-letter and word-by-word. It was slow and frustrating, but at least it gave Max a way to let his caretakers know what was on his mind and what he needed.

Max never wanted to use the communication board when I visited him. I knew he wasn't anywhere near content, but he seemed to relax a little if I just sat next to him, held his hand, and told him about my day. One evening, though, the board was on his lap when I arrived. I got the feeling he wanted to use it, so I began going through the alphabet.

Each time Max grunted I wrote a letter on a note pad. It took some time, but his message was clear: "Please don't let them feed me through a tube. Please don't let them hook me to a breathing machine. Please help me die."

I thought about my parents. Their lives had been snuffed out in an instant. They felt no pain, and they did not suffer. If not in life, at least they were lucky in death. Then, I thought about Max. He wasn't so lucky. Attached to a respirator and receiving nourishment through a tube, his life, forever empty except for agony and anguish, might go on for years. For all that time, his brilliant intellect would remain intact as a cruel reminder of whom he once was compared to what he had become.

I wiped the perspiration from his forehead and kissed him. "I love you more than you know," I whispered. "Of course, I will help you die."

Max's note told me what to do. I dismissed the caretakers early the next day. "I'll take care of him today," I said. I ground 40 sleeping pills into a powder and mixed it into a bowl of soft chocolate pudding. I helped Max swallow small sips of vodka until he'd finished a glassful. Then, I fed him the pudding. All the while, he was thinking love thoughts for me. They were red and yellow and smelled like flowers.

The combination of pills and alcohol worked very quickly. Max's eyelids fluttered before he closed them and fell into a deep sleep. Soon, he stopped snoring and his jaw dropped. At the end, I tied a plastic bag over his head. I didn't like that part, but Max wanted to be sure. At last, he was at peace.

I phoned the Foran brothers to arrange for a cremation. A suspicious caretaker phoned the police. A medical examiner did an autopsy.

They wrote about me in the daily newspaper. I was the subject of a front-page story, right between the mayor's plan for building more libraries and schools and the president's plan to provide better health care for senior citizens. They called me a bad name in the newspaper, because I unlawfully took the life of another person. They called me a very bad name.

I helped a loved one die whose suffering had become unbearable, and they called me a murderer. I helped a love one die whose life had already ended, and they called me a murderer. I helped a loved one die who would have been happy to take his own life if only he could have managed it, and they called me a murderer. The truth is they can call me whatever they like. I have no remorse. I am content with what I did. I would not hesitate to do it for him again. Perhaps they need to change their laws.

I have permission to live at the group home until it's time for my trial. Richard's mother and father got me a lawyer. I haven't met her yet, but she'll be with me in court. I'll have to explain why I helped Max die to a judge and jury. I wonder where they will find a jury of my peers--12 autistic orphans, each of whom fell for a brilliant, hairy, dangerously overweight, eccentric, poorly dressed, generous and incredibly lovely man who sucked on fat cigars and took his friends to France.

Richard tried his best to be brave after Max died. He told me crying is an OK way for people, even grownups, to show how sad they are. Once he let loose, it was much easier for him to talk about Max and all the fun we had at work and on our vacation. Of course, he knew I had helped Max die. He knew what the article in the newspaper said, and he knew I'd be put on trial, too.

"You should of let me help Max," Richard said. "I would of just told those police guys to take a good look at my slanty eyes, my flat nose, and the missing creases on my hands. Nobody blames guys with Down syndrome for nothing, 'cause they think we're retards and too stupid to know what we're doing."

Richard knows what he's doing, of course, and he isn't stupid. It's the people who enforce stupid laws who are the retards.

I haven't slept well since Max died. Often, I toss and turn until dawn. I never noticed it before, but Denyse snores and talks in her sleep. The neighbors play classical music on their stereo late at night, and stray cats prowl the alley behind our house, screaming and bickering over rodents. If I sleep at all, I either have nightmares about dead people or wonderful dreams about France. In either case, Max is the leading character.

Usually, my dreams wake me, and I can't fall back asleep. Without a job to go to in the morning, it doesn't matter if I sleep or not. So, I stay up and listen to my heartbeat or my blood or the dust landing on my nightstand. Sometimes I lick my alarm clock. It's made of metal, and it's cool on my tongue. It feels good.

Since I'm not sleeping well anyway, I've been watching a lot of television. Carolyn and I saw one of those late night talk shows the other night, the one that comes on right after the news. I can't remember the host's name, but he's that man with the funny looking hairdo he combs across his forehead. He talks with people every night about many of different topics. He really knows a lot of things, but not as many as Max.

Last night the topic was capital punishment. It's a topic like abortion, one of those things people are always arguing about. Some people think murderers and people who commit other crimes like kidnapping and rape ought to be executed. Others think people who commit those kinds of crimes shouldn't be executed; instead, they should be locked away at a maximum-security prison, in solitary confinement, for the rest of their lives.

The night Carolyn and I watched the television show, the host with the funny hair talked about a terrible man who had raped and killed seven women and who had done bad things to children, as well. There was a long search, a manhunt really, before the police finally caught him. The trial lasted only three days. Then, a jury decided the man was guilty, and a judge ordered the death penalty.

The terrible man's lawyers appealed the judge's decision. They were able to get other trials, and they hoped a different judge would be merciful and change the man's penalty from death to life in prison. They even asked the governor of the state and the judges of the Supreme Court to spare the man's life. It took almost 12 years before the lawyers gave up. The man was finally going to be executed.

Exactly how criminals are executed depends on where they live. Some states kill them by strapping them onto a chair and passing huge amounts of electricity through their bodies. Other states put them in a chamber and make them breathe cyanide gas. This man was in a state that would shoot poisonous chemicals into his blood to kill him. It's called execution by lethal injection.

The host of the talk show had a meeting with the man the day before the execution. The man was not angry, and he was not frightened. He said he would much rather die than live out the rest of his life in prison. "I have no contact with other people," he said. "I am isolated, worse than an animal, in a cage. I am not allowed to go outside for exercise. I never feel joy. I never feel the sun on my face. All I do is look at some old pictures of my mother and father hanging on the wall. I would take my own life if I could. I choose to die, because when you think about it, I'm already dead."

The host of the talk show was a witness at the execution, and he described what he saw. The terrible man was strapped to a long table so he couldn't move. A doctor and a priest were in the room with him. A needle was inserted in his arm, and he was asked if he had any last words. He didn't say anything. A machine was turned on, and the poison flowed through his veins to his brain.

The man gave one soft gasp and stopped breathing. He was dead in less than a minute. It looked as if he had drifted off to sleep, unafraid and comfortable, much like a young child taking his afternoon nap. This terrible man who raped and killed women and abused children and wanted to die got his wish. They helped him die instead of making him live out the rest of his wretched life alone, looking at pictures on the walls of his cell.

Isn't it strange? The people who turned on the killing machine helped a man die whose suffering had become unbearable, and they weren't called murderers. They helped a man die whose life had already ended, and they weren't called murderers. They helped a man die who would have been happy to take his own life if only he could have managed it, and they weren't called murderers. They might not agree, but in honoring his choice, they acted in a compassionate, humane way toward a terrible man who had hurt other people in the worst ways possible.

It's true that I helped a man die, too. But, he was a sweet man who never hurt anyone, a man who might have been the kindest, gentlest, most generous man there ever was, and a man who also chose death instead of a wretched life in his own dreadful prison. But, nobody honored his choice. How is it that people can be more humane and compassionate to serial killers, rapists, and child molesters than they are to Max? They really need to change the law.

This morning Penny had a meeting with a lawyer, the lady who knows Richard's parents. The lawyer's office wasn't too far from where Penny once worked. On her way to meet the lady, Penny heard the warning siren from the civil defense system. Two motorcycles without mufflers went by. A construction crew was laying tar on some potholes a few blocks away. A breeze from the direction of the city garbage dump passed over. The noises and smells were so awful they made her nauseous.

The lawyer's office was on the tenth floor of a building, so Penny took the elevator instead of walking. Penny heard music on the elevator. Musical instruments were playing, but no people were singing. The music was warm. It tasted like caviar, and it smelled like a bouquet of yellow roses.

The lawyer reminded Penny of someone else, someone from a long time ago. Penny couldn't figure out who it was for a time. Then, it came to her. It was Gramma Marie. The lawyer looked just like

Gramma Marie. She was wearing a blouse, and Penny could tell she had huge, pink arms underneath.

The lawyer asked Penny to tell her all about Max. "Go back to the beginning," she said. "Tell me how you met him and what you did at work. Tell me the kinds of things you did together, and what happened the day you helped him die. Tell me how you felt about him and why you helped him die."

Penny wanted to tell the lawyer everything. She spoke quietly and tried her best until the electrical storm exploded in her head again. Penny's head hurt. The pain was horrific. It came in alternating waves, from ear to ear, then front to back. At first she gasped; then she screamed; then it hurt so much, she could only whimper. It hurt so much, she wanted to die. "Please Mother, let me die."

There may be some interesting sights to see on this vacation, but so far Penny hasn't been allowed to go out. She stays in her boudoir with a tiny bathroom off in the corner of the room. It has a mirror but no bidet. There are no original oil paintings on the walls, only a no smoking sign and a picture of Mary and the Christ child. He died for our sins. Or, maybe for nothing at all.

The blinds are drawn, and the walls are green. A television sits in a niche across the room. A telephone and a pitcher of water are on the table next to her. There are no posters at the corners of her bed, no silken sheets, no fluffy white bathrobes, and no chocolate chip cookies. Penny can't find the balcony overlooking the garden, and no birds waken her in the morning. Un chateau must be full.

The waitress doesn't know a word of French. She's nice enough, and she brings Penny food every day. It's never what Penny orders, though. When Penny orders crepes, she should get them instead of burnt toast and rubbery oeufs. When Penny orders coq au vin, she shouldn't get macaroni and cold fromage. The service isn't very special. Penny will inform the maitre d' when she leaves for home next mardi or mercredi.

This time, Richard brought his parents to France. All three of them visit Penny almost every day. They bring her gifts and snacks. They want to hold her hand and hug her, but she doesn't like the feel of them. They shouldn't get so close. She doesn't feel much like talking to them, either.

At first, her voice is hoarse, as if she has laryngitis. Then, she begins to slur her words, as if she were drunk. Finally, she stops talking altogether except for a few words she repeats as if she were a parrot. "Hello, pretty Penny."

Chapter VIII
Richard

We got home from our vacation trip with hardly no trouble at all.
The airplane ride was smooth as ice except for a few times when it
got turbulent, which is another word for bumpy, up in the sky. You
don't have to worry too much about turbulence though, 'cause it's
just about the same thing that happens when a car you're riding in
happens to run over a bump in the road. And this time, when I heard
those loud noises coming out from under the plane, I wasn't scared,
neither. I mean, why would I be scared when I knew what the reason
was? You could say I'm a veteran at flying in airplanes now instead
of just a rookie.

The nighttime was really long on the airplane ride home. Max
was sure right about having to pay back for the extra daylight we got
on the ride going over to France. Boy oh boy. This time it was dark
almost all the way across the Big Pond. I didn't mind though, 'cause
with all the traveling around we did on our vacation, I was plum
tuckered.

I almost didn't believe it, but fact is, I slept all the way through
supper and one of the movie shows. It turned out perfect though,
'cause the flight attendant warmed up my supper for me after I woke
up. And, I'd rather take a good nap than see a movie show all over
again that I already saw. It's like what usually happens in a football
game or a baseball game you're watching on television. They show
that instant replay thing which is exactly the same the second time
around. I mean, nothing ever changes from the first time, so it seems
like sort of a waste of time to me. I have to admit it's better than
watching the commercials, though, 'specially the one with the frogs.

After a little while longer, I could tell we were getting closer to
landing, 'cause the ocean was gone, and there was some good old
solid land below us. I looked out the window at some of the buildings
down there. I recognized them, even though I was looking down at

the tops of them instead of the usual way, which was looking up from the bottoms. A few minutes later, I looked out another time and there they were again, the same buildings. Seemed to me like we were just going round and around, with the wings doing their tipping thing, without coming down too much.

The captain of the airplane, which is another word for the pilot, spoke up, loud and clear, over his microphone. He told all of us passengers to please be patient, 'cause we were circling the airport, just like I thought. There was a lot of planes lined up in front of us, a rush hour traffic jam in the sky almost, and we had to wait until it was our turn to finally land. The men that sit in front of those TV screens in the tall tower at the airport and make sure no one crashes into anyone else and are in charge of deciding which airplane gets to land next are pretty strict about anyone butting in line would be my guess.

After another little while, I'd say exactly 16 or 18 minutes, it finally got to be our turn at the front of the line. It's a good thing too, 'cause I was getting that crummy feeling in my stomach and that sour taste in my mouth that usually means you're getting carsick. You don't ever want to get carsick on an airplane if you can, 'cause there's no way to stop or even lean your head out the window. Alls you have is that barf bag tucked in the holder behind the magazines they give you.

For a minute or two, I was afraid I might be having my supper again, only this time coming up when it's not near as tasty as it is going down. Fact is, that's what happened to a nice old lady sitting just a few seats behind us. Boy oh boy, I never thought a nice old lady could make such a loud, nasty sound. It sounded like RALPH, only much louder, if you can believe it. And, pretty soon it was like her ralphing was catching, too, 'cause another nice old lady sitting right next to her started up with the same kind of noise, and then two more old people across the aisle got to doing the same thing, right along with the first two. It was like they were all taking turns, first with the ralphing noises and then with filling their bags, right up to the top, for sure. It didn't exactly smell too good up there in the first class part of the airplane. 'Course, I don't know for sure, but I'm almost positive that the second class part didn't exactly smell like roses, neither.

Penny and me, and even Max, got to laughing pretty hard at all that barfing going on, not that you should ever laugh when old people get very sick, or even a little sick. It just tickled us though, and right after I got tickled, I started to feel normal again. Next time I get carsick, I'm going to think of those same old people, just to see if giggling works again to make me feel normal. There's nothing like a good giggle, the kind that you can't stop no matter how hard you try, to make you feel normal. That's what I think.

Anyway, we were finally getting lower and lower, and then I felt the wheels of the airplane stick to the ground, after a little bounce and a rattle or two. I must admit that when the wheels finally stick to the ground, it's one of my favorite things about an airplane ride. Being a veteran, I'm not as scared as I used to be about flying, but it's still a good feeling when you get your feet back on earth. Like my dad always says, too: "There's no place like home, even though it's humble."

I think all the traveling around we did on vacation made Max a little tired, too. His muscles seemed a little weak after we got off the airplane and our suitcases finally came around to us on that spinning thing. I could tell his was a little heavy for him, so I helped him carry it out to the limousine. It wasn't that heavy for me, 'cause I'm a younger guy than Max, so I'm probably a little stronger. The younger you are the stronger you are, unless you're still a baby or a real little kid. That's how it works.

Was I ever surprised when I saw my good old mom and dad waving and walking up to us, with great big smiles on their faces, right after we got outside. They came to the airport to welcome everyone home. I was real happy they came to welcome us all right, 'cause it was the longest time in my whole life I ever went without seeing them. It's OK to miss your mom and dad, no matter how old you are, 'specially when they miss you too. I mean, you don't want to get all blubbery with bawling if you can help it, but there's nothing to be ashamed about if maybe a little tear or two leaks out of your eyeballs.

We talked for a while, all five of us, like old friends. Max shook Dad's hand, and he gave Mom a nice little pecker on her cheek. Penny gave them both hugs and kisses. Mom and Dad thanked Max very much for taking us on such a wonderful vacation. Then, they drove me home, and I told them all about everything we did and all the good times we had. Penny went home with Max in the limousine. It turned out real nice, 'cause everybody had some company for their ride home from the airport. You could get sort of lonely if you have to ride home from the airport all by yourself, with nobody to tell about all the good times you just got done having.

So, like I say, it was a wonderful time we had on our vacation. It was good to get home and go back to work, though. Me and Penny started right up on our jobs, almost like we never left. In a way, I think a good job is pretty much the same thing as riding your bike. Once you learn how to do it, seems like you're never going to forget how, no matter what. I'm hoping it's the same way for my reading and writing, too, 'cause I don't ever want to start all over at the beginning again. I mean, I would if I had to, but I'd rather not, if I can.

It was after supper but before bedtime, exactly three or four nights after me and Penny came home from Paris, France. Penny and me were practicing up on our French, but I was having a hard time keeping my mind on the new words. Fact is, I was hardly concentrating on the words at all, 'cause I was thinking about giving good old Ashley a ring, which is another word for a call, on the telephone.

I'd been thinking about calling her pretty much every night since we got home and sometimes during the mornings and afternoons, too. I was a little bashful about doing it, though. I mean, it's not like I'm a smooth operator, Romeo type of a guy that usually calls a lot of girls on the telephone. Truth is, if I went ahead and called Ashley, she would be the first one. But, when you think about it, there can never be a second one or a third one until there's a first one. That's only common sense.

I was a little afraid Ashley wouldn't remember me, or if she did, I'd run out of stuff to say to her on the telephone. I was even thinking about printing up a list of topics to have on my lap when I called her up. That way, when me and Ashley finished talking about one thing, I could just look down at my list and come up with something else, quick as a flash, so we could keep on talking, steady as she goes, without worrying about any of those quiet times when nobody can come up with something to say and everyone gets a little panicky, which is another word for very nervous.

'Course, maybe I'd get lucky and Ashley would have her own list of questions on her lap. You can never tell when a girl you're calling on the telephone for the first time will have her own list of questions on her lap. Then, alls you would have to do is take turns during your talk, first asking questions and then answering them, one right after the other, without getting panicky, or even a little bit tense, which is another word for nervous, too.

So, from about eight o'clock to nine o'clock at night I decided to give Ashley a ring, and then from nine o'clock to ten o'clock I was printing up my list of stuff to say to her. I had some good questions on my list too; stuff like "So, how's your mom and dad?" and "So, did you have a smooth airplane ride home?" and "So, how are things going at your job?" Those were some pretty easy questions, which is a good thing, I thought. You never want to ask a girl any kind of question that might be a stumper, at least until you get to know her a little better. If you ask a girl a stumper that she doesn't have any kind of answer for, there's a pretty good chance you're not going to get to know her any better at all is what I'm saying.

I figured that with some decent answers to all my questions, we'd be talking for a good long time, maybe around 17 or 19 minutes at least, before I asked good old Ashley if I could come over and visit her sometime. 'Course, that was my main question, the most important one on my list, which is why I was saving it for the end and slowly leading up to it, you might say, with some other questions. It's not that I didn't care about how her mom and dad were doing and how she was doing on her job and all the other topics on my list, but taking a little trip over to see her again was the real reason I was calling her up in the first place, all right.

Sometimes, when I'm thinking so hard about one thing, I forget about another thing. What happened this time is I got to concentrating so hard on my list of topics I forgot all about what time it was. So, when I finally called Ashley and her dad answered the phone, it turns out she was already sleeping, if you can believe it. I got a little panicky right about that time, 'cause I didn't have any questions on my lap for Ashley's dad. I handled the situation real easy, though, almost like I was a real veteran, or at least a smooth operator, at talking on the telephone.

Quick as a flash almost, I told Ashley's dad it was Richard calling, the guy that danced with his daughter at the nightclub in Paris, France. I asked him how he was feeling and how his wife was feeling, too. After he told me they were both feeling fine, except for some colds, I told him I hoped I wasn't interrupting something important going on at his house, and that I was calling Ashley to find out how she was doing since I saw her the last time across the Atlantic Ocean.

All the time I was talking to him, Ashley's dad was a real friendly guy and happy to do some talking back to me over the telephone.He wasn't grouchy or nothing like some people usually are when they have a cold; fact is, he was real happy I called, seemed like to me. He said, "And how are you feeling, Richard my boy?"

After I told him I was "very good thanks," 'cause I didn't have a cold or any other kind of sickness, he asked me how my friends Penny and Max were, and how the rest of our trip was, and how all of us were doing since we got home. Ashley's dad sure was an easy guy to talk to on the phone. It was almost like falling off a tree I would say.

Now that I think about it some more, most doctors are usually real friendly guys that are easy to talk to. If they're not, they probably won't have too many patients. I mean, no one wants to take their clothes off in front of a doctor that isn't too friendly. And, you don't want any kind of mean doctor coming at you with a needle, neither.

So, it turned out that me and Ashley's dad had a nice chat, like we were best buddies from way back in the good old days that didn't see each other for a long time. Before I said goodbye to him, I asked him to please tell Ashley I called her on the phone and to say hello to his wife, too. I thought his wife was real pretty and nice, and even if she wasn't, you should always make sure to say hello to everyone in the family, not just the one that happens to answer the phone when you call up to talk with his daughter for the first time in your life.

Ashley's dad asked me to make sure and call the next night. He said I should call a little earlier, so I could talk to Ashley while she was still awake. That seemed like a good plan to me. Then, it was time to hang up. When I said goodnight to him, Ashley's dad said I should take a couple of aspirins and call back tomorrow. I promised him I would, even though I wasn't exactly sure what the aspirins were for, 'cause like I say, I didn't have any kind of sickness, and you don't want to get into the habit of taking some medicine if you're not really sick.

While I was falling asleep, I kept thinking about how nice it was that Ashley's dad remembered who I was. I mean, I only met him that one time at the nightclub in Paris, France, and who knows how many other guys he met on his vacation? At least dozens, would be my guess, even though I was the only one that did some dancing with Ashley. 'Course, maybe they were at other nightclubs that I didn't know about, and so I wasn't the only guy that danced with her, but I still think I was. Sometimes, you just have a hunch about things that usually turns out to be right.

The next morning I told Penny I was going to give Ashley a ring first thing after supper. Penny thought it would be way cool to call her and a good idea for me to make some plans with Ashley for a visit. We were both very happy about it, even though Max wasn't doing very good, and we were starting to get real worried about how he was feeling and if he was as healthy as he used to be. You don't have to be a doctor of any kind to know when a person isn't as healthy as he used to be. Anyone could tell, just by looking at Max.

It was kind of scary, 'cause Max seemed to be getting weaker and weaker as the days went by. Penny and me kept on telling him to please go to the doctor, which a person should always do on a regular basis, 'specially if he's getting weaker and weaker as the days go by. Good old Max was plum stubborn about not going, though. Some people are like that, I guess. Maybe they're worried the doctor will find something terrible wrong with them that they would be scared of if they found out about it. 'Course, if you have something terrible wrong with you, you're still going to have it no matter if you find out about it or not, so you might as well go ahead and find out about it. That's what I think, all right, 'cause just as soon as you find out about it, you can get started quicker to do something about it and probably get better quicker instead of wasting time pretending there's nothing terrible wrong with you.

Anyway, after supper that night, I didn't waste any time, or dilly-dally around, like some people say. I scarfed down my dessert of chocolate cake quick as a flash, got my list of questions for my lap again, and gave Ashley a call, just like that. This time, I didn't have to worry about talking to her mom or dad, 'cause just like I was hoping, Ashley answered the telephone all by herself. I must admit that when she said hello, like most people do when they first answer the telephone, my heart got to pounding again, real fast under my shirt, and my mouth felt like it ran out of spit, too. "Cotton mouth," is what you call it when your mouth gets to feeling real dry and fuzzy like that, 'cause you're probably a little nervous about talking to a girl your age you only met one time in your whole life.

I told Ashley it was Richard calling, the guy that sat next to her at supper and danced with her at the nightclub in Paris, France. I could tell in a flash she remembered exactly who I was. There was no doubt about it, 'cause even before I got a chance to ask her the first question on my list, which was "So, how was your airplane ride home?" she came right out and said, "Hi Richard; I hope you can came over for a visit." I mean, there was just no way she would of wanted me to come over for a visit if she didn't remember exactly who I was. Girls don't usually ask perfect strangers to come on over for a visit is what I'm saying, 'specially if their teacher told them about Stranger Danger in school.

From the sound of Ashley's voice, which seemed kind of cheerful to me, I could tell she was glad I called her up. Boy oh boy. I sure heard a lot of her voice on the telephone that night. I'm telling you; even though she seemed sort of bashful when I first met her, she was a girl that sure could talk over the telephone, all right. Seemed like in no time at all, I forgot all about my list of questions. I forgot about my heart pounding so fast under my shirt too, 'cause it slowed itself down and just kept on beating away, steady as she goes. And, sure enough, my spit came back from wherever it went and washed away the cotton, too.

Me and Ashley must of talked at least 27 or 29 minutes on the phone. I finally got to do a little talking myself, mostly about how good I was doing at my job of janitor's helper, office worker, and chief of the one and only Rapid Richard's Delivery Service. Then, just about the time when I was getting ready to tell her how nice it was to talk to her and I would like to see her again some time real soon, Ashley said her mom and dad and her would like me to come over for a reunion supper, if you can believe it.

The next Friday night was the exact time they had in mind for me to come over for the reunion supper. 'Course, I was pretty nervous about that, 'cause I never went to a girl and her parents' house for supper before, even if it wasn't for a reunion. I got a little less nervous when Ashley told me that Penny and Max were invited, too. "Whew," I was thinking, which is what you feel like saying when you used to be nervous about something but you're not anymore. It's like you relieved yourself.

So, Max and Penny and me drove over to Ashley's house for the reunion supper the next Friday. I told Max which streets to drive on, so we found it real easy. It was one of those big stone houses with a garage for three cars and a curvy driveway in front made out of bricks. The house had three stories to it, which is another word for floors, and a ton of trees and bushes you call landscaping growing all over the place. There was a tennis court and swimming pool off to one side, too. As we drove up Max said, "bow coo bucks." In French, that means they were loaded with clams.

Doctors make a lot of money, I guess, 'cause there's always going to be sick people like Max that need their help to get better. The sick people finally make an appointment with the doctor, and after getting undressed and having a shot or two or some pills, the doctor sends them back home to rest up for a few days. Or, if they're real sick, like critical, which is right on the edge of dying, he might send them to the hospital for an operation of some type. Then, he sends them a big bill that could be for thousands of dollars if he pulled you back from the edge I was talking about. If you just have a cough or a wart or something else that's not so serious, then the bill is cheaper.

It works the same way that it does for lawyers, 'cause they send people bills too. There's even a receptionist sitting at the front desk that welcomes you when you come in for your appointment. "Have a seat," she says. "Doctor will be with you in a minute." Then, you have to be patient and wait for about 40 minutes, and all that time you're nervous about taking your clothes off in front of someone you hardly know very good. Sometimes it's more than 40 minutes and sometimes it's less, but there's always enough time to look through the pages of a magazine or two. Usually, those magazines in the doctor's office are all about golf, I've noticed. Sometimes they're about tennis, but usually golf.

Max parked his car near the end of the curve, and we all walked on the bricks up to the front door and rang the bell to let someone know we were waiting patiently to come in. The door was made out of heavy wood it looked like, with metal designs stuck all over it. It had some of that fancy glass made up of different stains that you see in church windows on either side of it. Big statues of lions, with flower pots sitting right there on their heads, were standing on both sides of the front door, too. Just as I was thinking it was the first time in my whole life I saw a front door with metal designs that had fancy glass on both sides of it and lions with flower pots guarding it, the door opened.

Ashley was standing inside the doorway looking just the same as I remembered her. She was nice and clean looking in a pretty dress that had a lot of bright colors on it, mostly red, I seem to remember.

A ribbon in her hair matched the red in her dress, and she had a white flower pinned to her dress, too. Ashley looked so nice I got to thinking maybe I should of put on some of my fancier duds, which is another word for clothes, too. I didn't worry about it too long, though, 'cause I felt pretty spiffy looking exactly the way I did.

Ashley gave a smile and a friendly howdy-do to Penny and Max by shaking their hands, and then she welcomed me too--only I got a big hug. I could smell her flowery perfume again, but fact is, I would of liked the hug, even without the perfume. I mean, perfume is a nice thing to smell, but any old kind of smell on a girl, as long as it's a clean one, is fine with me. That's the kind of guy I am.

It sure was a nice reunion supper we had that night. It started off with some appetizers and some drinks in their family room. This old geezer wearing white gloves that was working there but wasn't part of the family and always seemed to be smiling passed all kinds of little food things around with some shrimps and mushrooms on top. He passed around some liver pate and caviar on toast, too. I learned to eat those kind of things on my trip to Paris, France, not that I'm all that crazy about them. Then, the same guy with the gloves that smiles all the time popped a couple corks off of some bottles of champagne.

Max and Penny were mostly talking a lot with Ashley's mom and dad, and me and Ashley were mostly talking to each other. Like I said, good old Ashley sure had a lot of stuff on the tip of her tongue to talk about, even before we drank very much of the bubbly. I don't know the exact reason for it, but I've noticed that bubbly sometimes makes you talk too much, or at least talk more than you usually do. Dad always says it loosens up a person's tongue, which is usually better than having a tight one I would say.

This lady wearing a black dress with an apron over it came into the family room to tell us that dinner was ready to be served, so we all went into the dining room. 'Course, I waited until Ashley and her mom and Penny went into the dining room before me, 'cause ladies first is the polite way to be. In France, I saw a lot of guys help their lady friends sit down on their chairs before they sat down on their own chairs, so that's what I did, too. Ashley's mom said I was a perfect gentleman, which is the best way to be, all right. My dad and Max are the same way. So was Ashley's dad, I noticed.

Every time Ashley's mom thought it was time for some more food, she rang this little bell she kept close to her on the table. It was the same shape as the one the teachers used at my grade school, only it was much smaller and made out of glass. It made a soft sound, like a tinkle I would say, just loud enough for the lady in the apron to hear it. When the lady did, she came right out of the kitchen with one of her helpers, that was also wearing a black dress with an apron over it, to bring us something else delicious to eat. It was way cool; I mean, alls you do is make a tinkle and here comes the chow, just like that.

I think it was right after we finished the lettuce and tomatoes with the white asparagus, which surprised me 'cause I thought asparagus only came in pure green, and some of those little salty fishes mixed in I'm not too crazy about neither, that Ashley's dad stood up from where he was sitting at the front of the table to make a toast. Just as we were all holding our glasses up in the air, getting ready to drink to everyone's good health and happiness and more vacation trips and other good times, Max had one of those bad shaking fits with his hand. His hand shook so bad that he spilled some of his bubbly on the tablecloth. Everyone saw him shaking, and it looked to me like Max was angry at himself and a little embarrassed for doing it. 'Course I wasn't positive about it, but that's what it looked like to me.

Except for the shaking, the rest of the reunion at Ashley's house was a lot of fun. After a delicious dessert of apple pie or chocolate cake, if you liked that more than the pie, and some coffee or tea, her mom and Ashley showed Penny and me some of the pictures from their vacation. They went to a lot of the same places in Paris, France that we did. I recognized the Eiffel Tower, and the museum that covers a whole block with the pyramid where you go inside to see Mona, the French beauty queen, and the Arc just down the street from the building where Max's apartment was.

While we were looking at the pictures, Max and Ashley's dad

were talking to each other off in the corner of the home theater room, which is like a small movie show in your own house. I mean, they even had a popcorn machine, if you can believe it. Ashley's dad looked at Max's hand, the one that was shaking so bad during the toast. Then, he tapped Max on his knee a few times with one of those small hammers that doctors use to make your leg kick out, even though you're not trying to do it. 'Course, I couldn't really hear what they were saying to each other too good, except for the part when Ashley's dad told Max to make an appointment with his own doctor and not to wait too much longer.

The next thing that happened was that Ashley showed me some more of her house. It was way cool all right, just like I thought it would be after I saw the glass with the stains and the lions on both sides of the front door. I mean, you don't see that kind of fancy glass and lions with flowerpots on their heads in just any old house that people without bow coo bucks might be living in. It's not that it was a mansion or nothing, but it sure was close.

Besides the family room and the home theater room with the popcorn machine, there was an exercise room with a bicycle, treadmill, and rowing machine, a library room filled with college type books and a fish tank, a sewing room, a recreation room with a pool table that could also be a ping pong table, and a special room with glass walls and ceilings where flowers and plants of different types were growing. They even had separate rooms for the geezer with the white gloves and the lady with the apron to live in.

'Course, I told Ashley what a nice house it was and how lucky she was to live there. Then, it was getting pretty late in the night, so it was time to find everyone else wherever they were in some other part of the house and start getting ready to go home. That's when I got another one of those surprises of my life. Seems like those surprises never end, not that I mind having a good surprise every now and then. You got to stay on your toes at all times to be ready for whatever is going to happen to you next, all right.

I thanked Ashley for the good supper and for showing me around her house. I was getting ready to ask if I should call her up again sometime. Almost out of the blue I would say, she took the flower off her dress and pinned it on my shirt. Then, even before I could thank her for the flower, she put her arms around my neck and gave me a big, juicy smooch. And, it wasn't one of those short little peckers on the cheek, neither. This was a long one, right there on the old kisser. I mean, it lasted so long I thought I was going to strangulate if I didn't get me some air pretty soon. It felt pretty good too, I must admit, 'cause Ashley pressed the rest of herself against me during the kiss. She felt nice and soft to me, 'specially around her boobies, which is another word for breasts. And, she didn't have any hair above her lips, neither.

After that first supper at Ashley's house, things started to get real romantic between us. You could say it was getting plum lovey dovey, all right. Fact is, it was almost like one of those soap operas that are on the television, mostly during the daytime, when everyone has a girlfriend or is having secret meetings with someone else's girlfriend. I keep forgetting to ask my mom and dad or maybe Max why they're called soap operas; I mean, nobody sings classical music songs in a foreign language on them and they never talk about soap of any kind, so it's a real mystery to me.

Anyway, Ashley and me talked on the phone nearly every night, sometimes for longer than an hour. I sure never thought I could talk to anyone as long as that, 'specially on the phone, without a list of topics. I kept the flower she pinned on my shirt for a souvenir in the top drawer of my dresser, where my socks are, even after most of the petals fell off and the rest of it turned all brown. It didn't smell so good anymore neither, but it was the first flower I ever got from a girl, so that's why I decided to keep it as long as I could. I mean, it didn't take up that much space or nothing, so why wouldn't I keep my first flower?

I took the bus over to where Ashley lived once or twice a week for a date. I always remembered to bring her some flowers or some chocolate candy for a present. Once, when she opened her door and I was giving her some flowers, I told her she was more beautiful than a rose in the springtime. Ashley sure liked it when I said that.

"Oh Richard," she said. I could tell from her mom and dad smiling that they liked when I said it too, but they didn't say "Oh Richard" or nothing mushy like that.

Sometimes, Ashley's mom and dad drove her over to my house, too. They would visit with some of their good friends or relatives until me and Ashley finished our date. Then, they would drive her back home. At first, her dad always wanted to give me some extra spending money for our dates, but I wouldn't let him, 'cause part of being a grownup guy is paying your own way. Sometimes, Ashley and me had a Dutch treat, which is the same as splitting the money for a date down the middle. That seemed fair enough to me.

Fact is, Ashley is the first real girlfriend I ever had. 'Course Penny is a girl and she's been my best friend for a very long time now, but it's way different between me and Ashley. What makes it way different, without beating around the bushes any longer, is that Ashley and me do some sexy things together. I don't mind talking about it, not that I'm going to give out any secrets or get into the real personal stuff, which is another word for private or none of your business, even.

'Course, I already knew pretty many things about sex. My old friend Billy told me about a lot of things that him and his girl friends used to do when his mom and dad weren't home. And, Mr. Farber, my teacher in school, and a couple of my doctors made sure to explain the differences between a man and a woman's private parts, and what fits into what part and all that. Mom explained how you're supposed to hug and kiss your girlfriend in a gentle way before you go about making any babies, if you can, and Dad gave me some books to look at with some pictures that showed who goes in which position, like the man on the top or the bottom, whichever you choose, or even sideways.

At first, I was a little embarrassed about what was going on in those pictures, 'specially when I remembered that my own mom and dad did it to make me. 'Course, if you think about it, everyone's mom and dad did it, or they wouldn't be moms and dads. There's nothing to be embarrassed about is what I'm getting at.

219

Anyway, like I say, it wasn't like I didn't know anything about sexy things when me and Ashley started to do some of them. But fact is, I learned there sure is a big difference between hearing some other people talk about something and actually doing it yourself. What I'm saying is no matter how much someone tells you about how to swim, chances are you're not going to learn to swim very good until you get brave and finally dive into some water. Like a lot of people usually say: "Experience is the best teacher." You shouldn't dive into some water that's over your head, though, at least until you're excellent at swimming. And, you always want to watch out for big rocks sticking up, too.

I couldn't be sure, but it seemed to me that Ashley was a lot more experienced at sexy things than me. I mean, I caught on right away to the kissing on the lips and the tongue sticking in and out part real quick. It got to be real fun, 'specially when Ashley showed me how to pass a lifesaver back and forth from one mouth to the other. I was a little surprised at first, almost shocked I would say, and I was a little worried about germs too, but when you think about it, you're swapping all that spit anyway, so why not share a lifesaver or two, 'specially the red ones, while you're at it.

I was surprised, too, at how fast your breathing gets after just a few of those juicy kisses. I'm telling you that it's almost like the both of us are running a few blocks down the street, fast as we can, 'cause some kind of a mad dog, with long claws and pointy yellow fangs, which is another word for sharp teeth, is chasing after us. He's gaining on us too, and I can see that he's dripping a load of white stuff out of his mouth. Like I already told you, I'm not that fast of a runner, so it's a good thing I'm faster than Ashley.

Just when I think I'm starting to catch my breath and calm down a little bit, I start up with the fast breathing all over again, 'cause Ashley's doing something that feels good like breathing into my ear and licking it and sticking her tongue in and out. Boy oh boy. In no time at all, we both got wet ears, which feel nice and cool and is a fun thing to have as long as you make sure there's no wax or nothing else in there that you want to spit out, 'cause it tastes bitter on the tip of your tongue, instead of sweet as sugar, like a red lifesaver.

So anyway, one night Ashley and me are sitting real close together on the leather couch in the home theater room of her house. We're having some fresh made popcorn that's still hot and big glasses of root beer with lots of ice. In between eating and drinking, we're so close together that her leg is rubbing up against my leg and her head is leaning nice and easy on my shoulder. It's way romantic, even though some of her hair keeps getting in my nose and I need to sneeze about two or four times.

Ashley's mom and dad are out having a good time listening to some classical music tunes by the symphony orchestra so we got the whole place all to ourselves. The guy with the gloves and the lady with the apron are in the house too, but they're already sleeping or at least staying put in their rooms and minding their own business.

There's a romantic movie playing on the big screen television. It must be an old movie, 'cause it's in black and white instead of Technicolor. This guy wearing a bathing suit has a good built and a lot of hard muscles all over his body. He's laying on his back on some sandy beach and his lady friend that's wearing her bathing suit too is laying right there on top of him while some waves from the ocean keep splashing all over the both of them. Neither one of them is doing any talking; but pretty music is playing the whole time they're rolling around together, hugging and kissing as much as they can, without worrying in the least, it seems to me, about drownding or even getting sun burnt on some parts of their bodies.

In between a couple of my sneezes, I get the idea that what's going on between the man and woman in the movie, except for the getting wet part, looks like it would be a whole lot of fun in real life. Ashley must of got the same idea at just about the same time, 'cause before you know it we're going at it with the kissing and licking and heavy breathing stuff, and all the time we're going at it, the music from the romantic movie keeps on playing. That's the exact time when Ashley took my hand and put it on one of her boobies, if you can believe it. I mean, just when you think you got this sex business all figured out, something new happens to catch your attention.

In hardly no time at all, faster than a speeding bullet I would say, me and good old Ashley got to pulling off our clothes and almost in a flash we were plum naked, without our socks even, right there on the leather couch that felt cool enough but was a little sticky. At first, I was real glad that the only light in the room was coming from the television, 'cause I'm still a little bashful about anyone seeing the spaces between my toes or the rest of my body with all the soft muscles and flab hanging down from my chest and stomach.

Turns out that even though it was almost dark, I could tell that Ashley had some soft muscles and flab hanging down from the same parts as I did, so after that I didn't worry so much about it. I tried to get a quick peek to check up on the spaces between her toes, but it was too dark for me to see down there. I can always check up on them some other time if I still want to, I figure, not that it's such a big deal.

Well, like I said, I'm not going to get into the private stuff, except to say that Ashley is a real good teacher. When we do sexy things together, it's different than anything I ever felt before. It's not just my private parts and my whole body that feel good, neither. I get a feeling in my head that relaxes me and makes me want to be close to Ashley, and to be nice to her, and to take care of her too, so nothing bad ever happens to her.

Just when things were going along real good at my job and with my steady girlfriend Ashley, Max started to get very sick. Fact is, he was getting a whole lot sicker than he was before, and I had some terrible bad feelings about it way down inside of me. Penny and me kept telling each other that pretty soon Max was going to start getting better again, but he just kept getting worse. It scared me a lot when Max got so sick, and I was wondering why his doctor wasn't helping him too much, like doctors are supposed to do. I mean, if they send you a bill, at least they should help you get better. That's just common sense.

Some special kind of doctor that Max went to finally figured out what was wrong. I can never remember what the doctor called Max's disease, though. It's made up of a lot of those long words that doctors usually use that are hard for regular people to say. It doesn't matter very much what you call it anyway, 'cause Penny told me there's no medicine for it and no operation for it, and Max is going to die from it. It's the same disease that made Lou Gehrig die before he was ready. He was a real strong guy and probably the best baseball player that ever lived, except for the one and only Babe Ruth.

Penny and me went to visit Max at his house every day or night. Penny was much better at going there than I was, 'cause it made me so sad to see what was happening to Max. Except for my dad, he was the man I loved the most in my whole life, and when I thought about him dying pretty soon, which I couldn't help but think about, sometimes I just started to cry out loud and real hard, too. I tried to do it in places where nobody could see me, though.

When you love someone a lot, and that person can't even move anymore 'cause of some stinking disease, it hurts you real bad inside of yourself, almost as bad as if someone beat you up. And, the hurt doesn't ever go away, neither. It just stays right there, all day and night, making you feel plum miserable and more and more scared, all right. So, you can't help but cry is what I'm saying.

After a while, Max got so sick he couldn't even come to work anymore. He tried to keep coming as long as he could, but finally, he just had to stay home and rest in his bed or in a chair. I told him I would come for him every day and push him over to work in his wheelchair and back home again, or even carry him in my arms if he would let me, but Max didn't want me to. He just squeezed my hand as best he could, and he got real sad. Most of the time you can tell when a person gets real sad just by looking at him.

Finally, Penny and me had to pack everything up and close down the office; that's how sick Max was. We sure didn't want to close down the office, but sometimes there's just no choice, and you have to do things you don't want to do, no matter what. Doing what you don't want to do can be real rotten sometimes, but grownups have to learn to take the bad things with the good things in life.

'Course, when we closed down the office, there was no more job for Penny. I kept on working with John the janitor for a while, but in exactly a week or two the boss of the building wrote me a letter that said they didn't need me anymore. I still had a few packages to deliver now and then, but pretty soon I didn't have too much to do, 'cause hardly any new bosses of businesses asked me to help them.

Fact is, the one and only Rapid Richard's Delivery Service wasn't getting too much business anymore, so I just stopped wearing my shirts. I saved them though, 'cause maybe business will pick up and I'll need my shirts again. You can never tell when business will pick up again, and it wouldn't be good if I didn't have my shirts. They're like my uniform, and besides, Max gave them to me.

One night we went to Max's house for a visit and to help him with his supper. Penny cooked up a nice steak dinner with all the trimmings, 'cause steak was one of Max's favorite things to eat, just like me. We both like all the trimmings, too. I helped out by cutting everything up into tiny little pieces so Max could swallow his food and wouldn't choke on anything that might of got stuck in his pipes.

After supper, we cleaned up at Max's house and said goodnight to our good old friend. On the way home, Penny told me to be brave, 'cause she had a feeling something bad was going to happen to Max. Sure enough, that was the night when Max tried to commit suicide, which is another word for killing yourself. Some people say, "buying the farm" which I never understood the exact meaning of, just like soap opera.

Max didn't do very good at the job of killing himself, 'cause he woke up in his bed the next day. 'Course, I don't know what he was thinking when he first woke up. Maybe he thought he was dead, and he was up with the angels in heaven above. Pretty soon, though, he had to know he was still alive, right here with me and Penny on earth. He just had to know he was still alive, 'cause he couldn't talk anymore, and people in heaven above are perfect in every way. They don't have Down syndrome, and they can move all their muscles and body parts with no trouble at all. And, they can talk in perfect speech, too.

What happened next in the life of our dear friend Max is really awful, all right. When I think about it, it's like the meanest person on earth sat down one night with the idea of coming up with the most terrible thing he could possibly think of. Some good people on earth tried as hard as they could to stop him, but the mean person won. I'll go right ahead now and tell about it, without beating around any bushes. Now that I think about it, I wish I had some good things to talk about, 'cause I'm getting plum sick of the bad ones.

Fact is, Max didn't want to live his life anymore, and who could blame him when you think about what kind of life he had left? I mean, when you can't talk to your friends, 'specially the ones that love you more than anything in the whole world, and you can't eat anything but soupy stuff running through a tube some doctors stick straight into your stomach, and you can't move, even a little bit, 'cause your muscles are so weak you can't even take care of yourself in the bathroom or even breathe by yourself, I bet you might want to die, too? Be honest about it and tell the truth.

Well, even if you don't think so, Penny sure thought that dying would be better for Max, so she just went ahead and helped him do it. He was so weak from Lou Gehrig's Disease that he couldn't commit suicide anymore, so Penny did what he asked her to do and helped Max to die, just like anyone that really loves their good friend would do for him. For sure, I would of done it myself if Max asked me to. Even though I miss him something terrible, I would of done it in a flash, all right. I wouldn't of cared what anyone else thought about it, neither, 'specially 'cause nobody else in the whole world loves Max the way me and Penny do. I mean, what do they know about it?

It was almost impossible for me to believe it, but Penny got into some real bad trouble for helping Max die. Some policemen found out what she did, and they were going to take her to court and have a trial. There would be lawyers and a judge and some people on a jury that would listen carefully and decide if Penny would have to go to jail, if you can believe it. Can you imagine Penny having to go to jail?

There was this story that some stupid person wrote in the newspaper. Maybe it isn't right for me to call him stupid, 'specially 'cause I never met the person that wrote it, but I don't know what else he could be. Maybe it's a she, but probably it's a he, would be my guess. Anyway, whatever this person that wrote the story is, he or she said Penny might be a murderer, 'cause she did stuff that killed Max. It makes me want to scream out loud and punch the person that wrote the story in the nose; that's how dumb he or she is.

I must admit that even though I'm not an expert about the kind of people that are murderers, one thing a murderer just has to be is terrible mean. A murderer can be a black or a white person, a tall or a short person, a rich or a poor person, or a young or an old person. But no matter what else they are, it's for sure that a murderer has to be terrible mean. You could bet all your money on that is what I'm saying.

Only thing is, Penny doesn't have even one tiny bit of mean anywhere inside of her, not even a tad or a smidgen. Fact is, you could look all the way down to her bones, and you wouldn't find anything even close to mean. Alls Penny does is care about people and love them a lot, so there's just no way that she could be a murderer. That's just common sense.

I always thought people that have the job of writing stories for the newspapers went to regular class when they were in grade school and high school, and to college when they were older, and so they were supposed to be intelligent, which is another word for very smart. I sure was wrong about that, I guess.

I asked my mom and dad to please explain what kind of laws there are in the United States of America that would make Penny a murderer. They're both lawyers you know, so I figured they could give me a good answer to my question. I think they tried their best to explain it to me, but fact is, when they got all done with their explaining, nothing they said made any sense to me. How a person can have mercy and still be a killer at the same time just doesn't fit together in my mind. I was way more confused than I was before, and I almost got mad at them for being lawyers in the first place. Boy oh boy; nothing was making too much sense to me anymore.

No matter how hard I tried, I just couldn't understand what was going on. I mean, even someone with Down syndrome, someone that's not supposed to be too intelligent like other grownups, knows that a person should never be punished for helping another person that can't help himself anymore. It even says you should do the same stuff unto everyone else that you want them to do unto yourself in the Holy Bible, and the Holy Bible happens to be a lot more important of a book than any kind of law book that most lawyers usually read. Fact is, I heard once that the Holy Bible is the number one best seller of all time, at least since people started reading books, anyway. That tells you how much people believe what's written down in it.

When I was having a hard time figuring out what was going on, one thing that I was hoping and praying for with all my might is that our dear friend Max was resting in peace, dancing around with some beautiful angels in heaven above, looking for a new office, talking all kinds of languages, eating big bites of steak, going on trips to Paris, France, and playing his guitar, all perfect again. Truth is, that's my fourth wish, and if I can't have it, 'cause you only get three wishes in your whole life, then I'll give up on the one about changing how I look. I'll give it up just like that, in a flash, all right.

Penny knew some guys, brothers I think, that are undertakers, which is another word for funeral guys. She arranged for them to take care of Max's body after he died, and it was right after she took care of things that Penny got in the real bad trouble I was telling you about. And, if you think things were bad for Penny then, they only got worse. Things went downhill really fast, you could say. Dad said if the world was an apple, it would be plum rotten, with worms crawling in and out of it, even.

'Course, I wasn't there when it happened, but what I heard from my mom and dad is that Penny was in a lawyer's office doing her best to explain the reasons why she helped Max die. Right when she was in the middle of doing her explaining, she had another one of those fits like the one she had at Bonofaccio's Italian Kitchen on the celebration of our graduation from high school. You probably remember that's the night when her parents were run over and fatally killed by the bus. I'm real glad I wasn't there to see Penny have her second fit, 'cause the first one was plenty bad enough, and I'll never forget it anyway.

So now, another one of my best friends is gone from me. It's not exactly the same as when Billy went away, 'cause maybe you remember he moved far away with his mom and dad to another state near the edge of the Pacific Ocean. It wasn't exactly like that, 'cause Penny was still here. I mean, she was close by so I could go and see her, but what I'm saying is when I did, it wasn't like she was my best friend Penny anymore. She changed back to exactly the same way she used to be when she never smiled or talked to me. She got to spinning her charms around, over and over again, and she started licking metal stuff like the handle we used to hold on the yellow school bus.

'Course, when Penny changed back to the way she used to be, she couldn't live at the group home anymore. Tom and Carolyn had to take her to some place that seemed like a hospital to me, 'cause there were nurses there, and it had a bunch of rooms with beds in them. It was different from most other hospitals I'd been at though, 'cause the people that were living there didn't have any bad diseases like a heart attack, or cancer of the brain, or the one that Lou Gehrig and Max caught. Mostly, they did the kind of stuff I remember from the school bus on the way to high school, like rocking back and forth, banging their heads on the windows, and biting their fingers and hands. Fact is, some of the people at the place where Penny was living reminded me of Victor and Carmella that used to be in my special class. You probably remember them and Vladimir, the piano genius, too.

I went with my parents to visit Penny as much as I could. Some days when Mom and Dad couldn't go with me, I kept on going by myself, like a real good friend is supposed to do. I tried the best I could to make Penny feel better, even though she didn't want to talk to me. I talked to her anyway, usually about our jobs and about Max and about our vacation trip to Paris and some other parts of France. I called them the good old days, 'cause they sure were, 'specially compared to the bad new days we were having now.

At first, when I was saying stuff to Penny, I tried to hold her hand. She always pulled it away from me though, like she didn't want anyone, even good old Richard, to touch her anymore. She wouldn't look at my eyes neither, so there I was, like I wasn't a person again, no different than the wall, a coffee table, or the kitchen sink. Boy oh boy.

When Max and Penny went away from me like that, it was the beginning of a real bad time in the life of Richard. The apple got rotten through and through, all right. I might as well go right ahead and tell you about it, 'cause every story has an ending. A beginning and a middle are important for a story too, but unless there's an ending, it's not really a story. The only thing that you never know about until it happens is if the ending will turn out to be a happy one or a sad one. Maybe you could decide for yourself, 'cause everyone gets to have their own opinion.

I didn't have my job to go to anymore, so except for visiting Penny and my mom and dad, and talking on the phone and having some dates once in a while with Ashley, there wasn't much to do. At first, I tried to stay busy each day by going for walks, reading some books, or having some exercise, but, fact is, after a while, I was spending more and more of my time just laying around on a sofa or in my bed, watching TV, and feeling sad. Pretty soon, some things started happening to me that I didn't like very much. I tried to stop them, but no matter what I did, they just kept right on happening.

It's kind of strange, and I'm not exactly sure of why it is, but I've noticed that when you don't feel too good in your head, 'cause you're awful sad, then you don't feel too good in your body, neither. Fact is, I felt sick most of the time. It's not that anything hurt me real bad like a pain in my appendix or in my ear; it was more like a car sickness feeling in my stomach that wouldn't go away, even though I wasn't riding in a car or flying through some turbulence in an airplane. I thought I would feel better if I could barf, but nothing ever came up, except for the ralphing noise, even when I stuck my fingers down my throat.

I was really nervous and jumpy all the time, maybe anxious would be a good word for it, and I didn't know the exact reasons why. I had those sick feelings all the time, except for when I was sleeping, so I just tried to sleep as much as I could. When you're sleeping, you're unconscious, so you don't feel as bad as you do when you're conscious, which is when you're awake. That's how it works.

'Course, every time I woke up from my sleep, the sadness in my head, and being nervous, and the sick feeling in my stomach would come back to me real quick. It got so bad I usually didn't feel too much like eating anything, and pretty soon my jeans and corduroy pants were too big for me and so were my spiffy button down shirts and my boxer shorts that my mom and dad bought for me when I moved to my new house.

It's the first time in my whole life I ever wanted to be fatter instead of skinnier. If you ever have a choice, I think it's usually better to be fat and happy instead of skinny and sad. That's what I think, all right. Remember that too, 'cause it's a good thing to know about, and if anyone ever asks you, just tell them that Richard, a guy with Down syndrome that's had a lot of experience at being happy and sad, told you about it.

When I was getting skinny, another bad thing happened, too. I woke up in the morning, and I was laying in bed trying to decide the best time to get up and what to do with myself that day. I used to decide about things real quick, in a flash almost, but ever since I got so sad, I noticed it was taking me longer and longer to decide about things. First, I would think about doing this and then I would think about doing that, and pretty soon, I just didn't do anything except lay there in bed and think about not doing anything at all.

On one of those mornings that I was trying to decide when to get up and what to do, I felt some itches on my face. I reached up to scratch, like a guy usually does when he has something itching him, and that's when I felt some bumps. At first, I thought a few mosquitoes or bed bugs or maybe even a spider that bites your skin got at me during the nighttime. So, I jumped out of bed quick as a flash and looked at my face in the mirror. What a surprise I got. It was like a shock almost.

I guess I should of known it wasn't mosquitoes or spiders. Fact is, those bumps weren't any kind of bug bites or nothing even close. What really happened was a new batch of pimples sprung up while I was sleeping, and I'm telling you they were doozies, all right. They were the big juicy ones, red on the bottom with yellow pus balls and black dots on top, all over my face. Some of them were on my neck and back, too, just in case anyone might miss the ones on my face, not that anyone really could of, unless they were blind or needed some of those glasses with the very thick lenses, at least.

Well, I guess I was right when I used to think that everything has to be somewhere in this world. Pimples don't really go away when they finally dry up and disappear. They're always there is what I'm saying, just hiding right below the top of your skin, waiting around until you're terrible sad so they can pop out again and make you feel even worse than you already do, if that's even possible.

'Course, after that, I didn't feel like looking at myself in the mirror too much, and I couldn't find any tubes of that smelly cream I thought I saved to smear around my face, so I just went back to my bed for some more sleep. I had a dream about Max and Penny going up on the elevator to the top of the Eiffel Tower. I tried to get on with them, but there was no more room, and the door closed in my face. I kept waiting and waiting for them to come back down and get me, but they never did. So, I had to go home from the airport all by myself, with nobody around to tell what a bad time I just got done having.

Then, things got worse and worse, if you can believe it. Ernie tried his best to cheer me up, until I told him, in kind of a loud voice, I didn't feel like reading any of his books anymore or getting up out of bed anymore and to just leave me alone and not talk to me anymore. 'Course, in a little while, I felt real bad about yelling at Ernie like I did, and so I told him I was very sorry. He said it was OK and not to worry myself about it, and then he said he always talked to Carolyn and Tom when he got to feeling bad or sad, so maybe I should talk to them, too.

Carolyn and Tom understood how much I was sad and nervous about things, and they told my mom and dad. 'Course, Mom and Dad already knew I wasn't doing too good, 'cause like I already said, moms and dads know you better than anyone else in the world, and they can tell real quick, almost immediately you could say, when you're not doing too good. Mom and Dad could tell real easy, all right, 'specially 'cause I got to slouching over in my posture again and forgetting to keep my tongue in my mouth.

Mom and Dad talked to me a lot about what was bothering me, but then, when I was still feeling so crummy, with no energy to do anything, and mad at everyone most all the time, and no appetite for any food, and not wanting to go on any dates, and just wanting to stay in my bed and sleep, and not even wanting to go see Penny anymore, they took me to a special doctor called a psychiatrist that talks to you and helps you get happy again. I didn't mind too much, 'cause I was thinking that maybe he had some special kind of psychiatrist's medicine that does a miracle and finally dries up your pimples once and for all.

One thing I learned about psychiatrists, which was a good thing, is that you don't have to take your clothes off or get any shots when you go to their office for a visit. After you say hello and nice to meet you, alls you do is sit yourself down in a nice leather chair. It's one of those Lazy Man chairs that has a place to put your feet up if you want to get real comfortable. 'Course, right after that, the doctor sits down in his own leather chair which is behind his desk. Then, you start to talk to each other in a friendly voice, except you do most of the talking, seems like. I mean, every time you say something, the only thing the psychiatrist says is, "Tell me more about that." If you're not careful, you can get tired of doing all that talking real quick.

Like I say, there was this desk in between the both of us, and sometimes, when I was doing most of the talking, the doctor would write down some of the stuff I was telling him. 'Course, I couldn't be sure of the exact words he was writing down, but since he was doing the writing at the exact same time that I was doing the talking, I figured he must be writing down the words I was saying so he would remember them later on, after I left him to go back to my house. I think maybe the doctor should of used a tape recorder to help him remember what I was saying. That way he could of looked me straight in my eyeballs when I was talking to him, which is the polite way to be, instead of looking down at his writing paper all the time. Everyone needs to be polite, even psychiatrists.

When I first sat down in my leather chair and put my feet up, the psychiatrist asked me some easy kind of questions like my name and where I lived, when I was born, some things about growing up, and some stuff about my mom and dad. He asked me where I went to school and about the kinds of places I worked, too. I did real good on those kinds of questions, but after that they got a little harder, not that they were stumpers that I couldn't answer or nothing.

The psychiatrist asked me to tell him all about Down syndrome, which was kind of a surprise to me, 'cause I figured with him being a doctor and all, he must already know pretty much about the extra chromozones and all the problems they cause. Maybe he knew, but he kept saying I should tell him more and more about it anyway. By the time I got done with all my talking, he knew exactly how I felt about Down syndrome, which was being pretty darn sick of having it, all right. Fact is, the exact words I told the doctor was I was feeling down from Down syndrome. But, he didn't laugh at all. It would of been nice if he smiled a little at least, 'cause I was just trying to make a joke, which I didn't feel like doing too much of lately.

After he didn't laugh or smile at my joke, the doctor asked me to tell him exactly why I thought I was coming to him for visits. I had a pretty good idea of the reason, all right. Inside of me, I knew it wasn't as much for my pimples as it was for being depressed, which is another word for terrible sad. He asked me real quick to tell him more about being depressed, just like I knew he would.

I told him about being nervous all the time and not wanting to do anything except stay in bed and not even wanting to eat, which I always liked to do before, and the hard time I was having making up my mind about what to do and other stuff that used to be easy for me. Seemed to me, he was writing almost as fast as anyone could to get all the stuff I was telling him down on his writing paper. Once or twice he even stopped to shake his hand like you do when it hurts from writing too much.

While the doctor was making a list of the important stuff I was telling him so he wouldn't forget anything, it made me think of the time I made a list so I wouldn't forget my important stuff to say to Ashley when I first called her up on the phone. In a way, it made me feel good to know I wasn't the only person to make lists. Lots of people do it I guess, even doctors, and everyone knows they're almost as smart as lawyers, maybe even smarter, but I doubt it. Some doctors are probably smarter and some lawyers are probably smarter. I'll bet you all my clams that none of them are as smart as Max, though.

As long as I got on the subject of Ashley, I stopped feeling like calling her up on the phone and going over to where she lives for dates. Maybe I'll start up again after I'm looking better and feeling better, too. She calls me all the time and invites me over for another reunion supper with her mom and dad or to watch another movie all by ourselves in their home theater room with the popcorn machine and the ice cold root beer, but I keep telling her I don't want to, 'cause I don't feel too good. When she says she misses me, which she usually does, I feel sort of bad about not going over to her house to spend a little time with her, but fact is, I'm just not in any kind of mood for visiting her or anyone else these days. You can probably tell I'm feeling real crummy about myself, maybe worthless would be a good word for it.

After I went to the psychiatrist a lot of times, I would say at least four or six times, and I ran out of interesting stuff to tell him, he called my mom and dad and Carolyn and Tom to come to his office for an appointment all together. It was almost like another one of those family talks we used to have at the dining room table after supper at the house where I grew up, even though Carolyn and Tom weren't exactly my family, but they almost were.

The doctor explained to everyone, including me, that I was depressed, if you can believe it. I mean, after coming to him four or six times and me already telling him I was depressed the last time I sat down in the leather chair and got comfortable by putting my feet up, alls he did was repeat the same thing I already told him all over again. Seemed to me, we were right back where we started before I had the four or six visits and had to do most of the talking.

Truth is, for a while there, I got to thinking that maybe all those visits were a big waste of time. Maybe, psychiatrists don't really know how to make someone feel happy again, even though that's not a nice thing to say about a person that went to college all those years so he could become a doctor and try his best to help people feel better. By the way, I was smearing that cream on like crazy each night, but I still had my pimples, only worse than ever.

When I was getting ready to leave the family meeting with the psychiatrist, he gave me one of those little papers that nobody can read except drug store guys, prescriptions I think you call them, for medicine that was supposed to help me feel better. You carry your prescription straight over to the drug store and wait for a few minutes while the drug store guy counts out your green and white pills for you and puts them into that little jar with the lid that never wants to come off too easy until you know the trick of opening it.

I was supposed to take one of those pills, with a big glass of water, every night just before I went to sleep. 'Course, I did exactly what the doctor said about taking my pills, except a few times I washed down my pill with orange juice instead of water. Most of the time I drank water, but sometimes I had some orange juice for a little spice in my life.

I must admit that the pills didn't seem to help me feel too much better. About the only thing I noticed was that I started to have a lot of real scary nightmares, which is another word for bad dreams, almost every night, and I was even sleepier during the daytime than I ever was before. Seemed like I always had a bad case of the cottonmouth and the runs, too.

I told the doctor about my dreams and everything else, but he said not to worry and to keep on with taking a pill each night without missing even a single one. Sometimes it takes a while before they start to work he told me, except he never told me exactly how long that might be. By the way, he said the orange juice was OK.

Boy oh boy. While I'm waiting for the pills to finally start working, I been thinking almost every single minute about when I used to have my own room in the attic back at the house where I grew up across the street from my best friend Billy. Sometimes, when I'm real homesick like that, I look at Penny's picture in our high school yearbook, and I remember the time she sat next to me at the bowling alley and touched my face, and when she was my partner walking down the aisle with the nice music playing at the graduation ceremony, and when she smiled and talked to me for the very first time to make my third wish come true, and when we went to a baseball game that she never once saw in her whole life until I took her.

I think a lot about Max, too. He was a real good guy in my life, almost the best I would say. Of all the things about him that I liked so much, I think my favorite one is that he always expected me to do a good job, no matter what. It didn't matter to Max that my extra chromozones made me have some things wrong with me compared to other guys my age; he still expected me to do a good job, and so I did. Those were the good old days, all right, the days when I felt so happy about everything and so good about me. Maybe they'll come back soon. You can never tell when the good old days will come back soon.

I'm thinking about going over to the hospital to see my best friend Penny today. I got a plan that's way cool, too. Like I told you, Penny doesn't talk to good old Richard anymore, and she doesn't like it when he touches her. So, I'm thinking that maybe I'll tell her it's Dicky that came to see her. If Penny would only get better again, I wouldn't mind it if she called me Dicky. It doesn't matter that much what your name is anyway. Everyone could call me Dicky.

Epilogue

Our son came home last month, and yesterday, for the first time, he spoke of going back to work at the sheltered workshop. He plans to begin looking for what he calls a "real" job and his own place to live as soon as he feels better. Despite some reluctance, he visits his psychiatrist regularly, and the combination of counseling and medication is gradually taking hold. It's been a slow process, but the progress Richard has made is obvious.

Richard had a major setback, and it has been painful to watch him struggle with the anxiety, sadness, lethargy and lack of interest, inability to make decisions, and everything else that accompanies a serious depression. Given what has transpired in our son's life however, my wife and I believe his reactions have been appropriate and might have been anticipated. In fact, had Richard not reacted to the difficult and traumatic events in his life the way he did, it would have been even more pathological and a greater cause for alarm.

Our son, like millions of others, Down syndrome or not, suffers a debilitating mental illness for which he is being treated, and from which, we are confident, he will fully recover. Once again he has demonstrated, labels notwithstanding, that he is much the same as everyone else. As his beautiful friend Penny has often said, "There is no separate set of rules for the mentally retarded."

In her wisdom, Penny was certainly correct. Indeed, our son has done much to belie the outmoded thinking associated with mental retardation in general and Down syndrome in particular. He is literate, for example. Richard can use his reading and writing skills on the job and as an enjoyable pastime, as well. He has learned these things despite being labeled "trainable mentally handicapped," and therefore, according to the omniscient authors of textbooks and IQ tests, a person who will not benefit from instruction in basic academic subjects. "Your son is not educable," the experts told us.

He can work and live on his own as well. While the sheltered workshop and group home are important resources and backups, we have no doubt Richard will eventually rent an apartment and once again find employment outside the workshop. He will do these things despite being labeled "moderately mentally impaired" and therefore, if one were naive enough to believe textbooks in the field, dependent upon others for as long as he lives. "Your son will never develop to the level required for independent social and vocational functioning in the community," the experts told us.

Richard is a young man with the same strong drives as other healthy men his age. Although the quantity of his sexual encounters has surely been limited, from our conversations, at least to the extent that he is willing to open up to us, it is clear that he enjoys women and the pleasure that intimacy provides. He has an entirely healthy attitude toward his sexuality, and he understands its place in his life.

It's a sad commentary upon public awareness that large numbers of individuals, apparently unable to shed their oversimplified conceptions, still adhere to the hackneyed notion that people who are mentally retarded are either entirely disinterested in sexual encounters or are sexual predators, "creatures," if you will, whose limited intellect makes it impossible for them to control their "primitive" urges. Fact is, like true gentlemen everywhere, irrespective of their level of intellect, Richard respects women. He admires them and cherishes their company. He has grown into a loving and gentle young man.

Then, there are the feelings and compassion Richard has for others. He is acutely aware of mood, always concerned about the happiness of his friends. If she is interested, he will resume his relationship with Ashley when he his ready. Of course, he will continue to visit Penny, and he will watch over her, doing whatever he can to help her live with her autism. He will stay with her, always, as good friends do. Admirable isn't it, especially from a person who is mentally retarded and therefore still being characterized in some of the professional literature as unaware, or at best insensitive, to the needs of others?

And, Richard will always remember his dear friend Max Eberhart, a man who exhibited a rare combination of the best characteristics humanity has to offer. He was a fusion of brilliance and kindness, with equal parts contributing to the mix. Max gave our son the opportunity to show what he could do, never allowing undue sympathy or bias to affect his judgment. His contribution to our son's life was immense. As Richard will do, we too shall always honor his memory.

By the way, our son no longer cares if he's called Richard or Dicky. Just get past the label and get to know him. You will be better for the experience. That's what I think, all right.

Printed in the United States
1176200002B/3